HUNGER'S ROGUES

Also by Jacques Sandulescu

Donbas

HUNGER'S ROGUES

ON THE BLACK MARKET IN EUROPE, 1948

JACQUES SANDULESCU

HARCOURT BRACE JOVANOVICH
NEW YORK AND LONDON

Printed in the United States of America

Library of Congress Cataloging in Publication Data
Sandulescu, Jacques.
Hunger's rogues: on the black market in Europe, 1948.
Autobiographical.
1.   Black market—Europe.   I.   Title.
HF5349.E9S2   381 [B]   74-5280
ISBN 0-15-142991-X

First edition

B C D E

For A. Manolescu, without whom this would not be;
for Susu, Lenny, and all the little ones;
and for Kancho, Tadashi, and Shigeru. OSU!

1807392

A fig for those by law protected!
Liberty's a glorious feast!
Courts for Cowards were erected,
Churches built to please the Priest.
—ROBERT BURNS
"The Jolly Beggars"

HUNGER'S ROGUES

I was the last one on the rickety streetcar. It shook and clanked around a corner, slowed, and came to a stop. The end of the line. Picking up my cardboard suitcase, I got off and looked around in the dim winter twilight. Snow was falling, and for a moment I felt lost, as I had so many times in the last three years. Bare fields stretched away in every direction. We had long since left the outskirts of Hannover, and somewhere nearby was the little town of Buchholz, but that wasn't where I was going. Then I saw them: the long, low barracks with black smoke rising from their chimneys.

If you've ever been in camps—labor camps, prison camps, displaced-persons camps—you cannot mistake them. That was the dreary silhouette of the Camp. Transit Camp Buchholz.

I started walking the half mile or so to the camp gate. To whoever was in charge there I would be just one more DP youth, maybe a little taller and stronger than most, but just as skinny, wearing the black-dyed American army castoffs that had become the DP uniform. My wrists stuck out of the sleeves of the field jacket. I still limped a little. I was cold and hungry, as usual, and very tired.

I had left early in the morning from the camp in Bremen. It had been a long wait for the train to Hannover, and when it finally came it was so crowded that I couldn't sit down even on my suitcase. Hannover lies only about seventy-five miles southeast of Bremen, but train service in Germany then, at the beginning of 1948, was so crippled and overburdened that the trip took eight hours. I stood the whole way.

At the station in Hannover I'd had to push my way through the black-market crowd to find out which streetcar to take for Buchholz. Over two thousand people were milling around engaged in active trading—haggling for survival. I listened with the practiced ear of my eight months in Bremen and learned quickly that prices here in Hannover were 30 per cent higher. Meat, butter, sugar, cigarettes, fish, oil, soap, cigarettes, ration cards, coffee, cigarettes . . . the familiar round. I saw twenty Lucky Strike butts, stolen from ash trays or snatched from sidewalks, go for twenty-five German marks—one-fourth the average price of a fresh pack.

Now, remembering the station, I shivered and walked faster. I knew black-market crowds and how to get around in them, but I hated them. They reminded me of herds of hungry cattle, mindless and milling. The camp ahead, Transit Camp Buchholz, was my chance to get away from the Europe of beggar herds and ration cards, camps and more camps full of the lost and displaced. Here I would be screened for emigration, and if I passed I might soon be on one of the ships going across the Atlantic. To America, the land of plentiful chocolate bars . . . so cheap they were almost free . . . or at least to Canada and a lumber camp and fried eggs and bacon for breakfast every day. . . . Helplessly, my mouth watered and my stomach contracted. If I didn't pass the screening I might be thrown back into Europe's beggar herd. But there was no reason why I shouldn't pass. I had not

4

stolen from the Allies, like some of the DPs I'd known in Bremen. I had nothing to lie about, nothing to cover up. And I had escaped from Russia all alone in the middle of winter —the doctor who had treated my legs had said that was something to be proud of. I felt hopeful about Transit Camp Buchholz.

But the hope went out of me like steam when I saw the triple strand of barbed wire around the compound and the glint of the guard's rifle. This didn't look like the gateway to a new life; it looked more like the end of the line. The armed guard, the barbed wire reminded me of the prison camps in Russia, the camps I had escaped from. In Bremen we had lived in barracks, and there had been a fence, but not barbed wire, and a man at the entrance who checked comings and goings, but no armed guard. Here I was afraid I was going to feel like a prisoner again.

The guard motioned me into the guardhouse. Inside it was warm. A small stove glowed next to a table where three Poles sat playing cards. One of the players wore a sidearm and an air of authority. I handed him my papers and gratefully sat down in the chair they offered me.

The sergeant peered at the papers, then looked at me and back at the papers. He said something to the others in Polish. I understood him to be telling them I was a Rumanian, that they ought to call someone—I thought the name was Jony. It was a Rumanian name. I told them I spoke Russian.

The sergeant studied my papers some more. Finally he fished a pencil out of his pocket, scribbled something on a piece of paper, and handed it to one of the guards. "Take him to the supply room and get him his blankets, and then put him in Barracks 3. Tell the barracks chief to make sure he gets to the screening tomorrow."

At that word my hopes revived a little. At least I wouldn't have to wait weeks for the screening!

I followed the guard out into the cold and over to the first barracks, to the supply room. I caught a glimpse of the rooms there and saw that they weren't the run-of-the-mill communal rooms with rows of bunks; blanket partitions divided them into semiprivate compartments, and the smell of cooking made me dizzy. I learned later that the camp staff lived here—the guards, the cook, the canteen head and his wife, and so on. A burly supply-room attendant with blue eyes and a strong, broken nose silently handed me two blankets. Then we crossed the snowy compound, past the square wooden central building, which the guard told me housed the mess hall and canteen. A few DPs hurried like shadows from one barracks to another, hunched up against the cold.

Barracks 3, long and low, was divided into big rooms that opened onto a long corridor. The guard showed me the washhouse at one end. We went into one of the rooms, about thirty feet square. Seven or eight DPs sitting around the potbellied stove stopped talking and turned to look at us. Army cots, made up with army blankets like the ones I was holding, lined each wall, and the stove was in the middle of the room, bracketed by two rough tables with benches. (When the camp was full the cots were converted into double bunks, and a room like this could hold sixty men. Six rooms to a barracks, twelve barracks in the camp: at capacity, the camp held well over four thousand people. But because it was a transit camp its population was always swelling and shrinking as new shipments came in and others left for embarkation to the New World.)

The DPs were lounging on benches, on bunks, and on the floor around the warmth of the stove. They had probably been telling their endless, repetitive DP stories, the sole form of entertainment during the long afternoons, mostly lies about their exploits before the war or their trials during it. Now they looked me over. The guard showed me an empty cot under the room's single window and said I was to sleep there. On the way out he told the DPs, in Polish, that I was a Rumanian and had come from Bremen.

I put my blankets on the cot, shoved my suitcase under it, sat down, and took off my shoes. Putting my feet up on the dirty mattress, I closed my eyes and tried to listen. I was the odd man out again, the stranger. Three years of life close to the margin of survival had made my senses as keen as an animal's, and I could feel the suspicion, the unpleasant curiosity in the air. I had been in Bremen long enough to have friends and contacts, a good thing going for me. Now I would have to go through the testing process all over again.

They were whispering about Rumania. For most of the war Rumania had been an ally of Germany, and almost every DP hated the Germans with a bitter passion born of experience. Most DPs were Slavs—Poles, Lithuanians, Serbs, Czechs—whose countries Germany had invaded and occupied, and who had been interned and deported to Germany for forced labor in munitions factories or heavy industry. They had lived in prison camps, worked like slaves, and been beaten for any insubordination—and sometimes on a whim. The Nazis had considered them an inferior race, servile and stupid. What they thought of the Germans was beyond words. Not that I had much use for the Germans, either; indirectly, they were to blame for my troubles, too—they'd started the war. But what would these men think of me?

Suddenly the hushed whispers stopped. I opened my eyes and saw the men getting up and reaching for spoons and cans. Without a signal or a clock they knew, as one always knows in a camp, that it was time for their supper shift. I watched guardedly as one of them came over to me, but he only said, "We go to eat now. Until you get yourself a can and spoon, I have extra ones here." That broke the ice. I got up and walked with them to the mess hall, joining hundreds more DPs who moved across the yard in the cold and dark as toward some great, warm magnet. On the way we talked about food: how much better DPs were fed in American camps than in English ones, like Buchholz. It was said that there they even got their meals on trays, like American soldiers.

Our crowded mess hall was run by the usual routine. We lined up, each holding his cup or can, and shuffled forward as

7

the attendants ladled out the steaming potato soup. I looked at the men around me. For most of them lining up for food was the habit of years. Many lived from food line to food line. There was a fierce life left in some of the faces, and these were the ones who joked, "Pork chops tonight, Pavel?" "Oh, I'll settle for a nice thick Russian *borscht*." More of the faces were deeply lined maps of misery or closed books, blank and unreadable. What the war years hadn't been able to do to these men, the interminable waiting in camps would.

We ate the soup quickly, slurping it up, burning our mouths in our haste to get it into aching, growling stomachs. It was always gone too soon. Back in our room, the others made a place for me by the stove. Now would come the questioning. What other camps had I been in? What were they like? Why had I been sent here alone? (DPs who had been in the same labor camp or factory were usually kept together, and the solitary exception always aroused suspicion.) Where had I been during the war?

I told them how, at the age of sixteen, I had been arrested on my way to school and interned for forced labor as they had been, but by the Russians, not the Germans. I told them about my two years in the Russian camp and the coal mine. About the cave-in, and my escape. I talked about Vegesack and Halmerweg, the two DP camps in Bremen I had been in, and about my transfer here to Buchholz. One of them had worked in a German coal mine, and he asked me some questions about my work in the famous mines of the Donbas, the Donets River Basin. We spoke in Russian.

The man who had offered me his can and spoon took out a pack of cigarettes and passed it around. I said I didn't smoke. "How can you go without smoking? The nerves need it," he said. He blew a few smoke rings, and everybody watched them disappear near the pipe of our stove. This DP was in his forties, good-looking in a strong way, with dark blond hair and blue eyes. Life had given him a scarred nose, but the full, humorous mouth and strong chin were his own. He looked well able to take care of himself.

Was I nervous about the screening tomorrow? he asked. "No," I said. "Why should I be? I've been answering questions ever since I escaped from Russia. I have nothing to hide."

"The Canadians who do the screening here have gotten very suspicious," he said. "They've caught DPs in some terrible lies, so now they're screening very carefully. But you have no reason to lie. Everything should go smoothly for you."

He told me his name was Cheslav. I introduced myself as Vanya, the name I had been given in Russia.

As we talked I learned that Cheslav came from the heart of Poland, but when I asked what he had done before the war he gave me a sidelong look, as if he weren't sure I was serious, and mumbled, "What does it matter what anyone did before the war? I had it easy. I helped my father in his lumber business. Ahh, come on, let's get some sleep, so we can get in line early tomorrow."

I stretched out on my cot, aching with fatigue and discouragement. I had asked Cheslav casually how long he'd been in the camp. "Sixteen months," he spat. "The sons of whores don't tell you anything." I'd asked one of the others, and he grunted, "Just over a year." I thought of the long evenings ahead in their company, not knowing whether it would be six weeks, six months, or six years. Even if I passed the screening tomorrow I still had to wait for a medical examination and pass that. And then I had to wait for assignment to a ship, and I felt sure that no one was going to tell me anything, either. In my mind I saw the barbed wire, the guards with their rifles, the endless lines—for a plate of soup, to go to the toilet, to go into an office and answer endless questions. I was back to what I knew. Without the backbreaking labor of Russia, it was true. But in a way the work there had helped take your mind off the waiting and not knowing, the feeling of being guarded like a criminal when you hadn't done anything, until you began to think maybe you had . . . and the chronic, gnawing hunger.

For me the hunger had begun over three years ago. On a

winter morning early in 1945, as I was walking to school in my home town of Brasov, Rumania, I was arrested by a Russian soldier and pushed into a truck with several other frightened people. We were taken to a barracks on the outskirts of town jammed with milling, crying, praying people who had all been arrested as abruptly as I had, in their homes or on the street. Toward evening the Russians took us to the railroad station and transferred us to a train of thirty boxcars. We didn't know it then, but our destination was the Donbas, Russia's great coal-mining area in the Donets Basin. We were a shipment of labor prisoners.

Rumania had been allied with Germany until Russian troops started pouring across our border in 1944, when the government thought it wise to switch sides. It was too late. Russia behaved like an occupying power and treated the Rumanians like an enemy population, fair game for deportation and forced labor. Enemy or ally, it was all a matter of words. The fact was that Rumania was at Russia's mercy, and Russia needed laborers.

I had spent the war years in school, and my involvement with the Germans had begun and ended with the boy who appointed himself our school's Hitler Youth representative. One afternoon we were told to report to the school grounds, and there was this kid in his spanking-new brown uniform, very proud of himself, yelling out orders. He made us line up, called the roll, and started us marching and drilling. I didn't like it, and I didn't like him. He got louder and nastier by the minute.

Then I did one of the turns wrong and heard him holler, "You! Sandulescu! Down on your knees! Crawl after me on your elbows."

For a moment I wondered how to follow the order, but I knew how my father would rage at me if he found out I had done such a thing. So I turned around and walked off the parade ground, not looking back, while the "Hitler Youth Leader" screamed after me, "Traitor! Pig! Degenerate!"

That evening I told my father what had happened. The

next morning he came with me to school, and we went straight to the dean's office.

My father walked in without knocking and demanded that the flustered dean send for that boy. Someone scurried out, and in a few minutes a bold knock sounded on the door. The kid came in, clicked his heels, and greeted the dean— "Heil Hitler!" That did not improve my father's digestion. He turned to the kid. "Too bad your father doesn't do this," he said, and slapped him powerfully, once, twice, flinging him against the wall. Then my father grabbed him and shook him. "Now get back to your class and study hard. The Hitler Youth is not for you." The kid slunk out. He didn't look like the same boy who had come in.

The dean was halfway out of his chair, all puffed up and red like a rooster about to crow, but my father turned and pointed a finger at him. "Don't say a word," he said. "If I hear anything further about this, I'll close the school!" He would have, too.

That was the end of our Hitler Youth movement.

So I wasn't a political enemy of the Russians that day they arrested me. I was just a sixteen-year-old kid on the way to school at the wrong moment in history.

And now, in the boxcar, I pushed my way to the tiny window and saw my father among the others on the station platform, head and shoulders above the crowd of screaming, crying people. I tried to show him with my eyes that I could make it, that I wasn't afraid. As we looked at each other I saw him fighting back tears—something I had never seen before. A moment later I was shoved away from the window, and soon the train jolted into motion. We were on our way to the Donbas.

I was never to see my father again.

The hunger began right away. For three days the Russians didn't stop the train or give us anything to eat. Those of us who had been arrested at home had been able to bring a little food. I had only my three schoolbooks—and a pocketful of lei, the Rumanian currency, from my first black-market deal. There had been a vigorous black market going in Rumania since the Russians came in, and I had secretly sold my accordion, a present from my parents, to a Russian soldier, hoping that I could buy a fine new accordion and still have a profit left over. I hadn't been sure, but I had thought my father would be proud of me. Well, the lei were no use to me now. I couldn't eat them. Later, in Russia, I did trade the money—and the pages of my schoolbooks—for corn meal. The Russian guards used the paper to roll cigarettes.

The train rattled eastward, cold, dark, crowded, and sour. Every second or third day we stopped for food and water. Five people shared a loaf of bread a day, and each of us got a cup of thin cabbage soup and one spoonful of kasha, or buckwheat porridge. After three weeks, when the train came to its final stop among the coal hills of the Donbas, many were already very weak, and as we built our own kitchen and latrine in the terrible cold of the Russian winter people started dying. Grave digging was added to our other chores. After work each evening our reward was a fifth of a loaf of bread.

When we started to work in the mines our rations tripled. Stalin had decreed that everyone who worked underground should get a thousand grams of bread a day. The work was backbreaking. On a lumberjack's diet we might have thrived. On Stalin's diet we starved.

At sixteen, I was the youngest in the transport, but also one of the biggest and strongest. I was six feet, two inches tall, and when I was arrested I had weighed 180 pounds, though now I was losing weight rapidly. Later, in a second camp, my size and willingness got me a job outside the mine, on a high tower, tipping slag out of a car it had taken two smaller men to turn over. While the summer lasted, the chance to work in sunshine and fresh air helped me keep going. High above the mine entrance, I watched the weary, blackened men and women crawl out at the end of their shift and for moments felt closer to the birds in their freedom. But soon the summer ended, the short fall passed, and winter showed its teeth again. And when those cold Siberian winds swept the plains even Russians in sheepskin-lined fur coats hid from them. Up on the tower I had only a shirt and a light canvas jacket between me and the wind and cold. No padded overcoats for prisoners. It would have killed me.

I had myself transferred into the mine, and for the next fifteen months I worked underground, staying alive as best I could on my bread ration, a little soup and kasha, and now and then a tiny square of canned meat—from cans marked "USA." A couple of times I was allowed to visit Russian miner friends' homes in the village, and then I would have a real meal. Once I stole some potatoes from a storage cellar and was punished with extra work details. In desperation, my friend Omar and I even hit the captain's fat dog over the head with a lantern and made a stew out of him. Hunger gnawed at our insides constantly.

As I got weaker I grew less alert in the mine, and my reflexes slowed. One day my section of the mine caved in, and I got caught. For four hours I was buried, unable to move and barely able to breathe. I was sure I was finished. But Omar and my old foreman from the tower dug me out.

I was alive, but something was terribly wrong with my legs. I was sent to the local hospital, and within a few days my legs began to swell. Then the swelling broke and about half a gallon of pus ran out. After that, the sores wouldn't heal. They began to turn a dark green, and a few days later I heard the doctor say something to the nurse about amputation.

I decided to escape.

It was the middle of winter, around the New Year of 1947. I had no food, no physical reserves (I weighed 120 now), and no warm clothing. If I was caught I might share the fate of the two Rumanians who had tried to escape early in our imprisonment: they had been shot in front of the rest of us, as an example and a warning. But when I measured my chances against the possibility of having my legs cut off I knew what I had to do.

I got up in the middle of the night, wrapped my oozing legs tightly with rags and wire, and walked out of the hospital. At the train station I crawled onto one of the open coal cars headed west out of the Donbas.

Riding coal trains westward, I would dig myself a hole in the coal for shelter against the cold. When the pain from my legs grew less, when I didn't feel cold or hungry any more, that was the danger point. I would count to keep myself awake, and the next time the train stopped or slowed down I would roll off, drop to the ground, and stagger in search of food and shelter. Poor people, simple people living in shacks by the railroad, took me in and gave me food and a place to rest near a stove. They let me wash my foul-smelling bandages. From them I learned when the next train was due to go through for the west.

Two weeks out of the Donbas I had to make a painful decision. After I crossed the Dnieper River I could try to find a train southwest, toward the Rumanian border, or I could go northwest, toward Poland and Germany. I longed to see my father and mother again, to be safe at home, to have my legs taken care of by our good Dr. Negus, who had seen me through my childhood scrapes and sicknesses. But I knew those were dreams. Home wasn't safe for me any more, not in a Communist Rumania. If word got out that I had escaped from Russia I might be given a few weeks to heal and then shipped right back to the mines. In Russia I had heard talk of a divided Germany. Also, I remebered those cans that said PORK SAUSAGE—USA and SPAM—USA. I decided to try for Poland and then for the American sector of Germany.

Other kind people helped me—a trainload of German prisoners from Russia, a doctor in East Germany, a train engineer who let me ride in the locomotive near the boiler. On February 19, 1947, seven weeks after I walked out of the hospital, I slid down from a train engine and looked around. In spite of my hunger and the nagging pain in my legs, a surge of elation went through me. This was Kassel, Germany, safely inside the Western Zone.

In two days I would be nineteen.

My elation was short-lived. In the crowded station waiting room, the shabby, ill-dressed people began moving away from me, whispering. My bandages stank, and my clothes were black with coal dust. I didn't blame the people, but they were none too clean themselves. Shame and anger crept into my exhaustion.

The Kassel police took me to a Red Cross station. My German was poor, and I had trouble explaining where I had come from, what had happened to me. People kept asking questions. It was all so confusing that I had to think about what I had escaped from before I could feel better. During my escape I had been terribly alone, in spite of the people who helped me. But in that aloneness there had been a safety, a dignity. I had had to rely only on myself, on my own fierce will to live. Now I had stumbled into a Germany where I was one of hundreds of thousands of faceless refugees, all needing food, shelter, and medical care, all dependent for these things on overburdened, impersonal authorities. I was only just beginning to be aware of this.

The Red Cross nurses made an ineffectual try at rebandaging my legs. They gave me a pitifully small meal, a cot to sleep on, a handful of ration cards, and a ticket to Hannover, seventy miles north, where I was supposed to go to a refugee camp. At the train station early the next morning I saw the first of those peculiar milling crowds I was to see in front of the depot in every good-sized city. I wondered where so many hundreds of people could be going.

On the train to Hannover, an American Red Cross officer took pity on me and decided to try to get me into an American military hospital in Bremen, farther north. He took me to his base, where there happened to be a camp full of Rumanian prisoners of war waiting for repatriation. It was strange to hear my native language spoken, and the smell of ghiveci, the Rumanian vegetable stew, almost made me sick with hunger. While I slowly and carefully ate a plateful, the Rumanians told me what they had heard from home. Their stories convinced me that I had been right not to try to go back. My country was not the way I remembered it. Rumania was still occupied by the Red Army, and a disastrous inflation had set in. It seemed to me that the war had destroyed all the warmth and safety and well-being in the world.

I was taken to the American army hospital in an ambulance. When I got there the doctors refused to admit me. The Rumanian who had come along with the Red Cross officer as an interpreter said they thought I was too far gone, that I might die in a day or so, and since I didn't have any identity papers my death would cause them a lot of paperwork. But there was a refugee camp about three miles away, and they would have me driven there.

I refused the offer of a ride to the camp, and I refused the white-jacketed doctor's offer of clean bandages. I could see the distaste mingled with pity in his face. I wanted to get out of that clean white hospital. I didn't belong there, in my crusted, blackened clothing and the festering stench from my legs. I pulled myself together and got up. The Red Cross officer grabbed my arm, but I shook him off and walked out of the hospital, feeling the fresh, cold winter air in my face— my friend.

I tried to walk the three miles to the refugee camp. I didn't really know any more where I was going, to a refugee camp or back to the mine, where at least people knew me and I didn't have to explain anything, where a man could die without papers. I crawled into an old cement bunker to rest and stayed there for days and nights in a delirium. During all the weeks of my escape I hadn't felt so hopeless. In the moments when I was closest to death it didn't seem so bad to die. Then I would remember that I still wanted to live, and somehow I found the strength to make one more try. I managed to stagger within sight of the long, low barracks before I pitched into a snowbank and the world went black.

My escape ended there in Bremen a year ago. I came back to consciousness in the refugee camp. I had been found on the road and carried inside, and my legs had been cleaned and treated. American and Russian doctors notwithstanding, I was not going to die, and I wasn't going to lose my legs. I drank bowl after bowl of thick, steaming turnip soup. And slowly, under the care of the kind camp doctor, my legs began to heal.

As I regained strength I told the doctor about my escape and the harsh conditions I had left behind. He said that he couldn't understand how I had survived, that my constitution defied the medical laws. As skinny and worn as I was, I was recovering from a form of gangrene that usually led only to amputation or death. According to the doctor, I would have healed much faster with a diet of sugars, fats, fresh meat, and fruit, but in postwar Germany only the Americans had those.

The people who ran that first camp didn't have much, but what they had they shared. I was very moved when the doctor gave me his own pen so I could write a letter to my parents telling them I was safe. It had been so long that I wondered whether I still knew how to write.

Now, a year later, lying awake in another camp—my third —I still remembered the unspeakable relief of those first showers I had taken in Bremen. The water was icy cold, but it felt good to me. I had scrubbed and scrubbed, until gradually the dirt began to come out of my rough, blackened skin and flow down the drain. It was like the winter's end in Russia, when the snow began to melt and the ice broke up. People who have always lived ten steps from hot and cold running water cannot understand how dirt eats away at one's pride, how it corrodes the spirit.

At that time my mind, too, was bringing up and spewing out its black contents. I had terrible nightmares. In my sleep I was chased, grabbed, beaten by military police, dragged back to the Russian camp and the mine. Then I stopped being so scared of the life I had escaped from, the life in the Donbas, and became frightened of the white-jacketed doctor in the American hospital. Night after night I woke up screaming and drenched with sweat.

But gradually the terrors faded to nothing worse than bad

memories. I began to look around me, to take an interest in the present, in the comings and goings and whisperings of my campmates who traded on the black market. I had to orient myself in this chaotic new world. As always, it was my aching, grumbling stomach that reminded me that, though the worst might be behind, life in shattered Europe was still far from secure. And problem number one was filling one's belly. The camp rations were like everyone said: "Too much to starve, and not enough to live."

I began to learn about the black market. It was the real economy of postwar Germany, frantic, bustling, fermenting. Of course, it was illegal, but almost everyone traded on it at one time or another, on one level or another: disabled and older German men, boys too young to have fought for Hitler, soldiers of the occupation, the more adventurous DPs. They had to. The official economy of ration cards was too meager for anything but bare survival. If you wanted to eat, really eat, you had to trade. And then there were those who made their fortunes off everyone else's need.

The black market had begun almost immediately after the war. When Germany shuddered to a standstill in May 1945 warehouses were rapidly looted, stores stood empty, transport and communications were dead, and there was nothing to eat. Military governments were set up, and slowly, ponderously, the machinery of distribution began to function again. The new authorities issued new ration cards. In the last year of the war, Germans had received very little food through their own government; now the Allied military governments gave them even less. And often the rations couldn't even be issued because the food wasn't available. People starved. The DPs in their camps ate better than most Germans.

But the only ones who really had enough to eat, besides the soldiers of the occupying forces, were the German farmers in the countryside, because they raised their own vegetables and often some pigs or chickens as well. Wealthier city families began to sell their jewelry, watches, cameras, fur coats, silverware for a bag of potatoes or a pound or two of pork fat. Butter and sugar became luxuries. There were no jobs to speak of, so the unemployed German man or boy drifted into becoming a middleman between the rich city families and the farmers. Now and then the police would catch him on one of his trips back and forth, but the cops were as hungry as everyone else, so they generally confiscated his wares to eat or sell themselves and let him go back to his trading. The middleman had become the black marketeer of Europe.

After five years of war, with its anxiety, boredom, and horror, the black marketeer was usually a heavy smoker. Now hungry, always on the lookout, tense and alert, he needed desperately to smoke. And American cigarettes were the best in the world. I heard my roommates whispering about them —what they wouldn't do for a Camel, a Lucky Strike! It was not money, weapons, or well-fed health that made the American soldier king in this strange postwar world; it was the seemingly endless supply of tobacco he got from his PX. Americans paid for their women and everything else in cigarettes.

From late 1945 on, the American cigarette was the real currency of the black market, much stabler than the inflated German mark. The price of a pack of American cigarettes held steady at around one hundred marks, and the prices of meat, butter, sugar, oil, clothing were often quoted in packs or cartons of cigarettes. Two to five packs would buy a kilo (about two pounds) of butter, sugar, or pork, or a bottle or two of oil.

To really understand the significance of these prices and the driving motivation behind the black market, it is necessary to know in more detail just how scarce and precious these commodities were. Rations for German citizens were apportioned according to energy needs. Men doing hard physical labor got the most; then came pregnant women, factory workers, office workers, housewives, students. It is hard to remember today the exact amounts of food people got, but the rations for an office worker for one week would have been something like this: 100 grams (about one-fifth of a pound) of meat—*if* it was available (and then it might be only a couple of slices of Spam); 50 grams (less than two ounces) of butter or margarine; 150 grams (about five ounces) of bread per day, or two pounds of bread per week; and, for the week, three spoonfuls of sugar and three of jam—if they were available. Plus a little fat or oil and a few potatoes. Try to imagine having no more than that to eat *for a week*, and it is easy to understand why people traded on the black market.

Now, ration cards cost hardly anything—a token payment, a matter of pfennigs, though difficult enough for the unemployed to scratch together—but no one was ever allowed to buy more than his quota of cards, because there was so little food available. Often ration-card holders were turned away because there was no meat or jam. The town office that distributed the cards had a list of citizens' names and addresses, and once your name was checked off for the month you had all the ration cards you were going to get—legally. People sometimes tried to break into the rationing office just before the monthly distribution, or to forge ration cards. Both crimes were punished by stiff jail sentences. To get more food, the only alternative was the black market.

Meat, butter, sugar, and jam were available on the black market by the kilo—in quantities undreamed of under rationing. But the prices were hundreds of times as high as the price of ration cards. And the ordinary German couldn't afford black-market prices—unless he traded himself. Even if he was lucky enough to have a job he might earn only 100 or 150 marks a week—the price of one pack of American cigarettes on the black market. Trading, with all its risks, was the only alternative to slow starvation.

In almost every city—not only in Germany, but, so we heard, all over Europe—crowds gathered around the train station, in the waiting room or on the plaza in front, mingling, trading, searching for what they wanted. Prices fluctuated constantly, as in some crude, illicit stock market, which in fact is what it was. The more intelligent DPs, the ones who hadn't lost all interest in life, saw the black market as a way not only to pacify their growling stomachs, but also to keep themselves from rotting in the barracks while they waited for embarkation. On the lowest level it was a shabby treadmill, but among the black marketeers there were men of authority and nerve, men who took risks. There could be a kind of desperate adventure in it.

The camp I was in then, Vegesack, for DP youths, was in an old hotel by the Weser River on the outskirts of Bremen. As spring came and I could walk again, I enjoyed strolling on the boardwalk, making friends, breathing the fresh air, talking of the future. But I was restless. I wanted to get into the center of things, to learn more about the black market, to find my place in this world as I had found it in Russia, where work had been the measure of a man and I had been respected for my strength and willingness. As soon as my legs were strong enough I asked to be transferred to another camp, Halmerweg, in the center of Bremen.

Before I left Vegesack I got a letter from my parents. The kind doctor brought me the letter and then left the room, sensing that I wanted to be alone when I read it. The envelope was heavy with thousands of lei in stamps, a mark of the terrible inflation in Rumania. In the old days a seven-lei stamp had taken a letter anywhere in Europe. All sorts of feelings swept through me as I opened the envelope. I read the letter hungrily, and read it again.

My mother told me the bad news first: my sister Edith, two years older than me, had died in a camp in the Donbas not far from where I had been. The family had been notified of her death by the authorities. But thank God, my mother said, I was still living. And then she asked me all a mother's questions: did I have enough warm clothing, did I sleep well, how bad was my leg injury? I could feel her love penetrating all the way to my bones, like healing sunshine. What a luxury it had become.

My father's words were strong. He said that the worst was behind me; I was a strong man now, and I would go out into life and do well for myself. He only felt badly about not being able to help me, but his spirit was with me, I should never forget that. Ah, how I missed the old patriarch. I could still see him standing in that crowd at the train station, an *uriash amber,* as the Transylvanians said, a giant of a man physically and emotionally. His face had been close to the breaking point then.

He included the address of an uncle of mine here in Germany, a doctor, who lived in Giessen. I was to look him up, and he would take care of my legs. I wrote back that I might be moving to another camp, and that from now on they should write to me at my uncle's; I would get to Giessen somehow.

Then I was transferred to Halmerweg, right in the thick of things, and I set out to explore Bremen thoroughly. The area around the train station had been a luxury shopping district before the war, all expensive clothing stores and fine food shops. Now most of the windows were shattered and boarded up, the shelves were dusty and bare, and the black market seethed on the wide plaza. Some of the shop owners had probably been fat people, and I wondered if maybe now even they ventured into the thick of the black market trying to sell something of their own for a decent meal. Fat people weren't seen much any more, except for soldiers of the occupying forces.

I prowled around the edges of the black-market crowd listening, absorbing, sharpening my German. The traders both fascinated and repelled me. They had an animal alertness—they could smell an opportunity, and they had an uncanny sixth sense for danger. Quickly and furtively they passed packages or cigarettes back and forth, exchanged ration cards, counted money—and when a policeman came too close they knew it somehow and melted away into the crowd.

In Halmerweg I had a visit from the Red Cross officer, with

his Rumanian interpreter. I sensed how badly he felt about not having gotten me into the American hospital. As he left he gave me five packs of American cigarettes, even though he knew I didn't smoke. He also knew that on the black market a hundred cigarettes represented great wealth for someone as poor as I was. It was my starting capital.

My Red Cross benefactor advised me to get out of war-sick Europe and promised to help me get into a transit camp as soon as possible.

But in the meantime I began to build up a network of contacts. One man in camp, an escapee from Berlin, had found a job with a baker. Naturally he made off with as many fresh rolls as he could. He'd trade them for ration cards, which didn't get stale, and when he had a stack of cards he'd give them to me and tell me what he wanted for them. He was a small, frail guy and was afraid to venture into the black market himself. There were some rough types, real human sharks, in those crowds. They'd hit you over the head just to take the clean clothes off your back. But I was big, and Russia had made me tough. If it came to a fight I could take care of myself. For this buying service I got a good commission. I had the same arrangement with a DP who worked in a cheese factory and carried off his capital in the form of *Schmierkäse*, a soft cheese. Pretty soon I knew where to get whatever I needed and who else had my kind of setup. On a modest but respectable scale, I had become a black marketeer.

I didn't like to go into the trading crowds myself. The pressure of so many unwashed bodies, the mingling of stale, anxious breaths suffocated me and made my skin crawl. But I had made a good friend in camp, a brawling, high-spirited Hungarian DP named Jeno, and he didn't mind the crowds so much. We would go down to the station, I'd tell Jeno what to look for, and he would slip into the crowd and come back with a kilo of sugar or a pair of shoes. We became a team, and together we managed to eat fairly well.

You could take care of your stomach that way—there was

no other way—but you had to keep at it, trading your way from one meal to the next, and you had to be constantly on the lookout for the cops. When my transfer to Buchholz came through I was more than ready to give it up, to look forward to life in a new world where there would be jobs and meals. I knew it could take me weeks, even months, to establish the kinds of contacts in Hannover that I'd had in Bremen, and I hoped that long before then I would be on my way to America or Canada. I was sick of the constant insecurity, of the hunger that nagged at your back and drove you out into the crowd to trade and trade again.

Now it all depended on the screening. And the medical exam. And the whims of a new set of authorities.

That first night in Transit Camp Buchholz it was a long time before I fell asleep.

We got up early the next morning, splashed our faces with the icy water in the washhouse, and followed Stanislaus, the barracks chief, to the administration building, a long wooden L just inside the camp entrance. There were already several people in line for screenings in front of one of the office doors. Cheslav and I fell in behind them with the rest of the group from our barracks. As we waited the line grew longer and longer, until it stretched the length of the corridor. Other lines were growing in front of other doors. Cheslav pointed out the one where the camp officials made sure your issue of ration cards came through from your old camp; the one for the doctor's office; the line for DPs who had wives or relatives in other camps and were trying to get them transfered here; the long line in front of the office that made inquiries into the whereabouts of families or friends swept away by the war. Lines, lines, and more lines.

The men in our line were tense and silent. Their dark, drab clothing and unreadable faces made them look alike, but I knew that each one was, like me, hugging his own fierce hope of getting out of Europe, his burden of memories and secrets. Screenings were held only once every several months, so this was a rare chance to make a good impression on the authorities. Many had something to hide: theft, collaboration, a killing, a forged identity, a trail of lies. For example, men who had never been interned but had lived on the German-Polish border and so spoke both languages often slipped into the Western Zone, pretended to be Poles, and made up stories of terrible suffering in labor camps or concentration camps—anything to get to America. Most of these would be caught; one or two good liars might get away with it. I knew my own story sounded wild. It was impossible to escape from Russia in the dead of winter without food or warm clothing. Would the Canadian authorities believe me? Maybe it would help if I rolled up my pants legs and showed them the angry red fresh-healed scars.

Three men had gone into the office, and all three had come out looking grim. They avoided the eyes of the other DPs in line and hurried away to their barracks. The fourth man was in the office for close to two hours, but when he came out he was smiling. It was my turn.

I went into a sort of reception room. A pretty secretary in a trim uniform looked at my papers and waved me through another door. I found myself in a larger room facing a stern-looking, black-mustached captain who sat behind a long desk. His nameplate said CAPTAIN DAVIES. Cheslav had told me that he was one of the officials who traveled from camp to camp conducting the screenings. On either side of him sat an interpreter-secretary. Captain Davies's voice was deep and slow, but when he spoke the room hushed.

One of the girls asked me, in German, what language I spoke best.

"Rumanian and Hungarian. And Russian."

In Russian, she told me to hand the captain my papers. He

looked at them for several minutes while I stood in front of him. I was nervous now. The captain spoke to the girl in English, and she said I should tell them everything that had happened to me since 1944.

The captain watched me keenly as I spoke and the girl translated. In the past ten months I had told the story over and over to all the people who questioned me, but I still got caught up in it as I went along. By the time I got to the cave-in and my escape the words were tumbling over each other. The girl tried to slow me down once or twice, but the captain waved her to silence and kept his eyes on me.

When I finished I felt breathless and embarrassed. The captain said a few words to one of the girls. She typed something on my papers and gave them back to Captain Davies, who stamped and signed them. Then he reached out and shook my hand. I had passed the screening.

The girl wished me luck and told me that I would be processed for embarkation after I had passed the medical exam. I took my papers and thanked them, more with my eyes than with words.

Cheslav passed me at the door on his way in. The relief must have been plain in my face. He gave me a tight smile, and I gave him a look that meant good luck. In the corridor the other Poles from my room asked how I had fared, and when I showed them the stamped paper they shook my hand and clapped me on the back. Their enthusiasm was mixed with envy. I had arrived here only the night before, and already I had passed the screening.

At the medical office a nurse took my papers. She said that the examination would be in a week or ten days and that I would be notified a day ahead of time.

I walked out past the long line of DPs. Seeing their sad faces and bowed shoulders, hearing the subdued Slavic murmur of camp gossip, I suddenly wanted to shout, to scare some life into them. I felt happy and full of energy. Only a growl from my stomach announced that I had better head for the mess hall. So far, things couldn't have gone better.

Luck seemed to be on my side. Tomorrow I could make a quick trip back to Bremen. I had something to pick up there that I could sell on the Hannover black market, something that would keep my belly full and my wits occupied at least until the medical exam. After that, if my luck held, I wouldn't be around here much longer.

When I finished my bowl of soup I went back to the barracks, and there I found a satisfied Cheslav. He had passed the screening, too. I said I was glad for him. It didn't surprise me that he had passed; he seemed like a man of substance, a standout among the DPs. Only his decision to change his mind and emigrate to Canada rather than Australia, which involved a lot of red tape, had caused the terrible delays for him.

Finding the barracks chief, I made up a story about a suitcase I had left in Bremen. Could I go back the next day to pick it up? "The DPs have probably stolen it," he grumbled. "You should have brought it with you. Sure, go ahead, as long as you're back for the medical exams. There will be one less mouth to feed."

I knew that it would be best to take an early-morning train. By noon I would be in Bremen, and within hours I could make my pickup, get back to the station, and catch the next train to Hannover. I decided to get to sleep right after supper, so that I could get up early. This time I slept well.

I woke before dawn, dressed in the dark, and was on my way.

At the guard shack I asked a sleepy young guard how often the streetcars ran. "The first one is at five, so come inside. It's too cold to wait out there." I went in and sat with him at the low table by the window, where he could see everyone who passed. The stove warmed our backs. A dim light burned, and from the back of the shack I heard snoring. It all seemed much less ominous than it had the other evening. I had passed the screening, and I felt like a free man.

The guard asked whether I was the Rumanian from Bremen who had arrived just yesterday or the day before and had already passed the screening. News spread fast in a DP camp. "Yes. I'm just going back to Bremen to pick up my suitcase."

"Oh, it's probably been stolen by now," he said, just as the barracks chief had. He yawned widely. It was a pleasure to be on night guard duty, he said, when there was a card game going. The guards would play all night, hardly noticing the hours as they passed. A lot of money changed hands then. But if they didn't play cards the night seemed to drag on forever.

When I got up to go, just before five, we shook hands, and I walked off down the road. It wasn't really any harder to come and go than in Bremen. The armed guards were just a formality.

At first the streetcar was nearly empty, but as we approached the center of Hannover it filled up, then emptied at the station. I went in and found that a ten-mark bribe would get me a ticket on the express to Bremen, which was due in an hour. Without the bribe I would have had to ride the local, which crawled from stop to stop, groaning with people, and I would have spent half the afternoon getting to Bremen. The express would be packed, too—standing room only—but I would get there in five hours instead of eight. I was glad for the time to look around the black market before the train came. I might be able to find a contact.

Outside the station, even this early, a huge crowd of people mingled, pushing each other around, whispering, and trading. Suspicious glances were exchanged as the traders sized each other up—grimy people, dirty, shifty-eyed leftovers from the war, without work, without money, with little ambition left except to survive in this human refuse heap. Cigarettes, meat, marks, ration cards, sugar, butter, coffee, herring, dollars, soap, Lucky Strikes, Camels, dollars, more cigarettes. The black market, Hannover Hauptbahnhof.

I mingled with the crowd, keeping my eye out for a

particular type: the man who had others doing his looking, sniffing for him, pushing their way into the thick of the crowd to see what was going for how much, and reporting back to him. Prices changed constantly, and through his scouts such a man kept his finger on the pulse of the black market.

Then I spotted him—an alert, commanding little man in a tightly belted trench coat, who stayed at the edge of things waiting and watching while three or four men slipped in and out of the crowd and whispered to him. I walked over.

"Would you be interested in a camera?"

He turned toward me with the quick movement of a bird of prey and rapped out, "Where is it? What kind is it?"

Moving a little way off from his mob of informers, I described the camera, a standard make of thirty-five millimeters, and explained that I was going to Bremen to pick it up and he could have it by tonight. I saw that he was in his forties and that his clothes were old but well tailored, pressed, and clean. He had the keen bright eyes and sharp profile of a hawk, and as we talked, his eyes probed the crowd expertly.

"Good. I'll give you three thousand marks if it is in good condition. Do you live around here or in Bremen?"

"I used to live in Bremen, but two days ago I was transferred to the transit camp here at Buchholz."

"Very good. I need someone in a camp. If you come back I'll make you a proposition." He gave me an address not far from the station. "When you get off the train look for me here first, and if I'm not around go to this address and ask for Oskar. That's my name." We shook hands, and he turned his attention back to the swarm of traders.

At the station, the Bremen express had just come in. It was jammed, but I elbowed my way as best I could near a window. The air wasn't any fresher there, but because of the light it seemed less suffocating. The train started with a jolt, and hundreds of people swayed helplessly against their neighbors.

The countryside was covered with dirty January snow. Here and there the wind had blown it away, and the brown, tired-looking earth showed in patches. I somehow felt sorry for the earth, sorry for the packed train, the laboring engine—and I almost felt sorry for Siki. But not quite.

Siki had escaped from East Berlin, and I had met him in Halmerweg. He was a brash, nervy kid of sixteen or seventeen, something of a wise guy, the kind who always had to have the last word. A week before I was transferred to Buchholz Siki had come to me with a proposition.

A boy Siki had known in East Berlin had also escaped and had turned up recently in Bremen. Somehow, somewhere along the way, this kid had picked up a good camera, but instead of telling Siki about it he went out and tried to sell it himself on the black market. Not knowing anything about the local scene, the kid ended up in the hands of a notorious sharp practitioner named Hans. Hans told the boy, "I can sell the camera for you, but you must leave it with me so I can show it to an American friend of mine." It was a plausible enough story, since only the Americans were buying luxuries like cameras. The boy gave Hans the camera. The next day Hans told the kid he was sorry, but the American military police had caught him in the act of trading and had confiscated the camera. A few days later word got around the camp that Hans had a camera for sale.

Siki's idea was that the two of us should get the camera away from that bastard. I asked him how he thought we could do that. In his usual cocksure way, Siki said, "I've already told Hans that I know a rich American who wants just such a camera and that tomorrow I will bring him over to see it and we'll settle on a price."

I stared at Siki, wondering what this had to do with me, and then I understood. It was ridiculous. I hadn't been eating too badly on the black market, but I was still very skinny, and there were several deep frown lines in my forehead. Russia had left its marks. "Siki, do I look like a rich American?"

"Oh, I've thought of that. I got you some clothes for the occasion. We'll go to Hans's apartment, and I'll do all the talking. You only have to grunt an occasional 'okay.' I'll talk more English than I really know, but he's no English professor himself, it'll sound convincing. Then we'll say we're going to your ship to get however many cartons of cigarettes we've agreed on. On the way we'll just take the camera away from him. It's simple."

"Why did you choose me for this?"

"You're a big guy, very sure of whatever you do. All Americans are confident, and so are you."

"What do I get for my services?"

"Half. We'll sell the camera and split the take."

"I've seen Hans several times at the black market. How do I know he won't recognize me?"

"You don't spend that much time around there. Anyway, you'll be wearing sharp clothes, and it'll be dark. And Hans is very greedy. He'll just be thinking about the rich American and easy money."

Siki already had the clothes in his locker, a pair of sharply creased brown pants and a sport shirt. It was cold outside, but the Americans we saw seldom wore overcoats off their ships, so it wouldn't seem too strange for me to show up in just a shirt. Hans lived not far from the port where my ship was supposed to be docked.

I agreed to the scheme, and that night we met Hans in his apartment. The sharp-faced little man grudgingly handed me the camera, and I pretended to examine it while he and Siki haggled over the price. Hans was a tough negotiator, but Siki was tougher. It went back and forth for a while, and then Siki said something to me and gave me a significant look. I said, "Okay, okay," out of the side of my mouth, the way it was done in the gangster movies I'd seen as a kid, and the price was settled—fifteen cartons of cigarettes. I was still holding the camera, but Hans snatched it out of my hands and said, "Let's go to the Yank's ship and get this over with." He put on his coat and hat, and we left the apartment.

I knew the area we were walking through pretty well—mostly rubble and bomb craters, a shortcut to the port. It was dark, but my eyes soon adjusted, the one advantage I had from my two years in the mine. Hans was following me and Siki was just behind. They spoke to each other from time to time. As we approached a deep crater I walked to the edge and bent down pretending to tie a shoelace. When Hans came up behind me I straightened and grabbed the camera from him. He opened his mouth to yell, and I slapped him across the mouth with my open hand. Before he could pull himself together I handed Siki the camera and hit Hans again on the side of the head. Down into the crater he went.

Siki and I ran through the rubble and across the gaping ditches. We'd gone about fifteen paces when Hans got his voice back. "Police! Police! Help! Help!" I was amazed at how much noise the little weasel could make. He kept shouting, and we kept running.

Then a siren wailed and searchlights began sweeping the area. It must have been the guards from the nearby American army depot looking into the disturbance. Gazing around wildly in the dark, I saw a bunker with a boardwalk leading to it. I grabbed Siki and pulled him under the boardwalk. Our hearts thumped like gongs as we tried to breathe quietly. A detachment of German police had joined the hunt, and we could hear them crunching through the rubble, cursing and calling back and forth. Their flashlight beams crisscrossed less than a hundred yards away.

Twenty minutes later it was quiet. Siki wanted to leave, but I forced him back down on the ground. It was too quiet too soon. We waited in silence in the dark and cold mud for what seemed an incredibly long time. Siki started to say something, but I put my hand over his mouth. Then, not ten yards from the bunker, we heard whispering. Two policemen walked slowly away.

A few hours later we got back to our camp, and in the morning we went to see Rudy, a tailor I knew who did a lot of work for American soldiers. I'd done business through him often. He had a customer for almost anything.

Siki wanted four cartons of cigarettes for the camera, four thousand marks' worth. Rudy said three was the best he could do. But Siki persisted, and that annoyed me. I knew Rudy. He was an honest man, and if he said three cartons was it, then he really couldn't do any better. As Siki connived to get more out of him, it got embarrassing. I decided to leave the camera with Rudy and wait a few days before we settled on a price.

The next day a young Polish DP I had helped once in a mess-hall fight came to see me. He said he had overheard Siki bragging that he would get the better of the dumb guy from the Balkans, that he'd snatch the camera out from under my nose and sell it. I thanked the Pole for telling me, but before I could decide what to do I got my orders to report to Buchholz.

I told Siki I was leaving for another camp but would be back within two weeks for my share of the sale. Then I went to Rudy and told him that under no circumstances was he to turn the camera over to Siki.

Rudy laughed. "Oh, that one was here yesterday trying to get it. He said he had a buyer. I told him to bring the buyer here and we would come to an understanding. Don't worry. I'll take care of the camera until you come back for it."

And now I was on the express going back to Bremen for the camera.

The uncomfortable five-hour train ride finally ended, and I got out on the familiar crowded plaza in front of Bremen Hauptbahnhof. From the station it was only a few blocks to Rudy's place, and when I walked in Rudy hailed me.

"What a coincidence! Siki was here only half an hour ago. He said that you had gone to America and I was supposed to give the camera to him. I told him to show me a postcard from you in America and then I would give him the camera. He stormed out of here. He was furious." Rudy laughed.

I thanked Rudy, gave him thirty marks for his trouble, and took the camera.

On my way back to the station I wondered what would

happen if I ran into Siki in the black-market mob, but I didn't see him. I also wondered what had become of the kid from Berlin. Hans had stolen the camera from him, and we had stolen it from Hans. Then Siki had tried to double-cross me, so I was taking the camera away from him. From the way he'd talked about his friend from Berlin, I was pretty sure the kid had stolen the camera from a German in the first place. Well, I was about to break the chain of theft by selling the damn thing.

I got back to Hannover at about nine o'clock in the evening. Snow was falling, but the black-market crowd was as dense and active as ever. It wouldn't thin out until eleven, twelve, even one o'clock. My contact, Oskar, was nowhere in sight. I thought about going to look for him at the address he had given me, but it was late, and I still had an hour's streetcar ride back to camp. Besides, I was wary of venturing into strange territory at night. Better to look for him tomorrow, in daylight, in the trading crowd. I was running to catch my streetcar when I heard someone whistle sharply. I turned and saw Oskar running toward me.

"I'm glad I caught you," he said, and took the camera to examine. From the way he held it and turned it over in his hands to check the shutter and settings, I could tell he had handled many cameras. Finally he nodded and, pulling an old, bulging billfold from his pocket, he began to count out money—thirty hundred-mark bills. I re-counted them and put them in my pocket. With a fat pocket I felt much safer.

"Do you have to get back to the camp?" Oskar asked. "Come with me and I'll buy you something to drink."

I agreed. Oskar intrigued me. And he was a contact; my black marketeer's sense told me to be alert to every opportunity. Camp and sleep would have to wait. 1807392

After a five-minute walk from the station we entered a restaurant. The waiters and many of the patrons greeted Oskar warmly and with respect. He ordered me a bottle of dark *Malzbier* and left me alone while he went into the back of the restaurant.

I looked around. The place was about half full. Twenty-five or thirty people sat at tables eating, talking, and gesturing, and a few men were at the bar drinking beer. The atmosphere was lively, but as shabby as the rest of Germany in 1948. It was obvious that the place had seen better days. The floor showed where a rug had been not so long ago, and the walls had light-colored squares where several large paintings must have hung before they were removed and sold. The waiters' pants were shiny and patched, but impeccably clean, and the older waiters carried themselves with an unmistakable dignity. I guessed that this had been a very fine restaurant before the war. Even in poverty it had kept its pride and class.

Oskar was back at the table. He smiled. "You see," he said, "I own this restaurant." I looked at him with surprise. He beckoned to a nearby waiter. "Fritz, come here and tell him who owns this place."

The waiter arched his eyebrows, looked at me, and said, "*Ja, ja, das Restaurant hier gehört dem Herrn Oskar.*"

As we talked I saw another Oskar emerging, far more relaxed and convivial than the hawk of the black market. The lines of his face softened, his eyes danced, and he looked younger. On his home ground he could afford to let down his guard. But it was more than that. All good black marketeers operated on instinct, and Oskar had made a quick decision that he could trust me. I knew that if his instinct alerted him, if he sensed anything fishy, the warmth would vanish instantly from his face, and he would become the other Oskar.

He explained that he traded on the black market mainly to supply his restaurant with meat, oil, coffee, sugar, vegetables, and the like, so as to keep his service at as high a standard as possible. Then he told me about a very unusual setup in another DP camp near Hannover. The camp actually ran a bazaar where a DP could buy almost anything if he had the money. "They say the head of that camp is a crazy Corsican bandit who took it over from the English," Oskar said. "He gets whatever he needs from God knows where, and they have a sausage factory and a bakery going right there in the camp. It's like a little empire." He shook his head in amazement. The hitch was that only DPs with DP identification could get into that camp to trade. This was where I came in.

"Sometime," Oskar said, "I would like to cook a nice peacetime meal for some of my friends, and to do this with ration cards is impossible. Would you go shopping at that camp for me?"

"Of course. As soon as I get my identification cards I will gladly go for you."

We were interrupted by a slight commotion near the door. A slender, dark-blonde girl in her twenties had come in and was making her way toward our table, attracting appreciative attention. Some of the people seemed to know her.

Oskar said, "Ah, here is little Rita," and pulled out a chair for her. She sat down and put her hand on his arm, half possessively, half for reassurance, and looked at me with a wary curiosity.

"Rita, this is Karl," Oskar said, pulling a name out of the air. "He is going to shop for us at the big bazaar."

"Hello, Karl," Rita said, and smiled. She had a low, pleasant voice and a sweet smile, but she seemed nervous, like a bird that might fly away at any moment. She asked Oskar for a cigarette, and he offered her an English Player. She lit it, inhaled deeply, and shook back her hair, blowing out the smoke and studying me with clear gray eyes. At one moment she seemed young and fragile, the next very knowing.

She and Oskar chatted and laughed familiarly for a while. I was suddenly tongue-tied. What did I have to say to a fresh young girl, with the kind of life I led? She seemed to be Oskar's girlfriend, yet she kept glancing at me. I didn't know what was expected of me. When she shook her hair back with that nervous motion, or laughed at something Oskar said, I was aware of the fine slenderness of her throat. It looked vulnerable. I caught myself thinking that I would have to protect a girl like this. And I had enough trouble looking out for myself.

The wall clock said twenty minutes to twelve. Oskar saw

me looking at the time, and said, "Ah! I will get you a taxi back to your camp."

"But there are no taxis," I said.

"For you there is one." Oskar signaled to one of the waiters. He gave me a card with his telephone number. "Call me as soon as you get your identification cards." I said a brusque good night to Rita, who gave me her small, cool hand and another smile.

Oskar came outside with me to wait for the taxi. "You like Rita?" he asked, as we stood there in the snow.

I was caught off balance by the question. It sounded as if Oskar was offering her to me. But I was geared to take care of my belly and to keep myself warm and in one piece—that was enough. I didn't have the time or the energy to think about women, let alone other people's women.

"She is a very good-looking girl," I answered finally.

"Then I will introduce you to several fine girls," Oskar said, with an expansive gesture.

"I don't need a procurer."

"Oh, God, not that way! I didn't mean it that way. I know the people and you don't, so for me it is easier."

The taxi pulled up, an old black Opel. I shook Oskar's hand and promised to call him as soon as my identification papers came through. Then I climbed in and told the driver how to get to Buchholz.

It was strange and luxurious to be riding alone in a taxi, even an old one. I felt a little like an impostor, the pauper pretending to be a prince. When I stepped out at my destination, the mansion, the palace, would turn back into a dreary DP camp, and I would be exposed for what I was.

At camp I thanked the driver, said a few words to the guard on duty, and went to my barracks. I found my cot by the faint glow of the stove. Some of the DPs were snoring; others turned and whimpered restlessly in their sleep. In their dreams they were probably back in the war years, running, running to escape from a guard, or on the black market, hugging a hot item, hunted by the police. I knew those nightmares. I undressed and got into my cot, holding the three thousand marks tightly in my hand. Sleeping with one eye open was nothing new to me, either.

Now I had money and my first big contact. And the image of Rita kept floating disturbingly in front of my eyes. But none of that mattered. I probably wouldn't be in Hannover much longer.

I didn't know it, but my black-market career was about to begin in earnest.

On my way to the camp canteen the next morning the barracks chief stopped me and asked about my suitcase. I told him it had been stolen, just as he predicted.

"Sons of whores!" he exclaimed. "You can't turn your back on them. We DPs lost the war, and now we steal from each other. They screwed us all, and now we screw each other."

"I've seen our people do far worse than steal suitcases from each other," I replied.

"Our people." A year in DP camps, and it was the dispossessed I thought of as "my people." As if we had become a sort of nation of the lost and homeless, a nation of cutthroats and thieves, created by war and shaped by hunger and fear, that would leave its mark more surely than any real nationality. Yet what we shared most of all was the dream of escaping it, the dream of a "normal" life—whatever that was. We could hardly remember.

And still, this ragtag "nation" had its aristocracy, too, a rough-and-tumble aristocracy of the clever and strong—those who thrived on the anarchy of the black-market era and made their own kind of order out of it. I was about to meet one of them, and with that meeting to move onto another level of the DP world.

I was sitting in the canteen wondering how to pass the time until my medical examination, idly listening to two Serbs tell each other how good the beer had been at home, when I heard an explosive *"Cristosu Dumnezeu!"* ("Christ's mother!"), a rich Rumanian curse. I looked around and saw the bartender rubbing his head, which he had bumped bending down for something. And then I saw what I hadn't noticed before: he looked the way only a real Rumanian can look, small, with black hair, a Roman nose, high cheekbones, and lively black eyes.

He saw me staring at him and called over, *"Esti roman?"*

"Da sigur. Of course," I said.

"De unde?"

"Sunt din Brasov."

"I am from Bucharest," he said. "I was captured by the English." He drew two beers and brought them over to my table.

And that was how I met the canteen chief, Jony Mateescu. We were friends immediately, not just because we spoke the same language, but because I sensed in him a kindred spirit, a lively, lovable thief, and he must have sensed the same in me.

Jony told me he had been the captain of a Rumanian army division that was stranded in Germany when Rumania changed sides. The division had eventually surrendered to the English, and as the highest-ranking officer Jony had been put in charge of his men at the prisoner-of-war camp they were sent to. After a year the POW camp was dismantled, and Jony was transferred to a DP camp near Hannover— the one Oskar had told me about, the one that had a DP bazaar run by the crazy Corsican.

Jony had become the Corsican's partner. It wasn't until

later that I learned about some of the escapades they had gotten into together on the black market. For now, Jony just grinned and said his life in that camp had been pretty wild. "That crazy bastard can go three nights without sleeping. He drinks *rachiu* as if it were water. He's as strong as ten normal men. I had a hell of a time keeping up with him." He laughed. "You ought to meet him. You look pretty strong yourself."

I told Jony about my two years in the mine and how I had developed powerful arms and shoulders shoveling coal. I told him briefly about my escape, and when I finished he gave a long, low whistle.

"What you did is impossible," he said, shaking his head. "But then, of course you Transylvanians are savages. The ordinary laws don't apply to you, either." He laughed again. "Vasile will love you. Don't worry about going shopping in that camp. If he hears your story he'll try to *give* you everything you want. That's how he is."

When Jony had decided where he wanted to emigrate he had been transferred to Buchholz, the transit camp for Canada and Australia, while Vasile, who wanted to go back to Corsica, had stayed in his old camp. But before leaving Vasile's camp Jony had gotten married. When he talked about his wife and their three-month-old baby his face sobered and he looked troubled. A wife and child were a heavy responsibility in times like these.

Maria was a Rumanian girl, from Bukovina. When the Russian soldiers had come in burning, looting, and raping, Maria's family had urged her to flee westward with a German division. She found refuge in Vasile's camp, and there she met Jony and became his girl. He was not too well, and the wild life of drinking, smoking, and staying up nights with Vasile hadn't helped any. Maria took care of him. That was one reason he married her. The other was that she had become pregnant. Not long after they moved to Buchholz the camp doctor delivered their son.

The English captain in charge of Buchholz had known

Jony at the Rumanian POW camp and was sure he could be trusted with the responsibility of the canteen. Jony was also supposed to try to keep black-market trading in the camp at a minimum. But trading outside the camp was another matter. From his days with Vasile, Jony had an overview of the black market; he knew the what, where, who, and how much of almost any deal or commodity. And he needed to provide for his family. Being canteen head put him in an ideal position to act as a middleman for DPs who were emigrating and had something to sell. And he had friends and contacts outside the camp who kept him informed of any promising opportunity. His captain vouched for him, and the English authorities left him alone.

Jony didn't tell me all this that first day, but I could sense that he was a nerve center, a man with influence and contacts, confident, alert, and well informed. He was also an adventurous fellow, a pirate at heart, who had been only a little subdued by his responsibility for his family and by his poor health.

"I'm supposed to get a lot of rest," he told me. "The doctor found some spots on my lungs, and I can't emigrate until the X rays are clean. Listen, how would you like to help me out in the canteen? I can use an extra man."

He said that I could help tend bar and keep the place clean, but that the times I would really come in handy were on the nights they had dances, every month or two. A good strong Greek wine was sold then, besides beer. The Greek who supplied the wine lived in a shack behind the camp outside the fence, and one of the strands of barbed wire had been worked loose so that someone could climb through with a suitcase and bring back twenty bottles of wine at a time. The Greek charged 80 marks a bottle, and it sold in the canteen for 125 marks. Jony said that sometimes over a hundred bottles were sold at a dance.

The regular bartender was a Polish fellow named Max. Jony told me that Max had great charm and a fabulous sense of humor, and the DPs loved him, but on dance nights he invariably got stone drunk, abandoned the bar, and danced with the pretty girls until he began to stagger and had to be led off to bed. "That's where you come in," Jony said. "If you could take over the bar from Max it would save me a lot of work."

I liked the idea very much and told Jony I would be glad to help him until my emigration came through.

"Good!" he said, and we shook hands on it. "Come on back to Barracks 1 and meet Maria."

Jony's wife was a slight, pretty, dark-haired girl whose beautiful dark eyes flashed when she spoke, belying her shyness. She showed me the sleeping baby. Jony and Maria had a whole room of the barracks to themselves, and Jony had put up wooden partitions that made it almost a little apartment— a room for the baby, a living room with a few shelves, a table and chairs, and a couch made out of a cot, and a kitchen with a coal stove, where Maria had cooked a delicious black-market *ghiveci*. The three of us shared it for dinner, along with a bottle of the Greek's red wine, which was surprisingly good.

The warmth that was growing inside me had little to do with the wine. I had been afraid of a long, dreary wait in the barracks, weeks or months fighting the atmosphere of depression, hustling on the black market to stay really alive. That I might find something like a family in a DP camp had been the furthest hope from my mind. But Jony and Maria accepted me warmly and seemed happy to share their little household, and speaking Rumanian and eating *ghiveci* made me feel even more at home. What was more, I had a job, a place and purpose in the camp. And I had the feeling that around Jony the action would not be lacking. Suddenly the wait for emigration didn't look so hard. It might even be fun.

It looked still better that evening when I met Max, the bartender, and traded stories with him. Max had the devil in him, there was no doubt about it. He was a tall, straight, slightly portly fellow with a jolly face, a full mouth, and eyes dancing with mischief. He described himself as a *Heirats-*

schwindler—a "marriage swindler." He had been married once just before the war, in Belgium, and once during the war, in Italy, and now he claimed he was engaged to a German Mennonite who had some property in Canada—his overseas insurance, he called her.

Max, who had been born on the German-Polish border, was an incurable wanderer, and so somehow he had found himself in Belgium before the war. As he told it, he walked out on his Belgian wife the day she made the mistake of asking him to push the baby carriage. That rang some kind of alarm bell in Max's mind. He stopped in front of a hotel, asked her to wait a moment while he went in to get something, walked into the hotel and out the other side, and never came back.

In Germany again, he'd been stuck in the Wehrmacht. Basic training nearly killed him, he said. He wasn't the type. But he survived it and proceeded to spend the war years as something of a *bon vivant*, mixing drinks in the Special Services. Near the end of the war he went AWOL and turned up in Italy singing in night clubs. He had a beautiful baritone, which he demonstrated to me with a few bars of Italian opera. But times were gaunt in Italy, too. When the war ended Max heard rumors of the wonderful food the Americans fed their prisoners of war. So he slipped back into Germany, got hold of a German army uniform, and gave himself up to the Americans. Like Jony, he was put in charge of a group at a prisoner-of-war camp, and there he struck up a special friendship with the cook (he patted his stomach fondly). On his release, after a year, he went straight to a DP camp, claimed to be a Pole, and told stories of how the Germans had abused him. He was admitted. He was one who could lie his way through a screening with flying colors, especially now that he was known as Jony's man. He was also a born raconteur.

The barracks became only my sleeping place. I spent my days in the canteen with Jony and Max and ate Maria's cooking with them in the evenings. In a couple of days there was to be a dance, and Max introduced me to his helper, Mitya, a Yugoslav, who was usually the one to go through the fence to the Greek's for wine. Then he showed me a little room right behind the canteen where I could sleep on dance nights if I wanted. There was a neat cot in it, and it had a window.

Looking at the room, I suddenly had an idea. "Max, could I move my things and sleep here all the time?"

"Why not?" Max said.

I decided to move into the little room right away. It would be the first privacy I had had since I was herded into that boxcar in Brasov three years ago—not counting the terrible aloneness of the bitter cold nights of my escape. When I went to the barracks to get my suitcase and blankets the other DPs looked at me with envy—except for Cheslav, who had become my friend. Behind the canteen I made up the cot, put my suitcase under it, and looked around with an almost childlike pleasure. It was small and bare, but it was my room, my home.

That Saturday I helped out at the dance, and everything went just as Jony had predicted. Twenty minutes after the band started to play there were five hundred DPs milling around or sitting at tables, talking, shouting, dancing, and drinking. Soon we had to send Mitya for another twenty bottles of wine, and then for twenty-five more.

Like Jony and Max, the band members lived in Barracks 1. They included a drummer, a saxophonist, a trumpeter, a bass player, and a white-haired old pianist who, Max said, was a music professor from Riga. According to Max, all were DPs, Latvians or Lithuanians, and they played during the week at an English officers' club. They wanted to emigrate as a group and were waiting for their papers, but, like everything else that was the least bit complicated, it took time.

Except for the fine old pianist, the musicians were all drinkers. As the dance progressed they took off their jackets, rolled up their sleeves, and opened their collars, and their mellow jazz got mellower. The DPs got noisier or more silent and withdrawn, depending on their personalities. The merrymaking was awkward, and there was a dangerous undercurrent to it. I knew that if some of them got drunk enough all their hidden passions, their anger at the way life had cheated them, could explode into savage violence. I had seen it happen in Bremen, and it scared me. But no spark set off the dry tinder at this dance.

Within an hour, sure enough, Max was too drunk to help. He couldn't talk straight, but how he could dance! Some of the young DP girls were very pretty, and they had dressed up as nicely as they could, in whatever they had been able to make or find on the black market or salvage from better times. I felt sorry for them. They deserved a little lipstick and powder, but such things, like nylons, were luxuries and just not to be had. Max made them feel beautiful. He danced with each one, sweeping her around the floor in a dashing tango as if she were the only girl in the world—and then on to the next girl, and the next bottle. Finally his dancing turned to staggering, and Mitya helped him off to bed.

It was almost 4:00 A.M. before the dance broke up and the last DPs straggled back to their barracks. I had been busy behind the bar all night, selling more than a hundred bottles of wine, but one bottle was left, and I took it over to the old piano player from Riga. I had noticed what a beautiful light touch he had. Now he began to improvise on a dreamy, nostalgic jazz melody I had never heard before. His fine, expressive face changed with the music as his hands moved over the keys. A man like him, who for a few moments could create a soft world of sound more real than the harsh DP world we lived in—I wondered what the war years had done to him, but I knew how he had survived them. I remembered the sad songs the Russian girls sang as they worked in the mine. At times I had lived in those songs.

When the old man finished and got up to go back to his barracks I thanked him, and he told me the name of the melody. It was Glenn Miller's "Moonlight Serenade."

Later, in my little room, I lay awake for a long time, too happy to sleep and too aware of the unfamiliar silence. It was strange to hear only my own breathing—no ten or fifteen others around me in the dark. In just a few days everything had changed. I felt like a lucky thief. I had made a second escape—from the tedium of barracks life and the anxious treadmill of trading. And as always, given even a small margin of security, I began to feel the itch for adventure.

It was not long in coming.

The next morning I went into the canteen and found Max laughing and groaning, holding his head, and drinking beer to cure his hangover. Jony came in and complimented me on my work at the dance. He said that the most he had ever made in one night was five thousand marks, and last night we had taken in six thousand.

Suddenly he stopped and looked at me. "Can you butcher a pig?"

The question surprised me, but I said I could. Our neighbor at home had been the Balkans' foremost sausage maker, and during summer vacations I had watched and occasionally helped with the butchering. I was pretty sure I could remember how to do it. "But who has a pig these days?"

"We will have one," Jony said. "A friend of mine who chauffeurs for an UNRRA officer can use the car tonight, and he'll drive us to a village where we can buy a pig."

There was a law in Germany requiring every farmer who had cattle, pigs, or any other kind of livestock to register them with his *Bürgermeister* because of the shortage of meat. The state needed every pound it could get. But in the more obscure villages some of the pig farmers didn't report them all, and when they had a litter of little ones they would keep one or two for themselves or sell them into black-market channels. If they got caught the punishment was stiff, so the sale of a pig had to be undertaken by night and with the utmost caution.

Jony's friend, the chauffeur for UNRRA (the United Nations Relief and Rehabilitation Administration), had found a farmer who was willing to sell one. We would drive to his village tonight, butcher the pig, and bring it back. If all went well, we would keep some of the meat for ourselves, and the rest we could sell in the Corsican's bazaar.

"I think I have a sure customer," I said. "I told you about my contact, Oskar, the one who bought the camera. He would love to have some fresh pork for his restaurant, and maybe we could take him along to the bazaar, even though he isn't a DP."

"Consider it done," Jony said.

Early that evening Jony knocked. "We're ready," he said, and pulled out from under his coat a knife wrapped in a rag. I unwrapped it and saw that it was a shiny new Solingen, the best. Behind Barracks 1 a man was busy changing the license plates on an Opel. Jony said, "This is my friend Tannov," and introduced us. Tannov, a stocky Latvian, straightened up and shook my hand with a firm grip, as if we had known each other for years and were ready to tackle anything together. They both got into the front seat, I slid in back, and we drove away.

Tannov drove fast, like a gangster, or at least as I imagined gangsters did. Trees and lampposts flashed by, snowy fields and houses, whole villages with dark, sleeping side streets. Tannov stared straight on into the bobbing headlights, slowing only when we passed a jeep with two English soldiers. No need to brush with MPs. It was an hour's wordless ride.

We were all absorbed in the speeding car and the silvery landscape.

In another little village we stopped. We must have been forty or fifty miles from camp. Tannov got out and looked at a street sign with his flashlight, then drove slowly for another four or five minutes, made a turn into a side street, and stopped again. He and Jony got out. I was to wait in the car until we drove into the farmyard.

I rolled the window down and let in the fresh, cold air. In spite of the snow on the ground, the night was very dark, with only a thin, crooked slice of moon. A dog barked a few times; then all was silent.

In my mind I went over and over the butchering and quartering of a pig until I was sure I could do it. The last time had been five or six years ago, and that had been in another world, a world of unbelievable abundance, where sides of pork hung in ranks in our neighbor's slaughterhouse and sausages hung like fruit from the rafters of my father's store. Had I dreamed it all?

The gate to the farmer's yard squeaked. Tannov got in the car and drove slowly into the yard, stopping near a dimly lit barn in the rear. The farmer, urging us to be quiet, went into the barn first. We followed him, and the pungent smell of manure engulfed me. I saw two cows and a horse in separate stalls. Toward the back of the barn the stench grew stronger yet, and there were the pigs. Even before we reached the pigsty we could hear them shuffling around and grunting. There were five or six of them, weighing 150 to 200 pounds each.

The farmer touched one on the back to indicate the chosen victim. Then he picked up a well-balanced ax, took the flashlight from Tannov, and climbed into the pigsty. He tried to corner the pig by scratching its back and shoving it with his knees, but the pig was young and frisky and wouldn't stand still to be hit over the head. Before long the farmer was dripping sweat and cursing under his breath. The flashlight beam wobbled around, showing the restless backs of the other pigs. The struggle went on in almost total silence.

Suddenly the farmer swung wildly and missed, nicking the pig's ear. The silence was shattered by a terrified squealing that made all of us cringe and brought the farmer's wife running. "Ohhh, *mein Gott!*" she wailed. "The neighbors must have heard. Now we will go to jail." And she flapped her apron as if to shush the pig, glaring around accusingly. We were all frightened. I had a sudden ludicrous vision of the pig escaping into the yard, into the street, squealing in terror, while the farmer held on to its tail with one hand, dragging the ax in the other, losing his hat, but hanging on for dear life to the *Schweinefleisch.* Maybe the whole village would join in the chase for *Schweinefleisch.* After all, for most of them that was what the war had been about.

At last the pig's squealing subsided to snuffles and grunts. We listened, but there was no shout or footstep outside. I felt sorry for the poor pig, but if it had to die it might as well go as quickly and painlessly as possible. Taking the ax from the farmer, I climbed over the boards and scratched the pig's back till it stood still. Then I swung the ax over my head and brought it down with everything I had. There was a hollow crunch, and the pig fell over. Jony handed me the knife, and I turned the pig around and stuck the knife into its heart. Warm blood spurted out on my hand and sleeve, and the pig gave a few feeble kicks. I stepped back to let it die.

In three or four minutes the blood stopped running, and we dragged the pig out to the car. Tannov opened the trunk, and the farmer helped us lift the carcass in. I washed my hands and sleeve in the snow, cleaned the blood off my shoes, and got into the back seat of the car. The farmer pocketed the money Jony gave him, promising to send us word when he had another pig to sell. Jony and Tannov got in, and we drove away.

On the way I asked Jony whether he couldn't quarter the pig in the washroom of Barracks 1—just barricade the door and tell anyone wanting in that the plumbing was being repaired and he'd have to go to another barracks. Jony thought that was a good idea.

Now Tannov drove more slowly, to avoid attracting the attention of military or German police. In one of the smaller towns he pulled in to a gas station. As an UNRRA chauffeur he had ration cards for gas. While the attendant was filling the tank a police car drove up. Two German policemen stepped out, apparently taking a break, stretching their legs and lighting cigarettes. They greeted the attendant and looked casually at our car.

Tannov was standing near them, and one of the policemen said, "There is some water leaking from your trunk, or from the engine."

I knew it was blood from the pig, and I also knew that as soon as we drove away and they saw it was blood, not water, the chase would be on. From the look Jony gave me, he knew it, too. He got out of the car for a moment and spoke quietly to Tannov. When the tank was full Tannov paid for the gas and waited for the attendant to finish wiping the windshield. I was impressed at how calm he seemed. My heart was thumping so loudly that it wouldn't have surprised me if the cops had heard it and come over to investigate.

Tannov got in and started the motor. As we began to move he whispered, "I'll drive away slowly, and both of you keep watching the policemen. If they see the blood right away I'll have to do some very fast driving."

We drove off slowly, in the wrong direction, away from camp. The dark stain we had left on the ground still looked like water, but one of the policemen bent down to take a closer look. Suddenly he straightened up and shouted something to his companion, and they ran for their car. Tannov floored the accelerator and we raced away.

Luckily the road was straight. We flashed through the countryside, then through a village, and I looked at the speedometer: ninety kph. "It won't go any faster," Tannov said through clenched teeth. Another town rushed at us. At the last minute Tannov braked hard, turned down a side street, then another and another. Stopping suddenly, he shut off the motor and the lights, and we sat in the dark breathing hard. Within a minute we heard the police car tearing down the main street of the town, siren screaming.

The siren faded away, and we sat for three or four more minutes without saying anything. Then Tannov turned the car around and drove back toward camp while Jony and I kept a watch on the road behind us. Safely inside the camp gate, we all sighed with relief and then broke into shaky but triumphant laughter.

The camp was dark and silent. Tannov drove behind Barracks 1 and maneuvered the car up to the back door of the washroom. Jony hung an out-of-order sign on the entrance and went to get his stove going so we could heat water. Tannov and I dragged the dead pig into the washroom, and Jony blocked the door with two chairs. Each time someone knocked Jony called out, "A pipe is plugged up. There's a plumber working in here."

By the time the water boiled the pig was beginning to stiffen. Jony brought me the water, and I went to work. After I took out the guts I halved the pig with a small hatchet, and we hung the halves on two big nails on the wall. Jony had me cut off twelve or fifteen pounds of meat apiece for Tannov, him, and me. The rest we wrapped in a blanket and put aside. Maria had already begun cooking a stew with the organs and some of the meat, and the smell of frying meat and onions made us fiercely hungry.

We woke up Max and Mitya, for the feast was for all our little family. Maria had set the table with a clean white cloth. Jony opened two bottles of the red Greek wine, to go with Maria's two potfuls of delicious stew. Chewing a big chunk of meat and washing it down with wine, Max sighed, "If they fed us like this every day no one would go over the water."

When we couldn't eat any more, Jony opened another bottle of wine and Max started singing in his rich baritone. We all joined in. Sitting at a table with friends and wine and a stomach full of rich, warm stew, I felt miles away from the cold barracks.

We drank and sang until dawn.

5

A gentle hand touched my forehead and woke me. Bright sunshine was streaming through the little window above my cot. "Wake up, my boy," Jony said. "Tannov is waiting to drive us to the bazaar." He smiled. "And next time take all your clothes off before you go to sleep."

I washed up, put on my jacket, and asked Jony if I shouldn't lock the door to my room to make sure my share of the meat would be safe. "No, don't worry," he said. "Max won't let anybody in."

Tannov was standing by the car. "The meat is already packed in the trunk," he said. "Tell me where to pick up this fellow Oskar. Jony says we're taking him with us to the bazaar."

I told him to go straight to the plaza in front of the train station in Hannover, where the black-market crowd gathered. What took the streetcar an hour and a quarter Tannov made in fifteen minutes. At the station, he and Jony waited while I got out of the car and went to look for Oskar. Within three minutes I had found him, surrounded as usual by four or five seedy-looking types. He hailed me and shook my hand.

"Are you ready to go shopping?" I asked.

"You mean at the bazaar?" He stared at me. "But I—"

I waved him to silence. "Come on. I'll explain."

He said a few words to his army of informers, and they scattered into the crowd. As we walked toward the street Oskar started to ask me how I could take him into the DP bazaar, but then we came in sight of the car, and I saw two policemen standing there talking to Tannov. My heart stopped.

I whispered to Oskar, "That looks bad. We have about one hundred pounds of fresh pork for you in the trunk."

Oskar's hand shot out and grabbed my arm like a vise. He was immediately electrified, as he had been when I told him about the camera. We hurried to the car, and Oskar greeted the policemen in a tone of cordial authority and asked whether anything was the matter. Whatever his magic was, they grinned, said a few words to him, and walked away.

Jony and Tannov looked a little pale. I introduced Oskar to them, and the two of us got in the back seat. Oskar told Tannov how to get to his restaurant.

As Tannov drove, Oskar kept asking me, "Is it true? Do you really have fresh, real pork?" His eyes shone with excitement, like a young boy's on Christmas Eve. At the restaurant he jumped out and ran around to the trunk, staring thunderstruck when Tannov opened it and unwrapped the fresh meat for him. Then he grabbed me, kissed me on the cheek, and began dancing up and down, laughing with the rest of us.

"How much is this beautiful meat?" he asked Jony joyously.

"How does twelve thousand marks sound to you?"

Oskar ran into the restaurant, and in two minutes he was back with the money. When it was all counted and in Jony's pocket Oskar carried the meat inside.

He came out and said, "Now, I still don't understand how I can get into the bazaar with you. I am not a DP, and I have no identification."

"Jony used to be an officer of that camp," I told him. "We can take you in. It's no problem."

He looked doubtfully at Jony, but Jony waved toward the car, and Oskar, beaming, climbed in. Tannov raced the motor, and away we roared, Oskar still in ecstasy about his meat. "*Ach! Schweinebraten, Bratwurst, Schinken. Ach, Junge!* You saved me!" He leaned toward me and squeezed my arm with such insistent enthusiasm that I suddenly wondered whether he might be a homosexual. Then I remembered his girl friend, Rita. No, Oskar was just overflowing with energy. I asked him how Rita was. "Fine, fine! I will give her to you. She's yours. You have saved me!"

This camp was on the outskirts of Hannover in a different direction from Buchholz. A guard with a rifle stood at the gate, but when he saw Jony he grinned and saluted, and we drove right through.

The camp was laid out like a die showing a five. There was a big barracks in each of the four corners and one right in the center. As we drove in I could see the fluttering canopies of market stalls behind the central barracks. We parked the car and walked over to the bazaar.

In a lane between facing stands hundreds of DPs hummed and surged like a hive of bees. Spread out before us were pork back, beans, sugar, honey, flour, potatoes, barley, rice, meats, candy. We were pushed from stand to stand among the bargaining gibberish of Europe's lost nationalities. I stared in wonderment. That much food might sometimes be circulating invisibly in a black-market crowd, but to see it openly displayed as in the old days, all together in one place, was dizzying. It reminded me of the village bazaars I had seen in Russia, with the difference that every nationality was here and the trading went on in all the languages of Eastern Europe. And I was here without a guard, not as a prisoner with a few pitiful rubles of my "salary" saved to buy a jacket. I had money in my pocket and could do as I pleased. I bought two bars of soap, a tube of French toothpaste, and some hard candy.

I noticed that wherever the bargaining was loudest and most hectic Oskar was in the thick of it. He was weighed down with packages, but he kept buying more and more. I went over to him. "You don't have to buy everything. We'll bring you back."

"Yes, yes," he said. "But look at this, and this!"

Taking half his load, I carried it to the car. I had had enough of the shoving and dickering, and I knew Jony was buying the food for our meals.

Soon Jony and Tannov came back loaded down with food for their wives and families. Oskar was last, a bundle of packages. We put almost everything in the trunk, and then Jony asked Oskar and Tannov to wait by the gate in the car.

And said to me, "Now you must meet Vasile."

When we entered the guard shack it took my eyes a moment to adjust to the darkness. The apparition that came toward us was dark and wild, with a mane of uncombed black hair, piercing black eyes, a hawk nose above full lips, and teeth that flashed white as he grinned in recognition and shouted, "*Hahh*—Jony!" He was broad, powerful, and not quite six feet tall, but the force of his vitality was elemental; it struck me like a blow. When he and Jony shouted and embraced I thought Jony would be crushed. What hands and arms—they were lethal weapons!

Jony introduced me as his new right-hand man. The swarthy titan grabbed my hand and tried to crush it, but somehow I had anticipated that. As he tried to ruin my hand, to win this battle of strength, his eyes tried to conquer me, too. They were hypnotic.

Then, as abruptly as it had started, the struggle was over. Booming laughter filled the room, and he pounded Jony on the back. "You got a good man here, a good man!" I was also pounded on the back.

"Take it easy. Take it easy, you crazy Bulgarian," Jony gasped. "Don't kill him yet!"

Another volley of laughter from Vasile. It was contagious and so were the waves of garlic coming from his mouth. I guessed his age at around thirty. He took a bottle from under the table, brought three glasses, and filled them to the top, handing one to each of us. We drank to our health, and the liquid was as fiery and strong as Vasile. Vasile downed his in one gulp, saying "*Noroc, mult noroc*" ("Luck, much luck"). It was nice to have him say it in Rumanian. I felt the alcohol warming my insides.

Jony told Vasile that I would be coming to shop at the bazaar from time to time. Vasile said that was fine, and that I could sleep here, too, whenever I wanted. "Jony, you know everything I have is yours." He turned to me. "Listen, man, Jony here is my best friend—take good care of him. Whenever you come here just stop in to see me, and I will see that you get whatever you want. And you don't have to pay anything. If you are Jony's friend you are my friend."

We shook hands again, and as Jony and I went out to the car Vasile's laugh followed us into the weak winter sunlight like a gust from the underworld.

On the drive back Jony told me Vasile's story. He was one DP the war years hadn't beaten down; he was unconquerable, he would die of old age or murder. "You see how he dresses? It's winter and it's cold out, but he hardly ever wears a jacket. He has one somewhere, he just never wears it. His black shirt, the black pants, and the boots—he has others, but they're all alike."

Vasile's father had been a wild Corsican, a vagabond and circus strong man. When the circus was out of season he traveled through the Balkans trading, stealing, smuggling, working at odd jobs he liked, being royally welcomed in every gypsy camp. He spoke all the Balkan languages and knew that part of Europe like he knew his own hand—and a powerful hand it must have been when the old man was young.

In a tiny Bulgarian village, one summer during his wanderings, his fancy was taken by a girl, a spirited, black-eyed

59

beauty. But he was not the kind to settle down and farm. After a short courtship he just carried her off—and she took to the life of the open air like a duck to water. Of course, she was soon pregnant, and her pregnancy hampered the roaming, so he took her back to Corsica, and there he displayed her proudly. They stayed at home until Vasile, their pride, was born, and soon after his birth they took to the road again. That was how Vasile grew up; that was his education. Winters in Corsica, but come spring the little family was on the road, traveling with the circus or some wandering gyspy camp.

When Vasile was seven years old, his father left him and his mother in a room somewhere near Trieste one day while he went out to collect money that was owed him. A local moneylender who hated the old man crept to the room where mother and son were waiting. He burst in, knocked Vasile out, and brutally raped his mother.

Vasile woke up to find his father raging like a wild animal and his mother bloody, bruised, and moaning. She had fought the moneylender like a wildcat, but he had knocked her cold, torn her clothes off, and had his violent way with her. The raging father ordered an old woman to stay with her, kicked Vasile in the ass, and they went looking for the moneylender.

The man had gone into hiding in the woods outside Trieste. For three days they searched, asking questions of every band of gypsies, before they found him asleep in a shepherd's tent. Vasile watched while his father beat the man to an unrecognizable pulp, then grabbed the shepherd, beat him for hiding such a man, and left him, cringing and trembling, to dispose of the remains of the moneylender.

Back in their room, they found the old woman wringing her hands and the young wife and mother in shock. Hurriedly they started for Corsica, but she must have been hurt inside, for on the way she died. They had both loved her very much, and they mourned her, but their life was a rough one, and after a while it went on. There would be other women to love them, feed them, and enjoy them—but never one quite like her.

So Vasile grew up: father and son, bandits, smugglers, working a little now and then, celebrating often and boisterously, making trouble for the sheer fun of it. It wasn't an easy life or a secure one, but it was wild and free.

But Europe was darkening under Hitler's war cloud, and Vasile's fate took another turn. One day in 1940, after doing an errand for his father in a small Italian border town, Vasile got very drunk and fell into a crazy brawl in a roadside tavern. He came to his senses in a jail on the Austrian border. He had no papers, and he fought the German border guards like the wild young animal he was, so they beat him unconscious. When he woke up again he was on a train, under guard, being shipped to a labor camp in Germany.

He worked until the end of the war in German factories, fighting the Germans every inch of the way, getting bruised and beaten and kicked till he passed out—he had scars all over his body. He tried to escape several times and got more brutal beatings for it. But he never gave in. Finally Germany collapsed, and Vasile found himself in a DP camp under the English occupation army. Most of the inmates were Slavs, and they soon nicknamed him "the Black Bulgar" for his swarthiness.

It was the kind of situation in which Vasile was bound to take over. A few fights, a little strong-arm larceny Vasile style, and he was feared and respected both in the camp and on the black market. Then he looked at the furtive, cop-ridden black market, and he looked at the DPs sitting around their barracks with nothing to do, and he had an idea. He knew how Slavs loved to trade; it was in their blood, in their history. One fine day he set up a few tables behind one of the barracks and told a DP, "You can trade here." He told the next one the same, and the next. He promised them protection, for a price, and the trading spread through the camp like wildfire.

Soon an interpreter came running from the headquarters

of the camp's English officers shouting, "You can't do this! It's against the law."

Vasile roared with laughter, grabbed the man, spun him around, and booted him in the ass. The poor guy ran off to the administration building and came back with a British lieutenant, who told Vasile once again, through the quacking interpreter, that trading was against the law.

Vasile reasoned with the lieutenant. If the Slavs were allowed to trade peacefully among themselves they wouldn't have to go out and get into trouble on the black market, and there would be fewer fights in camp. They had nothing else to do. Why not let them trade? They had suffered enough in the last five years. He, Vasile, would see to it personally that there wasn't any trouble among them.

The British officer listened to reason, especially since it was backed up by such obvious force. I could see Vasile standing there, his white teeth bared in a grin, his strong hands on his hips, and with those powerful black-haired forearms. The officer said, "All right, let them trade. But the first time there is any trouble the trading will have to stop."

Not only did the market run well; it prospered, and within six months the English administrators moved out altogether and left Vasile in charge of the camp. He assembled a crew of guards, fellow ruffians, and ran the place with an iron hand, collecting tribute from every trader. He kept no books —everything was in his head. He could go for three days without sleep. Often DPs new in camp started trading on the sly, thinking they could cheat Vasile out of the tribute he called "my taxes." They were quickly beaten into obedience, and Vasile remained the bandit chieftain par excellence.

He had heard from his father. The old man was alive and waiting for Vasile at home in Corsica. But Vasile had decided that he wouldn't leave Germany until he had exacted payment for his wartime labor. He would take fifty big diamonds back with him.

Diamonds, Vasile knew, were better than money. His father had taught him that this precious stone could easily be converted into any currency because its value held, unlike flimsy paper money. Vasile carried his diamonds in a small pouch around his neck; to get them away from him you would have to kill him, and neither the elements nor Balkan cutthroats nor Hitler's henchmen had been able to do that. He had once shown twenty-seven stones to Jony, but later, after I got to know him well, he showed his treasure to me, and then he had thirty-nine. Just eleven more, and he would disappear into the night and reappear at home in Corsica, unconquered and free.

There was only one problem. He had gotten entangled with a beautiful Ukrainian girl, and she wanted to emigrate to the United States. Vasile wanted no part of any new world. For him it was Corsica and his old life. Jony figured that when the time came he would just carry her off, as his father had done with his mother. He was a very strong man, his father had molded him, and a woman would have to bend to his will. What would he do in the law-bound United States, or in Canada? His was a race that was fast becoming extinct. He had outlasted Hitler and his jackals, and if anything he had grown stronger. Jony told me a day had never passed that he hadn't heard that magnificent laughter boom out of the shack at the gate where the DPs came and went paying tribute to the king—Vasile.

I hardly noticed when we arrived at Oskar's restaurant and he ran in to bring a waiter out to help unload his packages. I shook Oskar's hand, and we promised to take him shopping again, but everything was moving past me as if in a dream. The alcohol and Vasile's story had made my head spin. I had to get off by myself and let the day's powerful impressions sink in. At camp I greeted Max, went to my little room, and lay down.

That laughter . . .

No one else but my father could laugh like that. I remembered how sometimes he would get up in the middle of the night, go down to the kitchen, and get out two pounds of pork back, a few raw onions, a gallon of wine. I would join him, and with a good sharp knife he would slice off pieces of onion and raw smoked pork back, chew them, his powerful jaw muscles working, and wash them down with a big swallow of wine. Then he would throw back his head and laugh and laugh until the rafters rang, and I would laugh with him, and down in the village people would wake up and look at each other and say, "Shh—the Sandulescus are laughing."

My father had been a dignified citizen, though he was an anarchist at heart and a titanic practical joker. Vasile and his father were undisguised robber barons. Yet they were alike. We were alike.

I fell asleep feeling as if something I had lost had been found again.

The next morning I woke up early, thinking about the precious meat still under my cot. I wanted to take it to my uncle's family in Giessen. He was my mother's brother, a doctor, and he had lived in Germany since he was a young man. Before the war the family had been wealthy, not only because of my uncle's substantial earnings, but also because the German girl he had married was the daughter of an engineer in the South African diamond mines. But in postwar Germany their wealth did them little good. Like everyone else not trading on the black market, they were completely dependent on ration cards, and the family of seven—my uncle and his wife, her parents (her father was retired now), her younger sister, Angelika, and two children, their daughter and Angelika's—was barely getting by. I had visited them a couple of times when I lived in Bremen, and once I had traded a family diamond ring for eight cans of a rich Danish cheese, about four pounds each, and some butter and sugar. I was their only black-market contact, so that was probably the last good nourishing food they had had. I knew how much fifteen or twenty pounds of fresh meat would mean to them.

I made my Giessen family a little nervous. Because I was a relative they trusted me, and they were eager and grateful for whatever I brought, but they found my black-market activities exotic and frightening. To them I was that wild, crazy kid, my father's son, and my aunt and her sister had made a big fuss over me, wanting to hear more stories about Russia, feeling the muscles in my arms. All that feminine attention had embarrassed and confused me, but I liked my uncle and felt he was a link to home. I wanted to help him and his family through these hungry times.

A week had passed since the screening, a week that seemed more like a month, and I still hadn't heard anything about the medical exam. In all the excitement of meeting Jony, Max, and Vasile, of moving out of the barracks and into my new job in the canteen, I hadn't forgotten about it. Now it occurred to me that as Jony's friend I was no longer just another DP. I might not have to wait for the medical authorities to notify me. Maybe I could get it settled right now and be free to travel to Giessen. I was confident that I would pass. I felt healthy enough.

I found Jony and asked him whether he knew the doctor from the emigration department. "Let's go there right now" was his answer.

When we got to the administration building, with its long, dreary lines of people waiting, waiting, Jony winked at me and went in alone. In a few minutes he came out with the doctor, who had his arm around Jony's shoulder. The doctor, a tall, cadaverous-looking Pole with a big mustache, shook my hand and said, "I am glad to meet another Rumanian." He took me by the arm and led me into his office. The nurse brought my papers in, and the doctor gave me a thorough examination.

As I was putting my clothes back on he said, "You are very healthy, considering the punishment you took in the Russian coal mines. Your legs have healed well, and your X ray is clear. But I'm afraid your blood pressure is a little too high. Try to get a lot of rest, and come back in six months."

Six months!

With just two words this doctor had sentenced me to another half year or more in the camp and on the black market! For the moment my new friends, my job, and my new little room were forgotten, and I was alone with my terrible disappointment. Jony tried to reassure me. "Listen, don't worry. I know this doctor, and his word is good. All you have to do is get more sleep, and next time you go in for an examination he'll pass you. Believe me." But six months! My vivid dreams of America were already receding, becoming dim and unreal. They had nourished me as surely as the food they were mostly about. Now the gray DP horizon was closing in again, and I would have to accept it as my reality. I would have to ask my uncle in Giessen about this high-blood-pressure business.

Jony gave me the special identity card he had carried for two years that said he was an official of a prisoner-of-war camp and entitled to the travel privileges of an English officer. With it I could travel anywhere in the Western Zone of Germany and Austria, and could get a ticket on any express train. Wrapping the meat for my uncle in fresh newspaper, I went off to catch the streetcar. It was a cold, gray day, and as I left, the guard shack and the barbed-wire fence seemed to say, *You'll be back. And we'll still be here waiting for you.*

At the station in Hannover, I bought a ticket on a military express due in about half an hour and then wandered toward the black market. To this day I don't know what got into me; maybe, depressed as I was by the doctor's bad news, it was an urge for self-destruction, because I knew how dangerous those mobs could be. But I went into that crowd of traders and swindlers with the package of fresh meat under my arm, wondering what they would offer me for it. And I asked one of the seedier ones what fifteen pounds of fresh pork was worth.

The man's eyes bulged. He leaned over and smelled the package, feeling it roughly with his fingers. I pushed him back, and he whispered urgently to another that I had *Schweinefleisch*. They came toward me as if I had a magnet under my arm. I had made a terrible mistake. The excited crowd pressed closer and tighter around me, and I knew I had to get away from them. When they started to reach and claw at the package of meat I tore myself loose and began shoving brutally with all my strength toward the station. They followed like a pack of hungry wolves. Sweating and shoving, I finally reached the military waiting room and showed Jony's pass to the guard. He noticed the mob behind me and gave me a curious look, but he let me slip through the door.

Sanctuary. They couldn't enter here. I was on the other side of the fence now—the pistol and the uniform were protecting *me*. The waiting room was clean and elegant, with comfortably upholstered benches and a little bar at one end. A radio played soft music. Several soldiers sat reading newspapers; three or four officers stood at the bar drinking. I had fifteen minutes until train time.

About five minutes before the train was due everybody got up and began moving toward the platform. I was still frightened of the carnivorous mob outside. As I followed the English soldiers out through the general waiting room eyes glowed at me and my package. I shivered like a dog in the cold and kept close to the English soldiers. Just then the train came in.

The military express was very different from the German trains. It wasn't crowded, and it smelled clean. I was safe here. I sat in a second-class compartment with several soldiers, who joked and laughed, passing a bottle around. Listening to the sound of their foreign tongue, I gradually relaxed and let the soft rattling of the flying express put me to sleep.

The conductor woke me for my ticket and said we would

be in Kassel within the hour. Kassel, where I had first arrived in West Germany—half-dead, but safe, out of Russia's grasp. As I came up out of sleep I noticed that the pig's blood had soaked through the newspaper and the package was making my pants bloody-wet. I pulled the jacket tighter around me. The military express was punctual, and in Kassel I changed to a dirty, crowded local for Giessen, still clutching the meat under my jacket. Now my shirt was bloody, too. I squeezed into a corner of a compartment and tried to stuff the sodden, disintegrating newspaper out of sight under my jacket. Again I drowsed off into uneasy sleep.

As the nostrils of a hunted animal quiver, I sensed it. The smell of blood and fresh meat had permeated the closed compartment, and a dozen questing eyes and noses had come to a stop on me. Some of them saw the blood oozing from under my jacket. "What is it you have that smells like blood?" the shabbiest ones whispered, coming closer. I shrugged my shoulders. Then they tried to touch the package under my arm. I couldn't squirm away; I was pinned in a corner of the compartment.

One of them saw the fresh meat where soaked newspaper had fallen off the package. He reached out and felt it. His eyes bulged, and he gasped, "*Frisches Schweinefleisch!*" and then, in a louder voice, he cried, "*Schweinebraten, Schweinebraten!*" Several others reached scrabbling for the meat, and as I looked at the faces surrounding me, the eyes glowing with greed and hunger, I knew I was in for it. Their hands were reaching as if they wanted to devour my meat and me, too. I had to get out of the compartment. I stood up, clutching the meat, but the insistent, determined, reaching hands were all over me. With the strength of desperation I wrenched myself loose and tore through the half-open door of the compartment.

The corridor was just as crowded. I lurched toward the next car, but the cry went up and swept past me—"*Frisches Schweinefleisch! Schweinebraten!*"—and every head flew up as I shoved and pushed my way to the front of the car. I made it, tore the door open, and slammed it in the faces behind me.

There seemed to be thousands of them reaching and screaming now. Through the glass door of the car ahead I saw more. They had already heard the cry of "*Schweinefleisch! Schweinefleisch!*" and their hands were reaching for me. I was surrounded. The others were pounding on the door behind me, but in their haste and shoving they had jammed against the door and couldn't get it open for a few seconds. Those seconds saved me. I looked up between cars and saw the train roof. Nobody was there! Holding the meat tighter, I climbed up on the roof and started running toward the engine, keeping my balance with one arm, enjoying the wind in my face and the momentary freedom. But I knew they would follow me. If I managed to fight them off at this end of the car, they would climb up to the roof from the other end and be on me.

I was right. Within seconds grasping hands appeared over the edge of the car in front. I kicked hard at the hands, looking down into crazed eyes, and with curses and shaking fists they had to let go. Then I heard a commotion behind me. People had climbed up on the roof from two or three cars back and were coming at me with the cry "*Schweinefleisch! Fleisch! Fleisch!*" I leaped to the next car and ran, clutching my meat as if it could save me. There were several cars ahead of me yet. I glanced back, and it looked as if the entire trainload were on the roofs now, coming after me.

I wondered whether it would stop them if I threw them the meat. Would they leave me alone then? Running, I turned and looked back again, and one look convinced me that it wasn't just the meat they wanted. They were after my flesh, too. I jumped onto another car and ran, then another and another—and there was the engine. Should I jump off the train? No, it was moving too fast. I had just saved my legs, and they would be broken for sure. I was getting ready to throw the meat at the mob, since nothing else was left to do, when "*Giessen, Giessen,*" the conductor hollered—and I opened my eyes. I was jammed into the corner of the compartment, damp with sweat and bloody moisture from the package. A few of my neighbors were staring at me. I must have been thrashing and moaning in my dream.

At my uncle's, the family hugged and kissed me and pulled me into the kitchen. They were asking excited questions when Angelika, my aunt's sister, saw the blood on my shirt. She gasped, "Are you hurt?" and opened my jacket to see where I was bleeding. As I took my hand away the meat fell to the floor with a smack. Angelika bent to pick it up, and when they saw what it was the exclamations and questions began all over again. How and where had I ever gotten so much fresh pork? I had to tell the whole story of our trip to the little village by night, of how I had butchered the pig, of our brush with the police and Tannov's wild driving.

Meanwhile, the grandmother began to cut up the meat and onions for a stew, and I asked Angelika where I could get some wine. She said she knew a local bar that might sell us some. I borrowed a fresh shirt from my uncle and asked Angelika to come with me.

The streets were quiet and dark, deserted. We held hands, and I told Angelika about the new camp, Jony and Max, my room, the Lithuanian music professor. She was my favorite in my uncle's household, a live, slender, dark-haired girl, just a few years older than me. A month after she was married her husband, an ace pilot, had been sent to the front, and he was killed soon after, leaving her with their baby. Her brother, too, had died in the war. But Angelika had made a strong comeback and was full of warmth and laughter. The first time I had visited the family, she had rested her hand on my shoulder while she talked to me. I was just a few months out of Russia then, and it was the first soft woman's touch I had felt. I had, in fact, fallen hopelessly in love with her for a few weeks, and, although that first passion had cooled considerably, I still liked being with Angelika.

We found the bar open, but the bartender grumbled at the suggestion that he sell us some wine. Fifty marks waved under his nose brought about a sudden and miraculous change, and he hurried to pull out two bottles of a good dry wine.

On the way home, Angelika scolded me for spending money so freely. "You don't know how hard people have to work to earn fifty marks, and you just throw it away on two bottles of wine," she said. "They should have cost ten marks at the most."

I reached inside my jacket and brought out the three thousand marks I had left from the sale of the camera, tied in a roll with string.

Her eyes widened and she gasped in admiration and alarm. "You shouldn't walk around with so much money! If somebody sees it they'll attack you."

"But nobody will see it," I said, putting it away grandly. "It's money to spend. The wine will give us pleasure. Listen, on some of the big black markets you can see much more than three thousand marks—you can see them in the tens of thousands."

Back at the house, the fried-meat-and-onion aroma permeated everything. While Angelika took the wine into the kitchen I went upstairs and had a cold shower. No one in Germany had hot running water any more—except, I supposed, the Americans on their army bases. But that didn't bother me. The first time I had visited them my aunt had offered to heat me some water on the stove. She couldn't understand how I liked to stand under the freezing water, scrubbing and scrubbing until my skin glowed. Nothing felt cold to me after the Russian winter.

Feeling refreshed, I went downstairs to my uncle's study and told him what the emigration doctor had said about my blood pressure. Without a word he took out his blood-pressure cuff and had me take off my shirt. After reading the jumping needle he said, "You need regular hours and regular meals, and then your blood pressure will be normal. You're as healthy as a horse. I don't expect you to start living a quiet life right now, but you should discipline yourself for about three weeks before your next examination, and get plenty of sleep. Then you'll pass. Now, come on. Let's go to the table. This is a special occasion."

It was 3:00 A.M. by now, but my aunt had set the table in the dining room with her fine things from before the war: a snowy white tablecloth, silver, china, crystal glasses. It was strange to know that all this had happened just because I had come bringing the fresh meat. The stew was delicious, the silver and china shone and clinked, and we laughed and drank wine, talking about the old days in Rumania, the gypsy music and the weddings that lasted for three or four days. It was almost like another time. Except that all of us ate a little too eagerly for a fine dinner party. And I had trouble remembering how to use all the knives and forks and napkins. I had been in camps too long.

It was dawn when we finally went to bed. For me, my aunt made up the bed in the spare room on the top floor with a big, fluffy quilt like one we had at home. I sank into the strange familiar softness and dreamed of running with Vasile over the roofs of a moving train. If I ran all the way to the end of the train I would be in America, but there seemed to be hundreds and hundreds of cars. Vasile tossed me a package. It was heavy and damp with blood, and I knew it was something important. I caught it, staggering, and he roared with laughter.

When I woke up it was two in the afternoon, and my uncle and Angelika were at work. I barely had time to kiss my aunt good-bye and leave messages for the others before leaving for the station to catch the crowded German express back to Hannover and the camp.

By the time I got back to camp it was dark. A card game was in progress in the guardhouse, and the guards merely glanced up and waved me through. In the cold night, the compound had a sour smell of wood smoke and hopelessness that I knew all too well. Coming from my uncle's, which was at least a home and a family, I felt the barbed wire and the barracks closing in on me more than ever.

But when I got to the canteen I knew right away that I was needed. The place was packed with noisy, drinking DPs. Jony came out from behind the bar and grabbed my hand, grinning. "You got here just in time! Now I can get some rest. We've been busy like this since afternoon." A new transport of DPs had arrived, and they were spending money like water on the Greek's wine.

I went behind the bar, and for the next several hours I was so busy that I forgot to be unhappy about the six months stretching ahead of me. And then something happened that made my dreams of America fade into the background.

Around midnight Max came to me with a well-dressed young man who immediately caught my attention. There was an air of style and confidence about him, in his clear, direct look, his sleeked-back hair, his clean and well-pressed suit, his *fragrance,* almost—in these days when most people wore frayed old dyed army uniforms and washed as best they could with a splash of cold water—that made me want to know more about him. Max introduced him as Alfred and said, "He needs a thousand marks right away, and he'll give you ten American dollars for them."

It was a very good price. This Alfred must have dollars to spare. Everyone was eager for them; if you could get hold of dollars and trade them on the black market for American military scrip, and if you knew someone who knew an American soldier—say, a German girl who went out with a GI— you could get all kinds of things from the PX that sold for a fortune on the black market. You could make a thousand marks to the dollar on chocolate bars alone. In the PX, American soldiers got twenty chocolate bars for a dollar, and they could be sold on the black market for fifty marks each. Yes, a hundred marks for a dollar was an excellent price. I took out my roll of money and counted out one thousand marks while Alfred watched keenly.

I gave him the marks; he handed me ten one-dollar bills and proceeded to spend six hundred of the marks right away on five bottles of wine. I watched him sit down at a table with another well-dressed man and two attractive girls. Alfred and the other man seemed to be discussing business, while Max hung around their table drinking wine and making jokes with the girls.

After the canteen closed Max came over and shook my hand. "Alfred is one of the biggest black-market men in the English zone," he said, "with operations from Hamburg to Kassel—and you impressed him. He asked me who you were and told me he liked the way you counted out the money.

He said he might need you for something and will be back tomorrow to talk it over with you."

"Is he a DP?"

"Sure—but a successful one! He has a pass for every DP camp in the English and American zones, and besides that he has some kind of phony or stolen identification that lets him travel all over the country in style. And you impressed him! Not bad for a scrawny kid from the Balkans." Max slapped me affectionately on the back and went off to bed, wobbling a little.

The next morning Jony came into my room and said, "Max tells me that a very important black-market man was in the canteen last night and asked about you."

"You mean Alfred," I said. "He has some kind of deal in mind for me. What do you think?"

"I know him," Jony said. "He's very big, and he's trustworthy. Let's see what he has to offer. If it suits you it would be worth going along with him. Alfred doesn't deal in small change."

I got dressed, and we went into the canteen. Max was already behind the bar, holding his head and groaning as usual, and we were laughing with him when Alfred came in, looking suave and in command. He shook hands with Jony and greeted me. Jony led the way to a table in the corner, and Alfred asked me to sit down across from them.

He leaned forward. "I want you to come with me to Kassel. I have to deal with an American officer at the base there, and your size and presence are very important to me. You make me feel confident. If the deal works out I'll give you ten cartons of cigarettes, and with you along I'm quite sure it will."

He spoke softly and straightforwardly, and he exuded confidence. I thought that he hardly needed me for moral support. But he wasn't a very big man physically, and I understood that he would be going into dangerous territory and wanted me for a bodyguard, a tough guy, or at least for the appearance of one. I already knew my answer, but I gave Jony a questioning look.

"If I were you I'd go," he said.

I turned to Alfred. "When do we leave?"

Alfred smiled and said to Jony, "With a spirit like that, how can I lose?" To me, he said, "So it's settled. I'll meet you here at the canteen at nine tomorrow morning." He shook hands with both of us and left.

That night I didn't sleep well. I kept wondering what kind of deal Alfred could have with an American officer. I didn't like the idea of going onto an American army base. The Americans were powerful. Oh, I was stringy and tough, and I could handle myself in a street fight with another DP, or even three or four of them. Those laws I understood. But the Americans had a kind of power that was beyond my grasp. It was shining and machinelike. It had something to do with cleanliness, and dollars, and cigarettes, and authority, and food. It made me think of that hospital with the white-jacketed doctor. At nine in the morning Alfred found me pacing uneasily in the canteen.

He had a car waiting to take us to the station. He had already bought tickets on the military express, and the train was on time. As it rattled along he told me in a low voice about the situation with the American officer.

Alfred had a diamond ring, and the American, a major, wanted to buy it. He had told Alfred to come to his base today to negotiate a price, but Alfred suspected that the major had a surprise planned and would try to take the ring away from him before the deal was closed. "That's why I brought you along," he said. "He's greedy, but he's not a hard man —far from it. I think your presence will be enough to scare him into behaving himself. All you have to do is stand there and look very sure of yourself. I'll handle the rest."

By two in the afternoon we were in Kassel. At the station Alfred made a phone call and then said we would have to wait twenty or thirty minutes, because the major was sending a jeep for us from the base.

The waiting room was crowded with the usual black-market types trading and milling around, darting suspicious glances at each other and keeping an eye out for the cops.

We passed the time trying to guess what this or that one had to sell or was in the market for. Alfred was much better at it than I was.

"You know," he said, "if someone went into a mob like that with ten pounds of sugar or meat they might literally tear him apart."

I said I knew.

"Even so," Alfred went on, "it's in such crowds that you sometimes find the best contacts. That's how I got started on the black market—just trading from hand to hand, looking out for opportunities. At the beginning it was a way to feed myself—the only way.

"You see, I was alone. I had been in a labor camp with my parents and my older brother. It's ironic—we were Germans, Mennonites, living in Russia. We had a nice home there until the Germans interned us and sent us to work in that damned factory.

"Toward the end of May 1945, when I was twenty-one, the factory shut down. And then my father made his mistake. He said to one of the guards, 'This is the beginning of the end.' The guard's face went white, and he left and came back with an SS man. I still remember the sound their boots made marching up to our barracks.

"They came in, and the guard just pointed at my father. The SS man asked, 'Do you have any other family here?' My father said no, but the guard pointed to my mother and brother. I don't know why he skipped me. The SS man ordered them to step outside. They did, and then I heard three shots. After the guard and the SS man left I looked out, and there they were—quiet and dead. I looked at them for a long time.

"The other workers had gone, so I hid, and that night I escaped from the camp. For three weeks I lived in the forest and ate grass. Once I stole some carrots from a farm, the only thing I could find. Then the shooting stopped, and three days later, in some little town, I found out that the war was over.

"My wanderings eventually brought me to Hannover, and there I got involved in the black market. I think about emigrating sometimes . . . but not this year."

I looked at him and saw the faraway look in his eyes and his small, hard smile. "Come on, let's go outside," I said. "We'll miss our jeep." His eyes cleared, and he quickly came back to the present.

Sure enough, there was an American army jeep idling in front of the station with an MP at the wheel. Gesturing toward me, Alfred said something to the MP, who said, "Okay, okay," and motioned me into the back seat. Alfred and I climbed in, and the jeep shot away.

The MP drove as if a car full of machine guns were after him. I was thrown back against the seat, tossed from side to side. The motor howled, the tires bit into the gravel, the brakes grabbed and squealed, but the MP stayed cool and nonchalant. The sleeves of his clean new uniform snapped smartly in the wind.

Alfred leaned over and said, through gritted teeth, "I think the major is trying to soften us up with this wild ride."

We had left the city behind. Now we were approaching a fenced-in compound of low, light-colored buildings. With a final squeal of the brakes the driver pulled up at the gate and saluted.

The MP guard who saluted back scared the hell out of me. His face was black, in startling contrast to his white teeth and white helmet, and he kept chewing and chewing on something. His shoulders were very broad in his crisp new uniform. He growled a few words at our driver out of the side of his mouth, and he didn't stop chewing for a moment. To me he looked ferocious. I thought, Well, this is it. This is the gate of hell. I wondered whether I still looked so sure of myself.

With another jerk and a roar our driver pulled through the gate and stopped next to a long building. He motioned for us to get out and follow him. I had a brief glimpse of a wide, clean-swept compound with new gray-painted buildings.

Loudspeakers playing American jazz. Men striding around in clean tan uniforms singing, snapping their fingers, chewing, smoking, confident, healthy. A lot of trucks and jeeps parked in a row. Then we went into the building. A corridor. Clean offices. Soldiers at desks with typewriters on them. Pictures of pretty girls in bathing suits stuck on the walls.

We entered a roomy office. The officer who got up from behind his desk probably wasn't over thirty-five or forty, but he was much too well fed and was slightly balding. A name plate on the desk said MAJOR WEINER. He reached out a plump hand to shake Alfred's hand and glanced at me uneasily. It was obvious that I was a factor he hadn't counted on.

Like a magician, from somewhere in his jacket, Alfred produced the ring, a two-carat sparkler, and the two of them began to argue over the price. They argued in English, in German, then in English again. I stood with my arms folded, glaring at the major and hoping I looked the way Alfred wanted me to. Inside I was quailing. Secretly I thought that at any minute two of those black MPs might come in, still chewing, and grab me. They'd put me in a can of meat, and I'd wind up back in Russia, the best part of some poor bastard's dinner. The major was almost shouting now. He had a high, fatty voice, and I noticed that whenever he talked about money a kind of wheeze came into it. Behind him on the wall was a big portrait of a grinning, bald-headed man with a lot of decorations on his shoulders. There was a name underneath it: IKE. To me it read "Ee-kay."

In German, the major asked, "Can't you leave the ring here until I get the price together?"

"You know that's impossible," Alfred said.

Now they were talking about how the price should be paid. American dollars? Military dollars? Alfred wanted cigarettes. Finally it was settled: sixty cartons of cigarettes—a black-market fortune.

The major told Alfred to come back in two weeks. Then he sat down looking displeased and telephoned for the Wild West driver. The MP took us to the station, driving slower this time.

I felt better as soon as we were out the gate, but Alfred didn't relax until we were safely on the train. Then he smiled and said, "You were just right, the way you stood there. By looking at you from time to time I got all the reassurance I needed. Jesus, he's a greedy bastard! We have to wait two weeks now, but I'll make him pay for our waiting."

On the streetcar back to camp I was quiet, thinking about Alfred's rough schooling. To see one's parents and brother shot to death was a strong experience, not easily forgotten. When we were close to Buchholz Alfred said, as if he had read my thoughts, "Please don't tell Jony or anyone else what I told you about myself. I haven't talked about it since it happened, and I don't really know why I did to you today. Maybe because Max told me how you were arrested and taken away to Russia. But it's best if you just forget I said anything. It is the past, and we must forget it."

We got to camp late and shared a bottle of wine in the canteen. Alfred said, "We go back in two weeks. I may be around here before that, but if I don't see you, then two weeks from today." We shook hands, and he left.

Max sauntered over and said, "He really likes you. Did everything work out?"

"No, Max. We have to go back to Kassel in two weeks. I'm tired now. I'll tell you about it tomorrow."

I went to my room. Tired as I was, sleep wouldn't come. I couldn't shake off the terrible picture of Alfred staring at the quiet bodies of his mother, father, and brother—Alfred just three years ago, but much, much younger. I had guessed his age at around thirty. He was so much in command, so self-possessed. I supposed that if you survived the worst life could do to you, you got strong. In a way the same thing had happened to me. Leif had toughened me well beyond my twenty years. And at the same time I was still a bewildered sixteen-year-old kid who had been arrested on my way to school and thrown into the stark reality of Russia, to survive as best I could.

This was a mad world. Alfred's parents had been Germans, and a German had shot them—for simply stating a fact. And now Alfred was offering me ten cartons of cigarettes, a small fortune, for just standing around and presenting an appearance I didn't feel at all. How could one look confident and positive in this insane world? I didn't like this diamond-ring deal, but I had come this far, and I was going to go through with it. I dozed, woke up, and dozed again. Then I dreamed that my parents were about to be shot behind a factory, and I woke up and couldn't sleep any more. In the morning I was still very tired.

I spent the next two weeks helping out in the canteen, listening to Max joke with the other DPs, and eating with Jony and Maria. I was edgy and miserable, though. I told Jony that I liked Alfred and would go back with him, but that from now on I intended to stay clear of deals with American officers.

Three days before the time was up Alfred appeared out of nowhere, fresh and energetic as usual. He found me in my room, sensed my mood immediately, and smiled and shook me gently by the shoulder. It warmed me. "Cheer up a little," he said. "Everything is going to be all right. I haven't got much time right now, but I'll be back in three days to pick you up." And he was gone. I felt much better, and spent the afternoon laughing with Max for the first time since the trip to Kassel.

The three days passed quickly, and on the morning of the fourth day Alfred was there, carrying a big empty suitcase. A car waited outside the camp, and we were on our way. On the train Alfred didn't say much. He seemed nervous, and that worried me. In Kassel he made a telephone call again and said a jeep would pick us up in twenty minutes. We ignored the crowd of traders in the station and waited outside. Alfred paced back and forth in the bright afternoon sun.

"Is anything wrong?" I asked.

"No, no," he said. "I'm just a little tense. I haven't had much sleep lately. I think everything will be all right."

The jeep roared toward us and screeched to a stop. A different MP was driving, but he seemed to take the same pleasure in punishing jeeps. After a short and rough ride we roared through the dreaded gates and pulled up outside the office building.

Major Weiner shook Alfred's hand—and the arguing began all over again. The major seemed to think that Alfred wanted too much for the ring. Alfred held firm. At one point he said to me, "All right, let's go." I picked up the suitcase.

The major half rose from his desk. "What makes you think you'll get out of this camp?" he asked.

"You promised us free entrance and exit," Alfred answered coolly.

This was just what I had been afraid of. Now my own survival was at stake. I wanted to get out of there, and fast. I put down the suitcase and took one step toward the major. I must have looked as if I meant business. Sweat popped out on his face.

"All right, all right," he squeaked. "Give me the ring."

"No," Alfred said. "The cigarettes first."

The major went into the next room and backed out dragging a case of cigarettes. Under his desk was a paper bag with another ten cartons. We hurriedly packed the fifty cartons from the case into Alfred's suitcase, and then Alfred reached into his jacket and handed the major the ring. I still expected a couple of man-eating MPs to burst through the door at any minute.

Weiner phoned for the driver. Alfred carried the paper bag and I carried the suitcase to the jeep. We climbed in, and the jeep took off for the station. We were free! I felt so much better as soon as we got off the base that I couldn't understand why Alfred seemed so tense. We left the jeep and went into the station. Alfred had our tickets ready, and before I knew what was happening he hurried me onto the next train to Frankfurt!

"But aren't we going back to Hannover?" I asked.

He didn't answer, but once we were safely aboard and the train began to pick up speed Alfred reached into his pocket and brought out—the ring.

"But I saw you give it to him!" I said.

"You saw me give him a ring that looked exactly like this one. I had a fine Polish jeweler make it up for me. It was a piece of glass. You see, if he hadn't been such a greedy chiseler I would have given him the real one. But after the way he carried on about the price I had to do it."

Now Alfred relaxed, and we laughed about the expression on the major's face when I had stepped toward him. "I meant it," I said. "I would have done whatever I had to do to get us out of there. Maybe he was just bluffing, but who knows? He could have picked up the phone and had a whole squad of MPs in there in thirty seconds, to grab us for dealing on the black market."

In Frankfurt we changed trains and were back in Hannover by midnight, in time to catch the last streetcar to camp. On the streetcar I asked Alfred where he would sleep that night. He said, "I have a room in the town of Buchholz, but it's so late. Can you find me a room in the barracks?"

"There is an empty one in Barracks 1, right next to Jony's," I told him.

At camp, Max was still in the canteen, but Alfred and I went straight to my room. There he gave me the paper bag with the ten cartons of cigarettes and said, "They are yours."

I opened one carton and took out two packs. Then I shoved the suitcase with the fifty cartons under my bed and said to Alfred, "They are safer here than in the barracks." I locked the door of my room, went over to the canteen, and gave the two packs of cigarettes to Max.

He beamed and kissed me on the cheek. "We were all worried about you. I am glad to see that everything came out all right. Now we can open a bottle of wine on the house." No sooner said than done. By the time Alfred and I had drunk a glass each Max was well on his way to being roaring drunk.

I took Alfred to the spare room in Barracks 1, and he went straight to bed. Back in the canteen, I had one more glass of wine with Max, who was still celebrating my return, and then I went to my little room and lay down. Drunk with wine and relief, I fell sound asleep, right over the treasure.

Early the next morning Alfred came for his suitcase looking as fresh and neat as if he had slept in a hotel. He took the suitcase, gripped my hand, and said, "If I need you again I'll look for you here." Then he was gone, as mysteriously as he always came and went by the labyrinths of the black market. I wondered if I would ever see him again.

I kept three cartons of the cigarettes for myself. The rest I gave to Jony, to help provide the food I ate with him and Maria every day.

8

I was working behind the bar, carrying cases of empty beer bottles into the storeroom and bringing out full ones. As I worked I listened to Cheslav and a friend of his, who were sitting at the bar talking to Max. They were talking about me. It seemed that a DP from our old room, a Pole named Jerzy, had been spreading stories about me, saying that I had lied about my whereabouts during the war, that I was probably a spy, and so on. Jerzy had been the loudest grumbler at the time I moved out of the barracks and became Jony's and Max's helper in the canteen. I remembered him, a little fellow with a thin mouth and a high, complaining voice.

Cheslav and his friend were agreeing with Max that Jerzy's gossip was totally harmless. No one would listen to him, because he was well known as a spiteful, backbiting type, and the DPs who had gotten to know me so far liked me. Cheslav was telling Max that in every camp there are a few who stand out, who develop outside contacts, whether from curiosity, courage, or just strong hunger that drives them into the thick of the black market to hustle and feel the pulse of the local trade. And, naturally, those few attract the envy of the greater number who hang back in the barracks gnawing on their bread rations and nursing their resentment at what fate has done to them. Cheslav was saying that envy in a strong personality could be dangerous, but in this case it was to be ignored. "A man like Jerzy doesn't have the guts to get out of camp and trade," he said. "So he thinks everyone is a coward like him. He figures Vanya here must have some special connections, because if he didn't he'd be sitting around the barracks complaining just like Jerzy, eh?" They all laughed.

I didn't say anything, but I was grateful to Cheslav for standing up for me. I admired him, too, for being another one who had refused to let the months of waiting get him down. I had seen what the waiting did to DPs like Jerzy, and I had dreaded its getting to me that way. My adventure with Alfred had come at just the right time. If he hadn't shown up when he did, I would have had too much time to think and brood about the months that stretched ahead of me. Getting the bad news from the emigration doctor had shaken my defenses against the atmosphere of depression that pervaded the DP world. And it was vitally important to keep those defenses strong, to stay active and on the offensive against the apathy and hopelessness. Once they began to eat away at you, you were finished.

But Alfred had come along. He hadn't taken me out of the DP world; he had lifted me up on top of it. I was fascinated by his aura of power and confidence, and yet he had started out just like me, trading to fill his stomach on the Hannover black market. With Alfred, without even thinking about it I had become a black marketeer again—on a different level. Watching the crowd in the station waiting room with Alfred, guessing what this or that trader had to offer, was very different from prowling around the edges of such a crowd looking for a kilo or two of sugar or butter, as Jeno and I had done in Bremen. Somehow it reminded me of working on the tower in Russia, high up in the free air, and watching the blackened, beaten workers crawl out of the mine.

Now I had three cartons of cigarettes, and I wanted to find something for myself on the black market. Not a grubby little transaction in the trading crowd in Hannover; something bigger, which would involve imagination and adventure. It would have to come to me through one of my contacts or through my own ingenuity. I didn't know yet what it would be, but my appetite was whetted, and I was determined not to sit around camp any longer than I had to.

While I was waiting another appetite was whetted—and frustrated—in a comic incident that paid off unexpectedly.

It happened after a trip I made to Bremen to buy some fish for Maria and Jony.

One evening after dinner, talking about food—a subject we never tired of, even when our stomachs were full—we had gotten to reminiscing about a smoked fish called *rusi* that we used to eat at home in Rumania. I remembered that in Bremerhaven, the American-occupied port on the North Sea about thirty-five miles north of Bremen, you could buy a kind of herring called *Bückling* that was very much like *rusi*. Feeling restless, I volunteered to go up to Bremen and get some *Bückling*. Jony and Maria were delighted, since our diet of pork back, sausage, and potato-thick *ghiveci*, rich as it was for the times, got pretty monotonous. So the next day I took the train to Bremen, found out the address of a packing house in Bremerhaven from someone selling *Bückling* in the black-market crowd, and hopped on the local to Bremerhaven. There I negotiated with the boss of the packing house, and, with the help of a pack of American cigarettes, seven hundred marks got me two twenty-five-pound cases of the oily, delicious fish. I filled myself with them while I waited for the train back to Bremen and hardly made a dent in the packed, gleaming rows. Edible gold, a fortune to my insecure stomach. Only a little smelly, so that some of the shabby passengers stared at my cases, reminding me uneasily of the mob that had followed me when I had the fresh meat.

I got to camp after midnight, dumped the two cases on the floor of my room, and went to the bar. It was one of those rare nights when the canteen was quiet. Only Max was there, talking in German with a woman I had never seen before. He hailed me and asked how the trip had been.

"Fine," I said. "I got what I went for."

"I saw, I saw. And I smelled! Here, you must be tired. Come and meet Olga. She lives in the town of Buchholz and comes in here from time to time to see what's new in camp. Sometimes she does a little business with some of the DPs."

Max winked, and I looked again at Olga. She was a big, athletic woman in her thirties, with a plain, crafty-looking face.

"Why don't you take her home tonight?" Max asked.

"Max," I said, "maybe she has somebody waiting at home who doesn't like the smell of fish!"

They laughed, and Olga said, "Oh, come on, take me home. I don't have anybody at my place."

Max grinned. "I've slept there. What a big warm feather bed!"

"Come on, Olga," I said. "I am very tired." And I took her by the arm. Over my shoulder, I said to Max, "If you see Jony tell him that I am back and we'll unpack the fish tomorrow morning."

I walked behind Olga. Even the guard at the shack seemed to know her, and he smirked at me as we passed. The path we followed over the fields was well worn, in spite of the recent snowfall. The brisk wind blew the fish smell from my clothes as we tramped along through a little valley among scattered trees.

We came to a street just at the edge of town, and Olga pointed to the first house. "This one is mine." She dug into her large pocketbook and came out with the key. Behind the house a dog started to bark.

She opened the door and with a finger to her lips motioned me to be silent. I followed her inside the dark house. She led me by the hand into one of the rooms and lit the lamp. It was a bedroom, large and clean, with a huge double bed in one corner, a small table, two chairs, and a chest.

Without a word she kissed me, pressing her full, strong body against mine. I responded eagerly, but she pulled back and whispered, "Shh. Sit down on the bed and take off your shoes."

I sat down. The bed was very soft, too soft. I took my shoes off and reached for Olga again, but she backed away, saying she had something to do in the kitchen and would be back in a minute.

Then, as if in an afterthought, she asked, "Where did you come from tonight when you came into the canteen?"

"I was in Bremerhaven getting some fish."

"What did you use to pay for it?" she asked.

"Money and cigarettes."

Olga went out, and I lay back on the deep, soft bed frowning. Her questions had made me suspicious. If she had asked them right after we met I wouldn't have thought anything of it, but now, for some reason, they made me very leery. In that soft bed and that silence, and as tired as I was, under ordinary circumstances I would have gone right to sleep. But now, as much as my body craved sleep, intuition won out over fatigue, and my mind stayed awake and alert. Another part of me was impudently alert, too, waiting for Olga; she had aroused a need for her ripe, healthy body. From the way she had acted, I had thought there was a strong physical hunger in her, too, but I was no longer so sure of her motives.

No noises came from the kitchen. By this time I was wide awake, straining to hear something. Then the door opened noiselessly, and Olga came into the room. Instinctively I closed my eyes and pretended to sleep. When she tiptoed to the bed I thought she had come to join me, ready to make love—but no, she was listening to my breathing! I made it as regular as I could. In a moment she tiptoed out and quietly closed the door. Now I was really alert. I didn't move. Somewhere in the house a door opened and closed. Then I heard nothing but the occasional creak of a floorboard.

But I couldn't stay this way much longer. Sooner or later I would fall asleep. I started counting seconds, up to sixty, one minute, then another minute, ten minutes. It was clear what Olga was up to. Unthinkingly, Max must have told her that I was carrying a lot of money. She had somebody hidden in the house, and when they thought I was sound asleep they would slip in and steal my money. What should I do? Wait here until they came? If I surprised them while they were robbing me there would be a fight, and the odds were against me; at best I'd get a sound beating and lose my money, and at worst they might even kill me.

Then I heard whispering right in the doorway of the room. I couldn't understand what was being said, but now I knew for sure that Olga wasn't alone. I grunted, made some noises as if I had turned in my sleep, and listened. Another whisper, a floorboard creaked again, and it was quiet.

I sat up in bed and in the moonlight saw Olga's pocketbook on the table. Slipping into my jacket, I tiptoed over and opened it. I felt a sheaf of papers inside and took them out, hoping they were money, but the moonlight wasn't bright enough to see, so I shoved them into my pocket. Then I picked up my shoes and tiptoed out of the room, moving slowly in the pitch-darkness until I found the front door. Softly, very softly, I opened it and stepped outside. I slipped on my shoes and walked quietly away.

After about thirty steps I started to run, across the little valley, up the hill, and all the way to camp. As I went past the guard shack, out of breath, the guard grinned at me. I grinned back and went to the canteen. It was dark. Max had closed up for the night.

In the light of my room I took the sheaf of papers out of my pocket—and whistled. In my hand were about twenty-five food ration cards: meat, sugar, milk, vegetables, everything for twenty-five people for a month. I laughed thinking of the faces of Olga and her accomplice, procurer, lover, or whatever he was when they sneaked into the room and found that their DP dupe had flown taking twenty-five ration cards with him. The extra food would be a godsend to my uncle's family in Giessen. Still grinning, I stretched out on my own familiar cot, narrower and lonelier than Olga's big, soft feather bed, but much safer. The voluptuous thief had left me with a slight ache of frustration; it was just another sign of returning life, for in the hunger and exhaustion of Russia it had been as the terse labor-camp proverb had it: "You'll live, but you won't want to screw." But things hadn't changed all that much. Olga's ration cards were a far bigger prize than her favors. I had definitely gotten the best of her.

The next morning, when I told Jony what had happened, at first he was furious. He knew Olga was a sly one, but he was surprised that she would try such a thing with me, when Max must have told her I was his new helper. He cursed her in his richest Rumanian and swore that she would never be allowed back in camp. I showed him the sheaf of ration cards from her pocketbook, and then he had to laugh.

"It serves her right," he said. "The thief got robbed. But she would have plucked you clean if it weren't for your keen instinct. If you want, I can stop her from ever coming into camp again, or I can mete out DP justice and have two of the guards give her twenty-five lashes."

"No, leave her alone," I said. "I consider myself repaid for my trouble."

Still, Jony vowed to give her a good talking-to and make sure she was cured.

I wanted to go to Giessen right away with the ration cards, some of the fish, and the twenty packs of cigarettes I had saved for my uncle, who was a heavy smoker. Jony dug up a sturdy old suitcase to pack the fish in and gave me his English identity card again. In Hannover, the card got me a ticket on the express to Kassel, and there I changed for the crowded local to Giessen and my uncle's.

It was in Giessen that I got the idea for my first solo venture on the black market.

After I opened the suitcase and everyone exclaimed over the rows of glistening fish, and after my uncle thanked me profusely for the cigarettes, I said that Angelika and I would go get some wine. The ration cards were still hidden in my pocket; I wanted to give them to Angelika when we were alone. Feeling mischievous, I told her I had a surprise and made her guess what it was all the way to the bar.

The bartender evidently recognized us and remembered my fifty marks, because he fell all over himself in his eagerness to sell us some more wine. We sat down at a table and asked for two cognacs, and while he was busy behind the bar I reached into my pocket and pulled out the ration cards. Angelika gasped when she saw what a thick wad they made. I gave them to her, and she counted them with trembling fingers.

"Do you know how much food this represents?" she said, almost accusingly.

"Of course. It is for twenty-five people for a month."

"But how did you get them? What will the people do without their cards?"

To stop her from worrying about twenty-five starving people, I told her how I got the cards. She laughed, shaking her head, when I came to the part about Olga's big, soft feather bed, the trap I had almost fallen into. While we talked the bartender brought us our two glasses of cognac and two bottles of wine, wrapped. I gave him sixty marks, and he bowed his way back to the bar.

Angelika cupped her hands around her glass and looked down into it, her cheeks pink with the excitement of my gift. "You know, I handle ration cards every day on my job at the grocery store. The poor people come in looking like ghosts of who they were before the war, and I collect their ration cards and dole out their little bits of meat and milk and sugar. I always wish I could give them more, especially when I know someone's baby is sick or her old mother is ailing. We haven't even got much of a black market here—the town is too small. When we hear about what goes on in the bigger cities, how you can buy meat and butter and sugar there by the pound, it just sounds unbelievable—like a dream. And then every once in a while you fall out of the sky from dreamland, just to prove that it's true."

I smiled and took her hand.

"To me," she went on, "the craziest thing is that they say the hottest items on the big black markets are cigarettes and coffee. Is that true?"

I told her that the American cigarette was virtually black-market currency and that coffee brought a high price, three or four hundred marks a pound.

"It's strange to me because people need food so badly," she said. "It seems as if they need their little pleasures, or their drugs, just as much. But then, they say cigarettes and coffee take the edge off hunger. I don't know, because I don't smoke, and it's been so long since I had a cup of real coffee that I can hardly remember what it tastes like."

I was still listening with one ear, but my mind had shifted into a practical gear. Coffee! Why hadn't I thought of it before? Even *Ersatz-Kaffee,* the substitute the Germans made out of scorched beans, was rationed; real coffee was rare and precious, and it came very high on the black market. But you could get it in Belgium. As much as you wanted, without ration cards. The only problem was getting into Belgium and out again with a lot of coffee. It was illegal for a DP to cross borders. He was stateless, a man without a passport, unclassified and quarantined, in this time of strict regulations imposed on the postwar chaos. A DP caught crossing a border could get thrown in jail, jeopardizing his chance to emigrate; a DP caught smuggling black-market goods across a border would be in for a really stiff sentence and would forfeit everything. But if he could make it without getting caught he'd have a small fortune. The question was how, how, how to cross that border into Belgium. There had to be a way.

Angelika broke into my thoughts. "You haven't heard a word I said, and you're scowling like an old bear. What on earth are you thinking?"

"Angelika," I said, "how would you like ten pounds of fresh coffee?"

9

I thought about the coffee all through dinner that evening, and I must have thought about it all night in my sleep, because when I woke up the next morning I had the answer. Who could cross any border in Western Europe without a passport? An American soldier! His uniform was his passport. Dressed as an American soldier, I could cross into Belgium, buy the coffee, and ride back with it. There was a good chance that no one would bother me, or even ask for identification, if I was wearing an American army uniform. The only problem was getting one, and Jony could take care of that.

Then I wondered whether I was crazy. Me an American soldier? One of those clean, confident, well-fed, finger-snapping fellows I had seen in Kassel with Alfred? What if I met a real American soldier and he tried to talk to me? Or, worse, if I met an officer and had to salute him? Siki, in Bremen, had thought I looked confident enough to dress like an American—and it had worked on Hans. My height was in my favor. But it wouldn't work on an American officer. I'd just have to trust my luck and hope I didn't run into one.

When I got back to camp I hurried over to Jony's. He sensed right away that I wanted to talk to him privately and suggested that we go for a walk. As we walked along the fence, looking out at the bare brown fields with their patches of tired snow, I could feel the first mildness of spring in the air.

"Listen," I said, "can you get me an American soldier's uniform?"

"Are you crazy?" Jony looked at me as if I had gone round the bend. "What for?"

I explained my idea, and he listened in silence. When I finished he didn't say anything for a few minutes.

"You know," he said finally, "you are a crazy bastard, but it just might work. It will take me about a week, but I'll get you a uniform."

The next morning he came into the canteen grinning. "It's all arranged. I have a friend in the American zone who cleans clothes for American soldiers, and I asked him to get me a tall soldier's uniform. He'll have it in a week." He also said he had contacted a friend in Belgium for the address of a place where I could buy the coffee. Now there was nothing to do but wait.

In the meantime, news arrived of another pig we could buy. Again I drove with Tannov and Jony to a little village, only twenty or thirty miles away this time. It was a cold, rainy night, and the farmer's wife made us tea, apologizing that she had no sugar. This pig was considerably bigger than the first one, but much more co-operative. After I hit it over the head and bled it out we hauled the carcass to the trunk of the car, paid the farmer, and drove back to camp uneventfully.

We cleaned and cut up the pig in the washroom of Barracks 1, and again finished the night with a luxurious pork stew and several of Max's drunken arias. The next day we planned to sell some of the meat to Oskar, for his restaurant, and then take him with us to the bazaar. I went to sleep thinking that tomorrow I would see Vasile again—the king!

In the morning we loaded the meat into the trunk of Tannov's car and drove to Hannover, to Oskar's restaurant.

As soon as I walked in he shouted, "Where have you been? I thought they had sent you to America already! I am glad you're still here."

Taking him aside, I whispered, "Pork, Oskar. We have more fresh pork for you."

He danced out into the street with me. Tannov had the trunk open, and when Oskar lifted up the blanket covering the meat he grabbed his heart as if he were going to faint. He ran inside and came out with a waiter, ordering him around and assuming Napoleonic airs; the waiter just grinned at him and carried in the meat. After Jony and Oskar finished their transaction I asked Oskar if he would like to come shopping with us. "To the bazaar?" he said. I nodded, and he ran back inside and returned with a fistful of money.

On the way to Vasile's camp, I asked him how the restaurant business was doing.

"*Ach, Gott,* the only way I make any money today is by trading on the black market. From this meat I give some to two other restaurants, friends of mine, and just for their families. As you know, from these stinking ration cards you can eat, you can exist, but you can't live. When I visit my friends tonight and they see the meat they will dance, too. I also have to feed some police commissioners and take care of my staff."

"Oskar," I said, "my share of the meat is still in the trunk, thirty pounds of it. I was thinking of taking it to my uncle, but I don't think I'll be able to get to Giessen soon enough. I will sell it to you." His mouth gaped open. I reached over and closed it for him, saying, "There's a chance we may get a lot of coffee, too, and if our plans work out we'll *give* you five pounds of it and let you buy all you want." Speechless, he took my hand and squeezed it gently.

At the gate of Vasile's camp the guard recognized Jony,

and we drove straight through. Tannov parked, and Oskar ran over to the bustling bazaar while we followed at a more leisurely pace. I was shouldering my way to a candy stand when suddenly a powerful hand grabbed my neck from behind. I turned, and there was Vasile.

He hollered, "Jony! Jony!" and the trading hushed. I would have thought that no one could stop the babble of arguing and haggling at that bazaar, but this giant shouted twice and it grew quiet. He really was king among them.

In a moment Jony appeared, and Vasile embraced him, almost swallowing him up in the bear hug of those strong, hairy arms. Vasile asked Jony to go ahead and do his shopping, and pick me up at the guardhouse on his way out. "I want him to come to the guardhouse with me for a drink or two."

As I walked with Vasile to the guardhouse he put his hand on my shoulder. Then he shouted with laughter, for no apparent reason.

I asked, "Vasile, why did you laugh?"

His answer was to laugh again, and it was so contagious that I had to laugh with him, all the way to the guardhouse.

There he pulled two chairs out from the crude table and said, "Sit, sit. I will tell you why I laughed." He reached under the table for a bottle and two glasses and filled the glasses. "I laughed because I was glad to see you. It made me happy. You see, I love Jony, and I am glad he has you in that other camp. You are young and strong, and I feel good when I think of it, so I laugh. A toast to strength!"

Looking into his fierce black eyes, I drained my glass with him. I thought my insides would burn out. "Do you have something to eat?" I asked.

"Sure, sure." He went to a cupboard in the back of the shack and brought out a sausage. He pulled out a knife, tested the blade against his thumb, and cut a piece of sausage as if he were cutting off an upstart's head. I bit into the sausage. It was gamy and good.

He saw that I liked it and said, "It is made right here in

my own camp. Eat all you want." He filled our glasses again, and we drank to Jony's health. The alcohol rose slowly up, up, up to my head while this powerful man in front of me poured glass after glass and we drank toast after toast and laughed and laughed.

At last Jony came, and I wanted so much to lie down, but I had to go with him. I heard Jony scolding Vasile, and then they both laughed and drank a toast to me. This time I was left out and couldn't understand why. I held out my hands for another glass, because it didn't burn any more. Vasile kissed me on the cheek. I felt his rough beard and laughed.

I went outside with Jony and got into Tannov's car, next to Oskar and all his packages. Suddenly I realized that I was drunk, really drunk, for the first time in my life. I mumbled to Oskar, "I'm falling asleep. When we get to your restaurant take my share of the meat. Give Jony whatever you think it's worth."

The next thing I knew, Jony was leading me to my room, and as we went through the canteen our good friend Max laughed, so I laughed, too. Jony took my clothes off and got me onto my cot. That was all I knew for a long time.

When I woke up my head wanted to crack open to let the pain out. Every time I moved, it throbbed. Now I understood what Max groaned about in the mornings. I went gingerly to the washroom in Barracks 1 and stood under the cold shower for as long as I could stand it. While I was under the shower someone came in, saw me, and swore under his breath, "Drunken Turk!" I rubbed myself briskly with a towel and got dressed. I was cold, but at least my head didn't hurt any more. Back in my room behind the canteen, I fell asleep again.

Later, when Jony woke me, he was holding five thousand marks, the money Oskar had given him for my share of the meat. I told him to keep it, saying, "Try to get some dollars or Belgian francs. I'll need them in Belgium for the coffee."

Jony had bought about thirty pounds of potatoes at the bazaar, and Maria had cooked a *ghiveci* for supper. I still felt a little peculiar, but the food brought me back to normal.

We talked about the trip to Belgium, and I said I hoped the American uniform would come soon, because thinking about it made me nervous, and the sooner I went into action the better I would feel.

"It should be here any day now," Jony said.

The next day it came.

Max's singing awakened me at noon. I walked out into the sunshine, which was melting the remaining snow and turning the ground to slush. Halfway to Barracks 1, I met Jony hurrying toward me. "I've been waiting for you! The American uniform has come in, and I got forty American dollars and some Belgian francs. Come on, try the uniform on. Let's see how it fits."

We went into his room, and there was the tan uniform, clean, pressed, and neatly hung over a chair. I got undressed and put on the pants and shirt. The cloth felt cool against my skin. Jony knotted the tie and adjusted it carefully. I put on the jacket and looked at him.

"Do I look like an American?"

"*Ma,*" he exclaimed. "*American adevarat!* You—a true American! You could pass for one anywhere. The pants are a little loose around the waist, but the shoulders are just right. Now I will get the camp barber to give you a good American-style haircut and a shave."

"But, Jony, I've never shaved in my life!"

"You have a lot of fuzz on your face," he said. "It has to come off."

He left, and I took off the precious uniform, covered it with a blanket, and sat down to wait. Jony came back with the barber, who got to work without a word, and in half an hour I was shaved and my hair was cut. It felt peculiarly short and bristly on the sides, but I looked in a mirror and saw that I really did look much fresher, cleaner, and younger. There was nothing to be done about the lines in my forehead.

"What about my shoes?" I asked.

"Very good," Jony said. "I had forgotten that."

He got some brown polish, and I took a rag and rubbed at the shoes for half an hour before I was satisfied with the shine.

Jony said, "Now, today you just relax. Go laugh with Max. But get to bed early, because you have a ticket on the nine o'clock train tomorrow morning. I'll come to the station and see you off."

When I went into the canteen Max stopped singing and looked me up and down, clucking appreciatively at the haircut and gleaming shoes. "Well," he said, "I see you are off for the coffee. Be very careful, and don't get carried away with the women in foreign capitals. We're going to have a dance this weekend, and we'll need you."

"I'll be here," I said, grinning. "Go on, Max, sing some more."

He launched into a bawdy French love song, followed by some Polish tunes and snatches of Italian opera, and soon he had the canteen half full of listening DPs. You could tell that they were cautiously, grudgingly feeling the effects of spring, like frozen ground that can't quite believe the winter is ending and it's safe to thaw out.

It was early when I went to bed, but I had a restless night worrying about tomorrow's dangers. I tossed and turned and woke and slept again, and then suddenly it was light, and Jony was there saying, "It's time to go."

I got up and put on the uniform. Jony adjusted the tie again, and we tried the hat. It looked best at a rakish angle.

Jony told me, "Wear everything now but the hat. I have a large raincoat for you to put on over your clothes. Stick the hat in your pocket. In the men's room at the station you can take the raincoat off, put the hat on, and I'll bring the coat home."

He gave me an envelope with the dollars and Belgian francs, the address of a warehouse where I was to get the coffee, and the name of Monsieur George. Then he looked embarrassed. "Oh," he said, "I forgot to tell you that there's an army identification card in the pocket of the jacket, but the photograph is of a Negro soldier. I guess it won't do you much good."

I took the card out of the inside pocket and looked at it. The soldier was a Negro, all right. If an MP stopped me, it was all over, though with the Belgian or German border officials I might be able to growl, flash the card, and get away with it. It would be best if I didn't have to show my Negro face to anybody.

When the streetcar reached the station we had about twenty minutes before the express train was due, and we went together into the men's room. No one else was there. It was time to work my transformation. Shrugging off the raincoat, I handed it to Jony and looked in the mirror to adjust the hat. When I turned around he was gone.

On my way out I almost bumped into two Germans coming in. I expected growls and shoves, but to my astonishment they stood back respectfully and let me pass.

Jony materialized out of the crowd, stood casually next to me, and said, out of the side of his mouth, "Okay, okay! Go get on your train."

I went out to the platform, and even though it was crowded nobody pushed me. This would take some getting used to. It was important to behave as if I had every right to the respect people were paying my magical uniform. *Ein Ami,* the Germans called an American soldier. I thought about the two Germans who had stepped aside for me. For all they knew, I might be the son of a millionaire!

The train came, and I got on, making my way toward the first-class section—Jony had me traveling in style, like a proper American. Soon I found a compartment all to myself. In a few moments the train started with a jerk, and there was no going back. When the conductor came in he tipped his hat, asked very politely for my ticket, punched it, and left "the American" alone. As the train sped through fields where green life was beginning to come through and it appeared that nobody else was going to come into the compartment, I relaxed and began to daydream about the kind of American I would like to be.

As a kid I had read about those big farms in Texas, called ranches, where cattle were raised. (Most of my ideas about America still came from either gangster movies or the romantic Western stories of the German writer Karl May.) Now I imagined that I was a soldier in Europe, and my parents were waiting for me to come home. When I got back to Texas the tables would be heaped with all kinds of good food. I would fill myself with these good things, and I would tell them about the war in Europe and the terrible devastation it had caused, about the camps full of homeless, uprooted people. I would tell them about the black market, too, how it grew and flourished like a weed all over Western Europe. I would answer all their questions. Then I would go outside, saddle my favorite horse and call my dog, and ride through the forest and the fields. I would visit the old Indian who lived on the reservation and tell him, too, about the terrible war across the great water. But how would I talk to him? My English vocabulary consisted of *okay, salt, water, jeep, sugar, chocolate, house, cigarettes, camera,* and a few other words. I would have to learn the language.

"Düsseldorf Hauptbahnhof," the conductor announced. In my dream world I hadn't noticed how quickly the time was passing.

As the train stood in the station I took the identification card out of my inside pocket and looked at it. Under the photograph of the dark face was the name Arthur Jones. So I was Arthur Jones! I wondered what kind of man Arthur Jones was, why he had left his card in his pocket, and whether he had gotten in trouble for it. I put the card away, and just then a nicely dressed man and woman came into the compartment. They eyed me curiously and sat down across from me. The train pulled out.

Now I couldn't dream any more. I was sure the man and woman were staring at me, and I tried to look as American as I could. The first-class compartment was very comfortable, with velvet-soft seat covers, but I was miserable. Mr. Jones's uniform didn't feel like such a good fit after all. It seemed to be tightening around my shoulders, and a trickle of sweat ran down between my shoulder blades. I cursed myself for not having brought along some American cigarettes. Then I could have taken one out and smoked it—but I didn't smoke! I probably would have started coughing, and that would have made people suspicious. Real Americans smoked their cigarettes smoothly, with style.

Glancing down, I got a shock. My pants were hitched up, revealing my shoes and my socks, which were gray, not army socks. I felt myself blushing as I pulled my pants down so that they covered the socks and most of the shoes. Then I couldn't bear to sit any longer, and I jumped up and went out into the corridor to get away from the two pairs of eyes that I was sure were looking right through my disguise.

Walking up and down the corridor, I looked for another empty compartment, but there were people in all of them. Finally I came back to my compartment and sat down. Right away I regretted having done that. With another jolt of panic I noticed my dirty fingernails and folded my arms so nobody could see them. Sweat dripped from my face onto my clothes. I longed to walk or move around. Sitting quietly was torture. I felt the urge growing to jump up and run and run, until I was somewhere far away from strangers with prying eyes, from this whole insane mission. Who needed coffee, anyway? I liked fresh cold water much better. And as soon as I thought that, I realized how dry my throat was. I longed for a glass of water.

We arrived at Gladbach. I had hoped that the man and woman would get off. Not only did they stay, but two more couples came in! Now the compartment was full. I felt the new passengers staring at me, so I turned my back on them and looked out the window.

They began talking in French. I remembered enough from my school days to understand when one of the women said, "He is probably going on vacation."

Another woman said, "I feel like asking him for a cigarette, but I don't speak English."

That froze me. If a civilian spoke to me he would expect

an answer. But what could I say? I looked doggedly out the window.

They were silent for a while. Then one of the men said, "I know enough English to ask for a cigarette, but I am too embarrassed."

"Oh, please, ask him for a cigarette," said the woman.

The man scolded her. I didn't catch what he said, but the subject was dropped.

In a little while the conductor came through the train announcing, "*Grenze, Grenze*—border, border." Now the real test would come. It was bad enough that I was a DP trying to cross the border illegally, but impersonating an American soldier—that seemed like a kind of sacrilege. I didn't know what the punishment was, but I was sure it was something terrible. If the border guards caught me they would turn me over to the Americans; and *they* would make short work of me for having dared to put on their uniform and pretend I was one of them.

The train stopped, and through the window I saw several uniformed border officials climbing aboard. The passengers in my compartment were getting out their passports; I kept staring out the window. I wondered what I should do if I was asked for papers or orders. At least I hadn't seen any MPs outside.

The door of the compartment opened, and someone asked politely for the passports. I turned around, trying to seem as bored as I could, and when the official saw me looking his way he saluted. I saluted, too, and turned back to my window. I wondered whether I had done it right, or whether my salute had made him suspicious. I stared through the window, seeing nothing, feeling every move that was made behind me. The official examined each passport thoroughly. Now he had finished with my side of the compartment and was starting on the other side. The rustling of paper and his "thank you" told me whenever he finished with another passport. Finally he said "thank you" for the last time, and I heard the door close. Slowly I turned back to the compartment. Everyone was busy putting passports away and looking at watches to see if the train was on time. I let my breath out. I hadn't even realized that I was holding it.

When the train got moving again one of the French-speaking women said, "He doesn't say a word. Do you think he is drunk or sick?" One of the men replied angrily, "What do you want him to do, sing and dance? Can't you understand that he is an American? He doesn't speak our language, and he doesn't know our customs." She mumbled something and was quiet for the rest of the journey. That man would never know how grateful I was. And the woman wouldn't have understood that I *was* drunk—with relief. I had made it past the border.

About five minutes after we left the little border town a French-speaking conductor came in and collected the tickets. Then we were left alone. The other passengers seemed to have lost all interest in me, and the release of tension had left me so exhausted that I dozed off. I woke up about ten minutes before the train pulled into Brussels.

The station was big, but not as big as the one in Hannover, and most of the commotion and babble was in French. I made my way through the crowds to a ticket window. The clerk spoke to me in English, but I smiled and asked, in French, "When does the next express leave for Hannover?"

"In about two hours," he said.

Outside the station, I found a taxi and showed the driver the address Jony had given me. We drove through a bustling business district and then a residential area. Brussels was in better repair than most of the big German cities I had seen, and it seemed to be recovering from the war faster. In a neighborhood of big commercial warehouses the driver slowed down, looked at the numbers, found the right one, and stopped. I paid him and went inside.

The aroma of freshly ground coffee enfolded me, and I had to admit it smelled wonderful. Dozens of burlap bags fat with coffee beans were stacked against the walls. After the scarcity of Germany, this warehouse looked like a mad fantasy, a black marketeer's opium dream.

I approached an elderly woman seated at a desk in the corner and said, in French, "I would like to speak to Monsieur George."

"*Oui, monsieur, dans cinq minutes,*" she said. She eyed my uniform curiously, but went back to her writing.

In about five minutes a gray-haired man came in and walked up to the desk. Nodding toward me, the woman said, "An American soldier wants to see you."

The man came over and said something in English, but I told him in French that I had some American dollars for him.

"*Bien, bien.* How many?"

I said, "I need some coffee. A friend of mine is stationed in Germany, and he asked me to bring it back for his girl friend."

"Sure, sure," he said. "Ten, twenty pounds—whatever you like."

"I'd like a lot more than that. About a hundred and fifty pounds."

He stared at me. "That's dangerous."

I took the envelope out of my pocket and showed him the dollars—four five-dollar bills and twenty singles. I knew I had to keep his mind on the dollars. "I also have some francs," I said.

"Fine. But if you get caught crossing the border with all this coffee, remember, you didn't buy it here. If I didn't need the dollars so badly I wouldn't sell it to you."

Then he gave me an odd look and asked, "Is the American army running out of coffee?" Without waiting for an answer, he went on. "You speak French correctly, but for an American you have a strange accent."

I shrugged. Monsieur George looked at me for a moment longer, eyes narrowed. Then he shrugged, too, and led me through a door into a large room where two workmen were busy stacking heavy sacks of coffee. He did some figuring on a piece of paper and told me the price for 150 pounds of coffee. It took all of the forty dollars I had, plus about 27,000 francs. That left me with 2,000 francs and a few military dollars. I asked if he wanted those, too.

He grabbed them out of my hand and said, "Of course. An American friend of mine will exchange them for me." He gave me some francs for the military dollars, and our transaction was over.

Monsieur George gave some instructions to one of the workers and went out. The workman brought over an old duffel bag, probably a leftover from the Liberation, and asked me whether I wanted to have the coffee packed in it. What a stroke of luck! It would be a good way to carry the weight, and a soldier with a duffel bag would hardly arouse suspicion.

"*Bien*," I said, and gave him 500 francs for the bag. He shoved the money quickly into his pocket, and began to weigh the coffee and pack it into the bag in five- and ten-pound parcels. When the bag was full he made up an additional package weighing about thirty pounds.

It seemed like hours, but the whole transaction had taken only forty minutes. I shouldered the heavy duffel bag, picked up the package, and left the store. Outside I caught a taxi back to the railroad station.

I hadn't seen any real American soldiers around, but nobody stared at me, and the Belgian police near the station seemed friendly enough, tipping their hats as they passed to acknowledge the casual salute I tried out on them—I was beginning to feel a little cocky. As I sat with my load in the station waiting room I did wish time would move faster. I wondered whether the people on the train would be able to smell the coffee. Then I remembered that the hungry black-market types with their keen noses did not ride in the first-class section.

The train was finally announced, and I lugged my contraband to the platform. I found an empty compartment and swung the duffel bag up on the luggage rack. The package I kept on the seat next to me. If all went well, I would be back in Hannover a little after midnight. This trip I was not only impersonating an American; I was also smuggling, engaging in black-market activity, and it would be very grim for me if I was caught. But I was more confident, because my disguise seemed to be working just as I had hoped it would.

Sure enough, at the border an official looked into the compartment, but, seeing only an American soldier, he nodded and left. I stuck my ticket in my hat, so the conductor would find it if I fell asleep, and soon I did doze off, with one hand on the package and one eye half-open whenever the train stopped, just in case someone came in who might cause trouble. But no one did, and I slept until a conductor woke me calling, "Hannover, Hannover in ten minutes." I was almost home.

And then, as the train pulled in, my heart sank into my shoes. Two English MPs stood on the platform. There was no way I could avoid them, and when they saw me they might want to talk. Not many American soldiers were seen in Hannover, since it was in the English zone. What if the MPs were curious about what I was doing here and wanted to have a chat with the Yank? I would have to get off the train and walk as briskly as possible, as if I had important business in Hannover at one o'clock in the morning.

I got off right in front of them. When I stepped down, the duffel bag slipped halfway off my shoulder, and I stumbled and almost lost my balance. One of the MPs stepped forward and helped me get it back into position, saying something unintelligible in his brisk, clipped English. I didn't look at him or smile; I just walked away, my heart pounding under Mr. Jones's identification card. But I felt sorry that I hadn't been able to thank the MP. Just before I went into the waiting room I looked back, and he was still looking at me, so I winked. He smiled and waved his hand, and I ducked through the door.

Outside, the huge plaza was empty. It looked strange without the usual black-market crowd. Carrying the coffee easily, I walked toward Oskar's, a few blocks off. On the way I met a young German policeman. At first he must have seen only a man carrying a huge package, but as I came closer and he could see the American uniform he looked very surprised.

After I passed him I glanced back; he was still staring after me. Quickly I moved on and turned into the side street where Oskar had his restaurant.

I knocked on the door, waited, then knocked much louder and rang the bell at the same time. Upstairs, a window rattled, and Oskar stuck his head out and called, in a sleepy, annoyed voice, "*Was wollen Sie denn?* What do you want?"

"It's me, Oskar," I called softly. "I've got something for you. Come down and let me in."

"*Ja, ja,*" he said, and withdrew his head.

In a few moments he opened the door, and I walked in carrying my baggage. The restaurant was dark. Oskar turned on a light behind me, and then he said, in a peculiar voice, "Turn around." The look on his face was comical. "Are you insane?" he asked. "Where have you been?"

I replied, "I just came from the station. I was in Brussels. An American soldier doesn't need a passport, so Jony got me the uniform and I went."

Oskar looked bewildered. We went into the kitchen, and I lowered the duffel bag to the floor, opened the smaller parcel, and took out a five-pound package.

"This is for you," I said, and gave it to him.

He opened the package, and then the aroma hit him. "Ahh!" He drank it into his body like a drug addict. "*Kaffee, Kaffee!*" Then he turned toward me and exulted, "*Ach,* this is so wonderful! You must let me do something for you—"

I interrupted him. "Yes, you can get me that taxi, so I can go home to Buchholz and get out of this damned uniform and into my own clothes."

"But you look so nice in that clean uniform. It fits you so well. You must keep it. Wait for a minute." And he bolted upstairs.

I looked into the parcel. Most of the coffee was packed in five-pound bags like the one I had given Oskar, but there were also a few little ones of about a pound each.

Oskar came back down. "Do you remember Rita? You met her the night you sold me the camera."

"I remember her very well," I said. "She is a beautiful girl."

"She is upstairs, and I told her to come down. I didn't tell her you were here. I want to see whether she'll recognize you in that uniform."

The stairs creaked, and Rita came in wearing a blue robe. It looked a little large for her; it was probably Oskar's. Her dark blonde hair was brushed back, and she had a sleepy look on her face. When she saw the uniform her eyes opened wide and she tightened the robe around her. Then she frowned, looked more closely at my face, and burst out laughing. "What a perfect American soldier! How have you been passing your time, besides bringing Oskar all that nice fresh pork?" She sniffed the air. "Coffee! So that's it. What a delicious smell!"

Oskar was smiling, watching her reaction. His brown hair was tousled, and he looked boyish. I was sure his black-market contacts had never seen him like this; with them he was sharp, quick, expressionless.

Abruptly he said to Rita, "Enjoy yourself here with him," and went back upstairs.

As soon as he was gone I felt shy, and I could think of nothing to do but reach into the bag and bring out a small package. Holding it out to Rita, I said, "Take this home. From the way you smelled it, I can tell you love real coffee. I don't like it much myself."

She took the bag, opened it, and breathed in the coffee aroma. Then she put it down on the table and came over to me. She looked into my eyes with her clear gray ones and smiled, which made deep dimples in both her cheeks. She reached up and kissed me, quickly and lightly. "Thank you for being so nice," she said. "You don't ask for anything in return, but I would like to spend some time with you. I am sure Oskar wouldn't mind. We could even use his apartment upstairs when he's on the black market."

She stepped closer and kissed me again, a little longer and harder this time. Waves of warmth went through me, and my hands went around her waist. Under the robe she was slender, warm, and alive. She took my hat off and mussed up my hair, playing with it with both hands.

"Can you dance?" she asked.

I shook my head. "I've never tried."

"With such a nice tall body, you will make a wonderful dancer. I would like to teach you to dance. How old are you?"

"I am just twenty, and before I reach twenty-one I would like to be far away from the black market."

Rita said, "You are only twenty? I am three years older than you. Why don't you stay here now? Oskar has to leave soon, and we can be alone for a few hours."

She put her head on one side and looked up at me. She was very, very lovely. She had been bold with me, and yet there was nothing indelicate about her. She was young and healthy, sweet and clean. But I didn't want to stay with her in Oskar's apartment—in Oskar's bed, for all I knew.

"I am tempted," I said. "But I want to get out of this uniform. We can meet another day, and we don't have to use Oskar's place. I have money. We can go anywhere you like."

"You can reach me here any time," she said.

Just at that moment Oskar came downstairs, and I stepped away from Rita, smoothing back my rumpled hair. Oskar looked from one to the other of us and smiled. Then he asked me, "Are you and Jony planning to sell the coffee to anyone in particular?"

"If you're interested I'll tell him," I said.

"Please do. Now I will call the taxi driver to take you back to camp. But first I'm going to make some real coffee."

Rita had gone upstairs, with a good-bye wink that made me blush. Oskar busied himself at the stove, and when the taxi driver arrived Oskar called him in to have a cup of coffee. The two of them sat at the table exclaiming with pleasure. I had a cup, too. It was black and bitter, barely sweetened with a saccharin tablet. How stupid the Germans were, I thought, to pay so much for a pound of this stuff.

The ride to camp was over quickly, and for the first time I was really glad to see the place. Somehow it looked warm and like home. I paid the driver, picked up my bags, and walked through the gate. The guard recognized me, but the uniform confused him. "Jony and I had a bet, and I won," I said, and left him to make sense of that.

The sky was beginning to get light. As I walked into Barracks 1, Jony came out his door and said, "I saw you arrive in the taxi. Thank God you're back! I haven't slept all night." He helped me lower the duffel bag from my shoulder, and we embraced. "We will never do this again," he said. "After you left I felt terrible. You are like my son."

We dragged the duffel bag into the empty room next to Jony's, and he started unpacking it. By the time all the packages were laid out on the floor the room was filled with the spicy fragrance of fresh coffee.

"You should have seen Oskar's face when he saw the uniform," I said. "He wanted me to tell you that he is interested in buying the coffee."

"Did you give him some?" Jony asked.

"Yes, and one of his pretty girls was there, so I gave her some, too. She wants me to spend the day with her sometime."

"And the night, no doubt," Jony said. I felt myself turn red. "Well, you know, we're having another dance here the day after tomorrow. Why don't you invite both of them?"

"Maybe I will," I said.

Jony locked the door of the spare room with a strong padlock and walked over to the canteen with me. It was dawn. I was tired, but peaceful and happy, as if I had accomplished something. Unlocking my little room, I saw my worn old black-dyed DP clothes laid out on the cot where I had left them. They looked wonderful. I started unbuttoning the new uniform. If Jony said it was all right to keep it I would dye it black. Then it would seem more like mine.

"I'll save half the coffee for Oskar, and this afternoon I'll try to make some contacts to sell what's left," Jony was saying. Then he noticed that I had folded the American uniform and was putting my own clothes on. "Aren't you going to get some sleep?"

"I will," I said. "I just had to feel my clothes on my body again."

Jony left, and I lay down on the cot in my clothes. It was like being back in my own skin. Before I fell asleep I thought of Rita and cursed myself for not staying with her. If I hadn't been so tired . . . Still wearing my clothes, I fell into a deep, dreamless sleep.

When I woke up, feeling refreshed, happy, and hungry, it was dark outside. Was it tonight, tomorrow morning, or to-morrow night? My stomach didn't care; it just complained. I got dressed and went into the canteen. Max grinned at me and said, "Congratulations! You slept all day."

"Hello, Max. Is it suppertime yet?"

"How did you guess? Ah, that's my boy. You have a fine timepiece in there, just like your uncle Max. Maria has some *ghiveci* on the stove for you. I just had a cup of real coffee at their place, and it tasted great. But never take another chance like that!" Max brandished the glass he was drying. "Jony showed me the uniform and told me the whole story. That took a lot of courage, but, boy, you have a fool's luck, too. Next time you might not be so lucky, and I'd hate to lose you."

At Jony's, I had to endure Maria's loving scolding while

the smell of the *ghiveci* made my stomach hurt and growl and my mouth water. "*There* you are!" she said, and kissed me on the cheek. Her black hair was coming loose, her cheeks were red from cooking, her black eyes snapped. "Thank you for the coffee! I've made some real Turkish coffee, black and strong. You must be hungry." I nodded vigorously. "But before you sit down I want you to promise me that you will never try anything like that again. Jony was very worried about you. When he came back from the station he told me where you had gone in the American uniform, and I was furious with him for letting you take such a chance. I love real coffee, and I'm glad we have it, but suppose you had gotten caught! Nobody knows what they would have done to you."

It was the longest speech I had ever heard from Maria. I gave her my promise, and then she brought me a steaming bowl of *ghiveci*. I would have promised her anything to get that *ghiveci*.

While I was eating Jony came in and joined me. Between mouthfuls he said that Tannov would take us to Vasile's camp the next morning to sell some of the coffee at the bazaar. Oskar could buy the rest, except for ten or fifteen pounds we would keep for ourselves.

"We have to talk to Vasile anyway," Jony said, wiping his mouth. "Listen to this. Everything happens at once. Mitya told me today that a friend of his who works in the UNRRA warehouse at Vasile's camp says that any day now a shipment of eighty bags of sugar, twenty-five pounds each, will be delivered to the warehouse for storage. I gave Mitya one hundred marks and he promised not to tell anybody else about it. Vasile is probably in charge of the guards at that warehouse, and he would know where the sugar is coming from and what's supposed to be done with it. If we can take it, he'd also know the safest way to sell it. We'll ask him about it tomorrow."

After supper we went to the canteen. The band was there rehearsing for the dance, and the bar was crowded with DPs. While Jony talked to Max about the dance I sat down by the piano and listened to the old man make his soft, nostalgic sounds. When the band took a break he smiled and greeted me.

I asked him whether he liked real coffee better than *Ersatz-Kaffee*.

"Of course," he replied. "Who doesn't? But it is much too expensive on the black market. Sometimes they let us have a cup or two at the officers' club after we play there."

"I have some for you. Wait just a minute." Asking Jony for the key to the spare room, I ran over to Barracks 1, opened the fragrant room, and brought back a one-pound bag of coffee. The band was playing again, and I sat by the piano. When the song ended I gave the bag to the professor.

He opened it and breathed deeply. Then he looked up and smiled. He had such kind blue eyes, and the network of fine wrinkles around them broke up and changed when he smiled. "God bless you, my boy," he said. "What can I do for you besides play the piano? After we finish rehearsing I will play whatever you like."

"Anything you play is very beautiful," I said.

The band ended its rehearsal, and while the other musicians were packing up their instruments the professor went on playing alone. The noise of DPs arguing at the bar and the clashing of music stands faded away as I listened to the dreamy sounds. The professor seemed to know one's mood, or maybe he created the mood. I wished, with a sharp pang that surprised me, that Rita was here listening with me. Most of the DPs were leaving. They liked the band better, probably because it was noisier. The old man bent his white head over the piano, moving his hands softly and surely over the keys. The music rose and came down and took you up again on soft wings. When it came down at the gentle end it was so soft that the last note could barely be heard.

Max and I thanked him, and the professor said, "I thank you for the coffee and for listening to me. I know you appreciate what you hear."

When he left Mitya began sweeping up. I went over to him and said, "Jony told me about the sugar. We're going to find out about it tomorrow morning. Be sure you don't mention it to anyone." Mitya said he wouldn't, and I promised to leave a pound of coffee behind the bar with his name on it.

The next morning Tannov picked us up, and in twenty minutes we were at Vasile's camp. At the gate, Jony went into the guardhouse and came out with Vasile. He embraced me roughly and kissed me on the cheek, saying, "It is good to see you."

Jony opened the trunk of the car and showed Vasile the coffee, explaining how I had gotten across the border and brought it back from Belgium.

"Good, good!" Vasile boomed, pounding me on the back. "I told you he is a good, smart boy."

He called two guards out of the shack and told them to take fifty pounds of the coffee to the coffee trader's stand in the bazaar. "Tell him it is mine, and sell it to him for me."

In a few minutes the guards returned and handed Vasile 25,000 marks—a generous price for the king. The traders knew it was not worth their hides to be stingy with him. Vasile gave the money to Jony, who then sent me over to the bazaar to buy ten pounds of sugar for Maria. I bought the sugar and got some hard candy for myself. Pushing my way out of the trading masses, I went back to the guard shack.

Jony and Vasile were standing outside talking about the sugar. According to Vasile, the UNRRA officer who was to receive the shipment very likely planned to steer it into black-market channels for himself, since he had been involved in black-market deals before. "It is the same one who was mixed up in the shoe scandal," Vasile said. "You remember him, Jony."

"Of course," Jony said, and explained to me, "They were caught selling a whole shipment of shoes that were meant for distribution to the DP camps. I've been thinking about this sugar operation. If the sugar is meant for holders of ration cards I don't want to take it. We can't steal from the people. They get much less than we do. But if this fellow has already stolen it, that's another story."

Vasile said he would ask some questions, and if it looked as though the UNRRA officer planned to divert the sugar onto the black market we would go into action and beat him to it. We shook hands and went to the car. Tannov was waiting for us.

On the way to Oskar's restaurant, Jony said, "Here, take ten thousand marks. And more is coming. You really earned it the other day."

Oskar wasn't at the restaurant, so Jony and Tannov waited there while I went over to the milling black market and found him. "Come on," I said. "Jony has about fifty pounds of coffee for you."

On the way back to the restaurant, he said, "Rita keeps asking me where you are. You should have spent an afternoon with her. She is really a very fine girl, and she talks about you constantly."

I said that they should both come to the dance we were having that night.

Jony and Tannov were drinking a bottle of wine, and a waiter had put a bill on their table. Before he even said hello Oskar grabbed the bill and tore it up. Then he shook hands vigorously with Jony and Tannov, and we went out to the car. Jony opened the trunk and showed Oskar the bags of coffee. "For you the price is two hundred marks a pound," he said. "There are about fifty pounds here." While they counted money I helped a waiter carry the coffee into the kitchen.

Before we left I reminded Oskar about the dance, and Jony said, "Yes, come see our canteen, and bring that girl I've heard so much about."

"How will we get into the camp?" Oskar asked.

"Just tell the guard that I invited you. I'll warn him to expect two friends of mine."

That night at supper Jony gave me another five thousand marks. "But, Jony," I protested, "my pockets are bulging. I feel like a millionaire!"

He laughed. "If you had to live on that money outside the

camp, without ration cards, with your appetite, it wouldn't last you two months."

By the time we went over to the canteen the band had already started playing, and the DPs were coming in out of the night in groups of five and more. Soon it was jammed, and within half an hour the musicians had taken off their jackets and ties, rolled up their sleeves, and everyone but the old professor had a glass within easy reach. The floor was swarming with dancers, and the air was a babble of all the languages of Eastern Europe. As the tempo of the music and the intake of wine increased, so did the gusto and body of the languages and the number of curses, like a rich, sweaty goulash with chunks of garlic in it.

Jony left to go to bed. Not long afterward a guard pushed through the crowd looking for him. I asked what he wanted.

"There are two Germans at the gate," he said. "They say Jony invited them to the dance."

Oskar and Rita! "They are friends," I told him. "I was with Jony when he invited them. I'll come with you to the guardhouse and pick them up."

Oskar and Rita were waiting in the dim light outside the gate. Rita was holding tightly to Oskar's arm, and they both looked strained. The sergeant was eyeing them with a cold hostility that made it obvious he didn't like Germans.

"Let them in," I called. "They are friends of mine and Jony's." When Rita saw me coming her face lit up with relief.

Grudgingly the sergeant let them pass. "You will be responsible for them as long as they are in camp," he warned.

Rita took my arm as we walked back toward the canteen. "I hope we aren't too much trouble," she said.

"Jony will tell the guards tomorrow that you are his friends, and after that you can come and go whenever you like. Don't worry about it," I reassured them. "Come on in. I want you to meet Max, and then we'll have some wine."

Mitya was sitting with some friends at a table near the bar, and when he saw that I had company he got up and gave us the table. Rita had taken off her scarf, so that her hair swung free. She was looking around wide-eyed at the crowd of dancing, sweating, swearing DPs. I guessed that the atmosphere of a DP dance was a rough introduction to the camp for her. The drab clothing, the sudden hoots of raw laughter, the brooding, solitary drinkers at tables here and there, and the slight edge of hysteria, of possible violence in the air, must all have seemed strange and frightening. Rita had on a frilly white blouse and a blue skirt, not new, but cleaner and finer than most of the DP women could afford, and somewhere she had found a touch of lipstick or rouge to redden her lips. I realized that I didn't know anything about her: what kind of family she came from, or where she lived or worked. I did understand this DP world and felt safe in it. A fineness like Rita's made me feel clumsy and ashamed. Maybe I shouldn't have invited her here.

I excused myself and went behind the bar, sending Max over to get acquainted with Rita and Oskar. When I took them a bottle of wine a few minutes later it was obvious that Max and Oskar had hit it off. They were laughing and joking like brothers, big Max and ebullient little Oskar.

Rita looked up and said, "Can't you sit down with us for a while?"

"I would like to, but I have to tend bar," I said, and escaped back to my observation post.

The band was playing a fox trot. I saw Max get up from the table, bow, and ask Rita to dance. They went onto the floor together, and Max swept her around for the next half hour. She looked very safe in his arms, and now and then I saw her throw her head back and laugh at something Max said, showing her beautiful, slender throat. She was a good dancer.

When they came over to the bar Rita was flushed and out of breath, and whatever her fears had been, they seemed to be forgotten. She said, "Your friend Max is the best dancer I've ever danced with."

Max came behind the bar and gave me a shove, saying,

"Go and sit with her for a while. She came to visit you, not me." I followed Rita back to her table.

Oskar was in his warm, expansive mood, so different from his black-market personality. His lean features could be very kind and full, and his eyes twinkled with humor. "I am enjoying every moment of this," he said. "Is every dance so lively? Where do the musicians come from?"

I explained that they were Estonians or Lithuanians who had met in the camps and hit it off, and that now they wanted to emigrate together but it was taking a long time to get all their papers straightened out, because three of them had been interned in labor camps in Germany while the other two had escaped from behind the Iron Curtain. I was having trouble keeping my mind on what I was saying, because Rita's hand had found mine under the table and she was gently playing with my fingers, watching me with a mock innocent expression.

A few minutes later I glanced over at the bar, and no one was behind it. Looking out on the floor, I soon spotted Max dancing like one possessed. I regretfully disengaged my hand, excused myself from the table, and went back to work. Between dances Max came over, rosy and panting, his round face shining with sweat, and said, "I'm sorry, but I just have to dance." He grabbed the girl nearest him and whirled her onto the floor.

The bar was so busy that Mitya had to go to the Greek's shack for wine several times. Oskar and Rita came over to talk to me between customers, and a group of DPs took their table. Suddenly Max reappeared, snatched Rita away from the bar, and danced with her again. He kept drinking more and more wine, and kept on dancing, until finally his dancing turned to staggering and Mitya had to lead him off to Barracks 1 and put him to bed.

But Mitya didn't come back, and later, when we needed still more wine, I asked Oskar if he would take charge of the bar while I went through the fence to the Greek's.

"*Aber natürlich*," he said. "Just tell me the price."

"One hundred and twenty-five marks a bottle," I told him. Oskar stepped behind the bar. I picked up the suitcase and turned to Rita. "Will you come with me?" She grabbed her purse, and we went out into the night.

After the crowds and noise and light of the canteen, the compound was very dark and quiet. The chilly wind felt good on my face. A few stars showed through the clouds. We walked without saying anything, holding hands, between the dark forms of the barracks. At the gap in the fence I crawled through first, still holding Rita's hand, and then helped her through. She caught the heel of her shoe on the wire and stumbled a little, and I held out my arms to stop her from falling. Suddenly we were kissing, clinging to each other. I dropped the suitcase, and we swayed in the night wind until we were very cold—on the outside. Between us surged all the heat and hunger of twenty and twenty-three years.

When we pulled back, breathless, Rita said, "Can we stay together tonight?"

"Yes, yes. Oskar can sleep in the spare room, and you can stay with me in my room behind the canteen."

She tried to capture her flyaway hair while I knocked on the door of the Greek's shack. He opened it, a bent, weather-beaten little man in his forties or fifties, with a mustache and gray-and-black beard stubble.

"That's some dance you got going over there," he said. Then he saw Rita, and his eyes changed to suspicion.

"She's with me. Don't worry," I said. When we stepped into the shack and he saw how she held on to my arm he smiled knowingly.

The room was smoky and dimly lit by a kerosene lantern turned low to conserve fuel. In one corner a small fire flickered, throwing weird shadows among the odds and ends of the Greek's trades: pots and pans, cases of dusty bottles, and a couple of big kettles for distilling.

The Greek took the suitcase. "How many you want?" He spoke a thickly accented German.

"Twenty-five."

He disappeared toward the back of the shack, into a closet or storeroom, while I counted out the 1,600 marks. When he came back with the suitcase I said, "That should be all for tonight."

Back at the canteen, we found Oskar very much at home. He had taken off his jacket and reigned in his shirt sleeves behind the bar, talking and joking with the DPs. He really did have some of Max's ease and charm, and the DPs seemed to have forgotten that Oskar was a German. When he saw me he winked and said, "What took you so long? I just sold the last bottle of wine."

The dance was ending now, and Rita and I sat holding hands, drinking wine slowly, and glancing at each other with shy anticipation. The wine was going to my head, and she said she felt sleepy, too. It was almost four in the morning.

I went behind the bar and said to Oskar, "If you want to stay, I have a room for you. Thanks for helping me out."

"*Ach*, it was nothing. For you I will do anything. Here is the money." He shoved the cashbox my way. I counted and recounted: 3,900 marks.

I took Oskar to the spare room in Barracks 1, where the smell of fresh coffee still lingered in the air. Oskar took a deep breath and said, "Here I will sleep very well and will dream of coffee. Good night, *Junge*." He looked at me kindly, and I knew he was thinking about Rita. I was grateful that he had the tact not to say anything about her. It bothered me to think about her relationship with him, but right now I was too happy to let anything bother me.

At the canteen, the musicians were ready to leave for the night, but I took the old professor aside and said, "I have a bottle of wine for you. Could you stay and play just a little for me and the girl I have with me?"

He said, "I am very tired, but for you I will play," and he began the "Moonlight Serenade." Rita leaned her head on my shoulder, and I remembered dreamily that just last night I had wished she was here with me listening to him.

Just as the professor finished and was getting up to go to his barracks Mitya came in.

"What happened to you after you took Max to his room?" I asked.

"I couldn't come back," he said. "My friend the guard showed up to tell me that the sugar came in late this afternoon."

"Good, Mitya," I said. "We'll know by tomorrow evening what we are going to do about it."

While Rita watched curiously, we figured on the top of the bar with chalk how much money the eighty bags of sugar would bring at the current black-market price: over three hundred thousand marks! But it would be almost impossible to dispose of that much sugar before an investigation of the theft was carried out, and it would also flood the black market and bring the price down. Mitya left, shaking his head.

I locked up the canteen and led Rita to my room. Propping a chair under the doorknob as a makeshift lock, I kept my back to her while she undressed and slipped into bed. Then I turned off the light, undressed in the dark, and sat down on the edge of the narrow cot. The blood was pounding in my head; I didn't know whether it was from the wine or because of Rita. I couldn't see her. Awkwardly I touched the rounded form she made under the blanket. She reached up and ran her hands lightly over my shoulders and chest, and the touch went through me like an electric shock. I found myself gripping her slender arms, kissing her with a crazy hunger that seemed to come out of nowhere and that met an answering hunger in her. She pushed back the blanket and pulled me down next to her, and suddenly the whole live length of her woman's body was pressed against mine, round and cool and soft and hot and demanding. . . .

Before I fell asleep I was aware of her warm, breathing weight in my arms. She slept trustfully, like a child, with her mouth a little open. With wonder I touched the silky softness of her hair, her ear and delicate neck. What a fragile thing a young girl was! And what a rough, predatory world we were living in! Its dangers were never far from my mind, and it was much more dangerous for a woman. A fresh young girl like Rita could so easily become the prey of an unscrupulous man, or of her own hunger. And I had nothing to offer her—no home, no job, no shelter. I had only my black-market life, with its wild risks and unpredictable windfalls. And my strength. At least I could protect her, and that made me feel happy and strong. Holding her safe in my arms, I fell sound asleep.

A soft knocking woke me, and I opened my eyes to bright sunlight. Rita was still sleeping. "Who is it?"

"Me, Jony."

I took the chair from the door and let him in.

When he saw the shape of a body in my bed he frowned and said softly, "Who is that?"

"Rita and Oskar came last night after you went to bed."

He smacked his forehead with the palm of his hand. "*Vai!* I forgot to leave word at the guardhouse. I hope they didn't give you any trouble."

"A little," I said. "The sergeant was pretty nasty. You'd better talk to him."

Rita stirred and opened her eyes. When she saw Jony, they went wide with alarm. She clutched the blanket under her chin.

I said to her, "Don't worry. This is Jony. I'm sure Oskar has told you about him."

"Yes, he did. Hello, Jony." And she smiled and reached a hand out from under the blanket.

He bent and kissed it in gallant Rumanian fashion. "Get up, now, and come over to my place," Jony said. "Maria is making breakfast for our guests."

He let himself out, and I washed, with cold water from the bucket I filled every night, and put on my clothes. I told Rita to take her time. I would wait for her in the canteen.

Jony was just leaving the canteen, and I gave him the money we had made at the dance and told him how Oskar had tended bar better than Max and I could have done together.

"He and Max are very much alike," Jony said. "Where did you put Oskar to sleep?"

I explained that he was in the spare room in Barracks 1 and we walked over together to wake him up.

When we knocked on the door Oskar opened it instantly, and his face lit up in a smile. "Good morning," he said. "I like your dances, but I was disappointed that you weren't there, Jony. Did he tell you I helped out at the bar?"

"Yes, Oskar, and I hear you're a natural. The DPs will be asking for you at the next dance. Get dressed and come over to my place, and we'll all have breakfast in half an hour."

"*Ja, ja.* And how is little Rita? Isn't she a fine girl?"

"Yes, Oskar, I like her," I said, not looking at him.

I went back to the canteen, where Mitya was busy sweeping, and knocked on my door. Rita answered with a musical "Come in." She had put on her blouse and skirt and was running a comb through her hair.

She turned with a mischievous look. "I hope you don't mind, but I used your toothbrush."

"Of course not." I kissed her and stroked her hair. She was so fresh and clean and sweet-smelling. . . . I kissed her again.

After a few moments she whispered, "Lock the door." I put the chair back under the doorknob and unbuttoned her blouse. Our love-making now was different, more exciting in a way, but more bashful and aware in the morning light. Afterward we shyly washed, laughing and splashing the icy water on each other's backs and necks. Her skin was smooth and creamy white. To me it was a luxury, like fine silk. It embarrassed me to touch it with my big hands, still work-hard from Russia.

Rita hurriedly straightened her skirt as we went through the canteen. When she saw Mitya she asked, "What were you and Mitya trying to figure out last night on the bar with chalk? What was he so excited about?"

"If things go well, we may get a lot of sugar."

"If you do could I buy some for my parents?"

"I will give you some," I said. "I won't forget you."

"My parents asked me to give you their thanks and regards. They are very grateful for the coffee you gave me."

In Barracks 1 we knocked on Max's door and got a re-sounding *"Herein!"* He opened the door, greeted Rita with a kiss on the cheek, and said, "How is my favorite dancing partner? Did you sleep well?"

"Yes, thank you," she said. "The dance was wonderful, Max. I would like to come to the next one. But we have to teach this fellow here to dance."

We went across the hallway to Jony's. Maria was a little shy, but Oskar's personality warmed the atmosphere. Fresh bread, butter, marmalade, and two big pots of coffee stood on the table, and sugar in a big white bowl beside the coffee. We were a little crowded, but we managed.

Oskar invited Maria and Jony to come to his restaurant for dinner the next time he bought some fresh pork from us. Maria told him she had been in Hannover only once. "All I remember is the huge black-market crowd in front of the station," she said. "It hummed like a swarm of bees I saw in Rumania when I was a child."

In her soft voice, she talked to Rita for a while. Listening, I learned that Rita's father was a doctor and that she had finished her education last year and was helping her father in his office. As we ate and talked and drank steaming cups of coffee, an old conviviality, shattered by the war, was slowly mending itself. Like all of Europe, we were convalescents, and life was coming back to us little by little.

Oskar had to get back to the restaurant, so he and Rita thanked Jony and Maria for their hospitality and said goodbye. Jony and I walked them to the camp gate, and I kissed Rita good-bye and promised to see her soon.

As we walked back I stretched luxuriously. "I'm ready for the action," I said, and Jony laughed.

"What about this sugar operation?" I asked him. "Did Mitya tell you the sugar had come in?"

"Yes, he did, and Vasile should be here later to tell us where we stand."

We waited for Vasile all afternoon. At five, when he still hadn't come, Jony got Tannov to drive us to his camp. We walked into the guardhouse and found Vasile taking off his jacket. He had just come in.

"I'm sorry," he said, "but I just got back from finding out about the sugar." Glancing at the guard on duty, he said, "Let's go outside where we can talk."

We walked behind the guard shack, and Vasile continued. "It is the same bastard of an UNRRA officer who sold those shoes. He got this sugar from the American army the same way, on the pretext of distributing it to the DP camps. So we have to take it away from him, and soon. I don't think he will dare to make much noise about it."

Jony said, "Vasile, we will need a truck, and I don't think I can get one in time."

"We'll have a truck," Vasile said. "I will get one. Now, what shall we do with the sugar? That's a hell of a lot of sugar. I am sure there will be an investigation. We can keep about five bags, but we will have to get rid of the rest quickly."

Jony frowned, thinking.

Suddenly Vasile smacked his hands together. "I have an idea! We will make liquor out of it! I have a still near my camp that can handle thirty-five bags of sugar. Jony, doesn't the Greek behind your canteen have a still?"

"He used to," Jony said. "I'll ask him tonight whether it's in working order. That's a good idea. It would be hard to hide so much sugar in either one of the camps. And we can sell the liquor in the canteen just as easily as sugar on the black market. The English captain never asks me where I get my liquor for the canteen. So it's settled. See if you can get a truck for tomorrow night."

We shook hands with Vasile, got into Tannov's car, and drove back to our camp.

The next day there was a hard spring rain. In the afternoon Jony came into the canteen shaking off the raindrops. "This is very good weather for tonight's plans," he said. "Visibility is low. Let's hope it keeps up. Tannov couldn't stay, so we'll have to take the streetcar into Hannover. We can leave at about five o'clock and stop at Oskar's for something to eat. From there we can take his taxi to Vasile's."

At five, when we got on the streetcar, it was still raining, but not as hard. The weather had not dampened the urgency of the black-market trading in front of the station, we noticed as we ran through the rain to Oskar's restaurant. He was delighted to hear that we wanted to have dinner there. Running into the kitchen, he cooked the meal himself: *Schweine-braten*, sauerkraut, and plenty of roast potatoes. After we ate our fill Jony asked Oskar how much we owed. Oskar acted insulted, so we just thanked him, and he sent for the taxi.

While we waited I said to him, "Sometime tonight we will stop by to see you. There will be something for you."

"You have brought me much pleasure," he said. "Fresh pork, coffee, and now what is it?"

"Sugar," I whispered. "We will give you fifty pounds. But please give at least five pounds of it to Rita. I promised her."

"*Natürlich*," he said, and then a customer called him away. Our taxi came, and we directed the driver to Vasile's camp.

A big solid shape loomed in the rainy twilight behind the guard shack. Jony and I looked at each other and grinned. It was a truck. Inside the shack, Vasile was sitting on a bunk, and when we came in he got up, obviously in good spirits.

"Did you see the truck outside? Guess how I got it."

Jony turned to me and said, "He probably took it from somebody at gunpoint!"

"How did you know?" Vasile boomed. "Let me tell you about it. I waited for a friend to bring me a truck, but by five o'clock no friend and no truck had arrived. I figured the best place to get a truck was on the highway. I had somebody drive me to the highway not far from here. He left me at one of the autobahn exits. I waited about half an hour, and when a truck came along I stopped it with my pistol. The German driver got out, and when he saw that I wasn't an English MP he tried to take the gun away from me. It was over quickly. I only hit him two or three times and then left him sitting against a lamppost right at the exit. Now, my friends," he whispered, "let's go out to the truck."

Once outside, he continued to whisper. "The guard on duty at the warehouse likes to drink. Before he went on duty I gave him a bottle of *rachiu*. By now he is probably sleeping, so we will only have to tie him up good, and he'll never know what happened. This way, if he is questioned later he can just tell the truth. No one will never find out that we have the sugar. Let's wait about forty-five minutes more, so there is less risk of the guard not being peacefully asleep." We sat in the truck, talking until we got cold and had to go into the guardhouse, to be near the stove.

Vasile said, "As soon as we have the sugar in our possession I will get the still going. I will keep only one bag of sugar for myself. The rest goes into the still. Did you find out if the one at the Greek's is working?"

Jony replied that it was, and that the Greek had said he could handle thirty or thirty-five bags.

"If everything works out," I said, "those two stills will be very busy for the next three or four days. Think of all that liquor, and I don't even drink!"

"This might get you started." Vasile laughed. "Let's have a drink now, before we start out."

From under his cot he pulled out a bottle and passed it around. Remembering the last time, I declined, and Vasile's booming laughter filled the shack. He tossed down another healthy swallow and shouted, "Now we go!"

The three of us went out and piled into the truck. Vasile yelled for the guard to open the gate, and as he drove through he started singing a wild song. I thought, "This crazy bastard doesn't know the word fear. He is one of the last great bandits."

As he drove I turned and watched his pirate's profile. Its broken, crooked nose gave him a fierce and determined look. If I were one of the guards at the warehouse, I would help Vasile load the sugar on his truck just so he wouldn't get mad at me. I had never seen him really angry, and I didn't want to.

Jony was sitting in the middle, and between us he looked like a midget. When he saw me staring at Vasile he chuckled and said, "We are in the best of company for this undertaking. Have no fear."

"I don't have any fear after looking at him. I fear for the guards."

Vasile growled, over the noise of the truck, "Just let me get my hands on them."

At the end of a winding side street, we stopped outside a forsaken-looking warehouse. Moving quickly, Vasile took some wire out of his pocket and vanished around the corner of the building to get in through the back. Jony and I rolled the windows down and waited about ten minutes. There was no sound, and then suddenly the door of the truck was flung open and Vasile stood there—laughing. He got in and drove up close to the door, and we jumped down and went into the warehouse.

The only light inside came from a dim bulb. The ceiling could barely be seen, just a network of dusty spider webs. Against the front wall, near the door, were the piles of sugar bags, and next to them were two trussed-up bundles—the two guards, bound with wire, with empty bags over their heads as blindfolds. Vasile took a flask out of his pocket and poured some whiskey over them; they would reek of drunkenness when they were discovered in the morning. We went to work quickly and quietly loading the sugar into the truck.

As I lifted the sacks I could feel the precious grainy stuff sliding and sifting under the cloth. I had been so starved for sweets in Russia that it suddenly seemed a pity to turn all this good sugar into poisonous liquor. But the liquor would turn into good money—money that would bring us candy and all kinds of other good things.

Within twenty minutes we had all the sugar on board, and the two guards hadn't stirred. Vasile shut the door of the warehouse. We climbed into the truck and drove off, and a few minutes away from the warehouse we started laughing. It had been so easy.

"Vasile," Jony asked, "what happened with the guards? Were they asleep?"

"I knocked softly on the door in the back to find out, and one of them came and asked who it was. So I said, 'Open quickly,' and he opened the door a crack and stuck his rifle out. I grabbed the rifle, yanked him outside, and hit him over the head with his own gun. Then I went in. The other one saw me coming out of the dark, but I was carrying the rifle, and he was too drunk to notice that I wasn't his partner. By the time it dawned on him it was too late, and I hit him over the head, too. And that was it. I dragged the other one in and bound them both. Tomorrow they will have sore heads." He laughed so hard that the cab of the truck shook.

At his camp, Vasile went into the guard shack and came out with a shabbily dressed old man, who climbed into the back of the truck. Soon we stopped in a dark, narrow street in front of what looked like a garage. Vasile asked us to help him unload half the sugar. This was the still he had told us about, and the old man was the operator. Opening up the musty room, the old man turned on a dim light and got busy with his still right away, while we carried in the sugar. We were soon back in the truck driving toward our camp.

On the way through Hannover, Jony asked Vasile to stop

at Oskar's restaurant, and I gave Oskar two of the twenty-five-pound bags.

We talked about how much our two thousand pounds of sugar would have brought on the black market—about three hundred thousand marks. But then we figured the DPs and black marketeers would pay just as well for alcohol—the rawest rotgut stuff, anything that gave them a few hours of release and oblivion.

And there was Vasile, too, who drank the way a car drinks gas, as if the alcohol just fueled his incredible energy. "Soon you will have plenty to drink," I said.

"Yes, and it will warm my insides."

The Greek was waiting for us at Buchholz. He had his still ready to go, and he was thunderstruck when he saw how much sugar we had. Within five minutes we had emptied the truck.

As the last bag was unloaded, Vasile clapped his hands together like a gunshot, saying, "Ha, ha, my father would be proud of me! Tomorrow I will discover the theft myself. I will untie the guards and ask them what happened. Then I will report the missing sugar to the UNRRA officer, and we'll see how loud he screams. UNRRA, what a laugh! Now I will drive this truck somewhere near my camp and leave it and go about my business. By tomorrow evening I will let you know what UNRRA had to say." And he roared off in the stolen empty truck.

Jony and I each took one bag of sugar with us and told the Greek to save us five more. The Greek got busy with the still, and Jony and I went through the wire to the canteen.

Early the next morning the Greek woke me excitedly and demanded all the empty bottles I could find in the canteen. I helped carry two boxes of empty beer bottles to his place. He walked unsteadily and spoke thickly, and when I walked into the still and breathed the air I knew why. The alcohol fumes were overpowering. Five deep breaths, and you were intoxicated. For some reason, it seemed much easier and more natural than drinking. I stayed for several minutes inhaling the air, filling myself up with it, and then went back to my room feeling exhilarated. Here were fumes strong enough to intoxicate all the DPs in all the camps in Germany. Enough fumes to drive away all Europe's memories of the miserable war. The coal miners of the Donbas could pass through that room, breathe deeply, and forget their miseries. Then the Red Army could follow. Maybe all the armies of the world would get drunk, stop fighting, and make Vasile the big General of Peace.

With this happy thought I dozed off, and was awakened by a knock on the door. I groped, opened it, and met a drunken Max, happy and grinning.

"Come, come, my friend," he said, and staggered through the wire back to the Greek's. As we opened the door those beautiful fumes rolled out, even more pungent than before. I took several deep, deep breaths.

Max was laughing. "This is my kind of air."

The Greek had a scarf tied around his mouth, and he was staggering around among countless bottles full of a clear liquid. He gave us one and said, "Here, taste this, my friends."

Max took the bottle and drank from it. Then he shook himself, said "Brrrrh," and gave the bottle to me. I tasted it, but it burned like hell. I told Max I would stick to breathing.

I don't remember going to my room, but I found myself there, lying on my cot, with peaceful thoughts and no desire to get up. The room went round and round in a pleasant way. Later Jony was there, and he told me not to go back to the still or I would never sober up. Patting me reassuringly, he said, "You just go to sleep. I will come and wake you up this evening."

I must have slept again, because much later I remember Jony and Max being in the room. They were talking about bottles, and Jony was cursing Max for being drunk.

"This is serious," Jony was saying. "The Greek needs more bottles. He is going like an engine. Everything is full, and he still has over twenty bags of sugar left. Tannov will bring some canisters over, but not till later."

Max grinned and replied, in a slurred way, "Until we get the canisters let's just empty some of the bottles ourselves and take them back for a refill."

Jony shook his head. "Don't you go near the Greek's place. Go to sleep, and I'll do something." Then he turned to me and asked, "Can you help me later, if I need you?"

"Sure, sure. I feel all right now."

I got up and helped Max onto my cot. He could be easily maneuvered when drunk. I took his shoes off and put his feet up on the blanket, and before we were out of the room he was snoring.

We hunted up another dozen empty bottles and took them over to the Greek. I didn't go inside, and Jony put a handkerchief over his mouth before he did. He came right out with the Greek, who pulled his scarf down and took several deep breaths of fresh air.

"It is a long time since I work the still like this," he said, rubbing his face wearily. "I tend it all night. This is a marathon run, but it will be all right. Just get me those canisters when Tannov brings them. Until then, these empties will do." He pulled the scarf up, turned, and went back in, looking like a Western bandit with the scarf over his mouth and nose.

By the time we got back to the canteen I felt less drowsy; the fumes were wearing off. A few DPs wandered in and sat down at the bar, and I opened beers for them.

Suddenly Vasile burst in. "*Hahh!* I am glad I found you two," he shouted. Then he looked toward the DPs at the bar. "All right, all of you clear out. I will pay for your beers."

He must have been in his still inhaling the wonderful intoxicating air and sampling the new liquor. There had been no time for him to sleep, because he had had to "discover" the theft, free the guards, and report the loss to UNRRA. Yet he was fresh with an energy that electrified the air. The DPs wasted no time getting out of the canteen and out of his way.

When they were gone Vasile said, "There was a lot of

noise about the stolen sugar. Notices are going to be sent to every DP camp in the area stating the facts about the sugar. If the thieves are caught they will be shot. And do you know who is sending out those strict notices? The same officer who was planning to channel the eighty bags of sugar into the black market for himself!" Vasile roared with laughter, pounding the bar so that the glasses shivered and jumped. "But in two days there will be no sugar left, nothing but alcohol! How is your still going?" he asked Jony.

"Full force," Jony said. "Every empty bottle from the canteen and from my kitchen is full. By tomorrow night I think we will be done."

Vasile wanted to see our still, so we went off through the wire fence to the Greek's. I waited outside while he and Jony went in. They came out shortly, Vasile smacking his lips and grunting, "Very good, very good." Then he left to go back to his camp, saying, "Tomorrow we will celebrate having all this fine liquor, and we will drink a toast to the UNRRA officer."

The next morning Jony was called into the English captain's office. The captain showed him the notice about the sugar robbery and asked him please to report anything he heard about sugar traffic. Jony earnestly promised to do so. Meanwhile, in the Greek's shack behind the camp thirty-five bags of the stolen sugar were rapidly disappearing into hundreds of bottles of a clear, innocent-looking liquid. The weather was still chilly, and the wood smoke pouring from the Greek's chimney attracted no special attention.

That evening the still finally came to rest.

Word arrived that Vasile had rented a hall near his camp and was preparing to give a private party. He was sending some cars over to pick us up.

When the cars arrived it made me uneasy that the drivers were already drunk. They were loud and unsteady, and after we all got in they roared off toward Vasile's camp, slewing from one side of the road to the other and slamming on the brakes with happy abandon. I was beginning to have an ominous feeling about this party. DPs were highly explosive, and so much liquor could hardly fail to light the fuse. Once all their pent-up violence and anger were released, there could be no stopping them. I had a hunch that we were heading for disaster.

The rented place where the party was being held was a big, echoing high-ceilinged hall that must have been a gymnasium before the war. Tables and benches had been set up, and on a big table in the corner were spread out the proofs of Vasile's largesse: healthy chunks of pork back, garlicky homemade sausages and big hunks of black bread—not German bread bought with ration cards, but the genuine heavy, sour Russian black bread, the kind that had kept me alive for two years, baked by some Ukrainian women in Vasile's camp. There was a rush for the tables, and for the first twenty minutes or so everyone stuffed his mouth with pork back and black bread, jaws working away. A hall full of hungry DPs could eat ten bakeries and ten sausage shops empty in that time, but two women kept bringing more pork back and bread from a room at the back, and they kept the table full. The supplies seemed endless.

After about twenty minutes, though, I was eating alone. All the rest of the DPs had turned to the liquor, and they were drinking with single-minded determination. The band from our canteen, except for the old pianist, had come in one of the cars, and it was playing. Some of the drunks were dancing, and some of them were staggering around shouting and telling stories of the great drinking sprees they had been on before the war. Some were just quietly drinking themselves into a stupor. I didn't want any alcohol—I didn't need any. I had been in the still inhaling the air and sampling the bottles when the Greek finished the run. I was none too sober.

Jony wandered by, and I grabbed him and got him to sit down with me. He was about as sober as I was. Vasile was sitting on the next table in the middle of a flock of girls. His favorite, the blue-eyed Ukrainian, was sitting on his knee, drunk. The musicians were playing badly. They were drunk, too.

It started with an argument among three or four DPs. In drunken brotherhood, they had asked two girls to sleep with all of them at once. The girls had refused, and in the ensuing quarrel over which girl should go with whom the erstwhile brothers started yelling and swinging at each other. Bottles cracked over heads, and liquor and blood flowed freely. Just when it looked as if the fight would turn into a free-for-all Vasile jumped into the thick of it. I knew that no one had drunk more than he had. Two or three bodies went flying, bottles crashed around, liquor spluttered through the air—and there was silence. Vasile went back to his table. Two of the DPs began dragging limp bodies into a corner.

Then there was a loud, officious knocking on the door. It flew open, and there stood two German policemen looking around at the confusion. The people who lived in the neighborhood must have complained about the crashing, shouting, and music coming from the big hall. We weren't within the boundaries of Vasile's camp, so the local police had the authority to investigate.

The two cops didn't realize that they were risking their lives. They were Germans. And they were about to walk into a hall full of people who hated them savagely, who would be happy to hold them responsible for all the sufferings of the past ten years, and whose inhibitions had been removed by alcohol. The policemen saw only a hall full of shabby-looking drunks. That was their mistake.

The first one barked, "*Was ist los da?* What's going on here? We will lock up you drunken swine, all of you."

His partner had come in with him to assess the situation. At the sound of their German, the crowd grew ominously quiet.

I saw one of the more drunken DPs easing himself around behind them, swaying. They saw him, too, but because he was so unsteady they didn't pay any attention. He got close, and I noticed that he had a full bottle of liquor behind his back. He raised the bottle and swung it down on the second policeman's head so hard that the cork flew out like a projectile. Alcohol splashed everywhere, and the cop staggered. His partner spun around at the noise, and as he turned three or four bottles flew at him. The first hit his shoulder, the second grazed his head, and another missed and exploded on the wall.

It was the signal for bedlam. Pent-up screams tore out of chests stagnant with hate and frustration, and the mob of DPs swarmed forward and over the police officers. The DPs would have their blood, now, for all of Hitler's wrongs. I felt the violence in the air, thick and heavy and fearfully contagious, and I knew that only one thing could save those policemen's lives—Vasile. No sooner had I thought of him than there he was.

He dived into that howling mob of furious bodies like a tornado. Bodies flew right and left, chairs smashed, bottles splintered, and at the center of the storm stood Vasile, bleeding and growling and laughing and hitting, like a bloody King Neptune in his element. The sea of struggling bodies closed over him for a moment, and then he reappeared dragging the two unconscious policemen by their collars toward the window at the back of the hall. The DPs in the writhing heap on the battlefield were now fighting among themselves over whether or not they should let Vasile take the Germans away from them.

Vasile got the two policemen to the window, cracked their heads together—you could hear the sound in all that bedlam—and heaved up first one and then the other and hurled them out.

But the DPs couldn't stop fighting now. They grunted and howled and struggled, and then somebody smashed the light bulbs. In the dark I heard high-pitched screams of fury, and I felt stark fear. Jony and I ducked under a table, abruptly sober. He muttered, "We should never have come here, God damn it."

Then Vasile was there. I felt his strong hand close on my

arm, and he said, "Just follow me." I clutched at his shirt sleeve, and Jony held on to me. Through the dark hall we went, winding a safe path among the struggling and fallen bodies, the infernal screams and groans.

When we got outside Vasile said, "This is for me! You are not used to it, and, besides, you are both drunk"—this from Vasile, who had drunk enough for ten of us. Pointing at me, he said, "You take care of Jony. He is too small. I will go back in and restore order."

He turned and went inside. It took real courage to tangle with that demented mob. Jony and I looked at each other, and then went across the street to wait and see what happened.

We heard curses and howls of pain and anguish. The crash of breaking chairs, more shattering glass. Then Vasile's voice boomed, "The next one I catch on his feet, I will break his neck."

The noise dwindled away to silence. A weak light was turned on, and the guests started coming out the door. The party was over. The musicians staggered out, most of their instrument cases broken, and made their way unsteadily toward the next street, where the cars were parked. Others limped off into the night holding broken heads and bloody noses.

The last one out was Vasile, with a bottle of liquor in his hand. His face was a little bloody. At the door he tipped the bottle up, took a big swig, and threw it back inside. And then he laughed.

We walked toward his camp, where his Ukrainian girl was waiting. He had gotten her out first, even before us. She looked at his bloody face, gasped, and began wiping the blood away, saying, "I knew there would be trouble tonight. Now if you don't go to sleep I'm going to leave this camp tonight."

"Now I will sleep for one whole day. I am really tired."

He had said he was *really* tired. Jony turned to me and said, "I never thought I would hear him say those words."

Vasile found a driver to take us home and then went off with his girl to sleep. All the way back to our camp Jony and I were quiet, thinking about this incredible man, his power, endurance, and quick thinking. If he hadn't acted so quickly the two policemen would have been literally torn to pieces, and two dead bodies would have brought on a severe investigation. Vasile had saved them the only way he could, and it had worked. Someone had hit him over the head with a chair and he had laughed as he bled, as if it felt good, as if the blood running down his face relieved the pressure of energy inside him.

Chairs and bottles had been broken, blood and alcohol had flowed freely, and incredible violence had been released. But there was no major damage done. The party was over.

After the events of the last week I was exhausted. Vasile's explosive party was the last straw, and, glad as I had been to see the camp when I got back from Belgium, I needed to get away for a while.

I thought about spending a couple of days with Rita in Hannover, but that wasn't far enough away. Besides, I wanted to savor the memory of our first encounter, to make it last, like a cake of real soap or a piece of hard candy. And I was wary of getting too involved with her. In normal times, Rita was the kind of girl I would have fallen in love with. But in Russia, where I was occasionally drawn to one of the girls who worked in the mine, I had learned to deny myself that luxury. Love brought responsibilities that I, a prisoner, was in no position to handle. Now I was a DP and a black marketeer. Was that much better? No, I didn't want to visit Rita too soon or too often. Better to keep things casual, once-in-a-while.

With a little over ten thousand marks in my pocket, money was no problem, and I thought about taking a week or two off and just going somewhere. If Jony would lend me his military pass I could travel around easily enough. When I proposed the idea to him he said, "By all means take a trip. Get it out of your system. But be careful."

So I put my toothbrush and towel in my little cardboard suitcase, and took two bottles of liquor and the few pounds of sugar and coffee I had saved for my uncle. With Jony's pass in my pocket, I embraced him and Max, kissed Maria on the cheek, and promised that I would be back safely in a week or ten days. When they asked where I was going I said, "I'm not sure yet, but I've been thinking about Vienna. I would like to sit at a café and relax. I'm curious to see whether the famous *Gemütlichkeit* has survived the war."

The streetcar took me to Hannover, and soon I was on a packed, laboring train to Giessen. The ride seemed endless. It was tiring to be shoved from place to place constantly guarding my packages. Most of the passengers looked like black marketeers, furtive, skinny, ill-dressed, and pale. I was sure most were involved in deals of one sort or another just to survive. Only a few were seeking fortune or adventure. When the rationing ended the others would get jobs and go gratefully back to quiet, normal lives. The black market would vanish. Or, rather, it would go underground, and the profiteers and pickpockets, the moguls and the misfits, all those who couldn't or wouldn't fit into society or who preferred to prey on it, would merge with the underworld of organized and disorganized crime. And the others—the respectable citizens—many of them would find out that filling the hungry belly didn't stop the itch of greed, and they would learn to lie and steal and swindle in respectable ways. But all that lay far in the future. This was Germany 1948, and the black market was open, desperate, and nearly universal. It was like a disease, and on the local train to Giessen you were in strong danger of catching it.

It was late when I got to my uncle's. The children were in

bed, but the grownups hugged and kissed me and exclaimed over my black-market gifts. It was five years since they had drunk a cup of real coffee or had a shot of good, strong liquor. My aunt was happiest about the sugar. With ration cards it took six months to accumulate a few pounds.

They had a surprise for me, too—a letter from home! I tore it open eagerly. My parents said they had written to me often in the camps, but that they suspected I had been transferred and many of their letters had never reached me. My uncle had told them about my last two visits, they wrote, and they were overjoyed to know that they could be sure of reaching me at last. They said they were fine and I shouldn't worry about them. They kissed me and wanted to know more about me. How was I living? What were my plans?

It made me ache with sudden homesickness. I wished I could write them everything about my life here. I knew how my father would relish hearing about my black-market exploits. And how he would have loved Vasile—no one else in the world could laugh like those two! But my mother would worry if she heard about the chances I was taking. I couldn't tell them. And what if my letters were opened? I knew they couldn't tell me everything, either. Life in Russian-occupied Rumania was no bed of roses, I knew that. We were writing to each other through a veil of reassurances. I am glad I didn't know, then, that we would be doing so for the next twenty years. (I would not be able to go home again until 1966, five years after my father's death.)

My aunt and uncle and Angelika and I sat talking and drinking my fiery liquor late into the night. I had to tell them my stories: how I had gone to Belgium for the coffee dressed as an American soldier, how we had stolen the sugar from the UNRRA thief, and about the mad days of alcohol making. My uncle and his family were highly entertained. But I couldn't help thinking about my parents, wishing I was telling it all to them instead.

It was near dawn when we went to bed, and I slept until noon. When I woke up I lay there for a while thinking about where I should go. The idea of Vienna appealed to me more and more.

I thought about buying a decent suit of clothes. In Vienna, I would be conspicuous in my black-dyed uniform—the only place such clothes were really at home was a DP camp. But the only things available on the black market were old military uniforms, and the civilian clothes you got for ration cards were made of a mixture of paper and fiber. I could have bought a ration card for a suit, but it would have fallen off my back in a week—if it lasted that long. This was ridiculous! Here I was with a lot of money in my pocket, and I couldn't even buy myself a decent suit.

I thought about all the clothes I had had at home and wondered whether my mother was still keeping them for me. Shirts, underwear, socks, sweaters, suits—all of fine quality. Before I was taken to Russia I hadn't given them a thought, but in the coal mine and the labor camp, I would have deeply appreciated even the one sturdy outfit I had now.

I put it on and took a walk toward the station to find out about trains to Vienna.

The weather was warm and beautiful, and I stopped in a little park to sit on a bench for a while and breathe in the soft spring air. At Buchholz I hadn't really felt the arrival of spring, maybe because it was farther north than Giessen, and chillier, or because I rarely had a chance to go for a walk by myself. There, we were awake most nights and slept through a large part of the days. I wished I could be alone in a forest or a meadow, lying on the grass and drinking in its scent, or on a high mountain, feeling the wind on my face and savoring the clear, crisp air, with all the dirty deals and the sick, sad darkness gone from me.

It was getting late. I jumped up and walked on to the station, and there I found out that a train to Munich left at eleven that night. I would have to change in Munich the next morning and would arrive in Vienna in the late afternoon or evening. I bought a second-class ticket and went back to my uncle's.

Over coffee at dinner, with only an hour left to share, the

time passed quickly in reminiscences of Vienna before the war. Angelika had spent some vacations there, and my uncle had friends in Austria, medical colleagues, whose addresses he gave me in case I needed a place to stay. After warm good-byes I walked through the dark, deserted streets to the station.

My train was on time. I was tired and had no packages to protect this time, so I let the monotonous rattle of the train lull me to sleep. I was getting used to sleeping on trains. The conductor woke me only twice to look at my ticket, and then it was early morning and the train was pulling into Munich, the city where Hitler had gotten his start. He had promised to bring prosperity to Germany, and now the black market seethed and milled in Munich's big railroad station.

On the train to Vienna I found a window seat and rode all day long dozing on and off or looking out the window at the soft, rolling landscape of southern Germany and Austria. The countryside, covered with a haze of green, showed few signs of the war or the terrible poverty that had followed it. The land healed quickly. It was the cities that were bomb scarred and black with misery.

It was evening when the train got into Vienna. Climbing off, I looked around in the late twilight. The city was big and broad, and at first glance it seemed more intact than Hannover or Bremen. I hoped it had good food. I hadn't eaten for close to twenty-four hours, and I was ravenous.

Near the station, where the usual black-market crowd was gathered, I found someone who would exchange my marks for Austrian schillings at the black-market rate, and I also asked directions for the Café Mozart. It was a name I remembered from before the war, when I had heard of its legendary pastries topped with whipped cream, the finest in any Viennese café. My mouth watered at the thought of clouds of sweet, soft whipped cream, even though I knew such things had probably vanished with the war.

My contact said the Café Mozart was open and not far from the station. I found it in minutes. A few people sat at tables outside in the fading light, bundled up in their coats, drinking coffee. Some of them seemed to be waiting expectantly for someone, something. I went inside and looked around for a table. The café was very busy.

A waiter came over, and I pressed some schillings into his hand and said, "I want to eat a good meal. I have no ration cards, but I have enough money."

"*Na ja*," he said. "We can take care of that." He led me to a table.

In a few minutes he brought out a big bowl of beef broth, several fresh rolls, and a whole ersatz liverwurst. It wasn't Sacher torte, but to my hungry stomach it tasted wonderful.

When I finished eating I sat and looked around as I drank some tea, feeling the pulse of the place pick up as evening came on. The usual kind of shabby, hand-to-hand trading had been going on outside the train station, but here bigger deals were evidently being made. A group of four or five would occupy a booth, drinking beer or endless cups of coffee, keeping a sharp eye on the rest of the clientele. One was almost always a little better dressed than the others. This was the big man, who sent his messengers around to other groups to find out what was new or promising on the black market. Deals were made and packages passed under tables.

In the back of the café was a group whose big man wore a beret, sturdy knickers, and a handsome tweed jacket. I heard one of his boys address him as *Herr Baron*. Once he got up and walked to the door of the café, passing my table. He was an arrogant-looking high-colored man in his late forties or fifties, smoking an American cigarette. He sauntered back to his table and spoke to one of his group in a strong accent that I couldn't identify. I ordered more tea and settled down to watch the scene.

At the table next to mine were three men dressed like woodsmen, in torn and ragged boots and coats trimmed with coarse black fur. They had ordered some hot brew to go with the sandwiches they kept taking from a sack under their table, and they were talking in what sounded like Czech. From the little I could overhear, they had made it through the Iron Curtain bringing something that they hoped to sell for a nice profit. They were waiting for a middleman. I felt like asking them what they had, but they would probably be suspicious of a stranger.

Two gypsies carrying violin cases came in and went straight to the baron's table. He nodded to them with the air of one accustomed to commanding servants, and they took out their violins and began to play. Over the noise in the café, I heard snatches of the music—Hungarian gypsy melodies, as passionate and flamboyant as anything I had heard at home in Transylvania. It made me homesick. The baron sat back obviously enjoying the music, but when he spoke again to one of his group I noticed that his strong accent wasn't Hungarian; it might have been Czech. The gypsies played on.

In a little while someone from the baron's table got up and came over to the three Czechs next to me. He whispered something, and the three went over to the baron's table. After a short conference they came back, paid the waiter, and left with one of the baron's men.

Then the waiter materialized at my elbow. "Excuse me, sir. Would you mind if a young lady joined you?"

I looked at him, and he smiled, showing several bad teeth. He was a heavy, florid man, with untidy white hair, probably in his sixties. I was pretty sure he was asking me about the girl because I had given him the tip. He probably thought that if I liked her he would make himself some more money. A little pimping wasn't the worst thing people did these days to keep themselves alive.

I shrugged. "There's room," I said. "If she doesn't mind, it's fine with me."

The waiter bowed and vanished, and a brunette in her early thirties came over, smiled hesitantly, and sat down. She was a little on the plump side, but she seemed graceful enough, and her face, though plain, was delicate. Heavy black penciled lines emphasized her eyes.

"Are you from Hamburg?" she asked.

"No, I come from Bremen," I said, covering my tracks instinctively.

"Do you have a place to stay?"

"Yes," I lied. "I am staying with a friend." I had no idea where I was going to sleep that night. If it wasn't too late, I supposed I could look up one of my uncle's colleagues. If worst came to worst I could sleep on a bench in the train station, but then someone might try to rob me. If I took the prostitute up on her offer she and her pimp would almost certainly try to rob me. Well, I wasn't tired yet. I had slept on the train. And I still wanted to look around and see what the cafés had to offer.

"That's good. It's very hard to find a place. I see you like Hungarian music," she continued, in a sweet, toneless voice. "Would you like to go to another place, where they play better?"

"I don't find anything wrong with this place," I said.

"Oh, there's nothing wrong with it," she said. "But the baron over there in the corner is always being watched by the police, and because of him this place gets raided from time to time." She leaned forward and whispered loudly, "They suspect him of dealing in penicillin."

I had heard about the penicillin racket in Bremen, a cruel and unscrupulous business. The Americans gave shipments of penicillin to the German authorities for distribution to hospitals. Somewhere along the line some of it was stolen, only to reappear on the black market, where hospitals, desperate for the drug, bought it at exorbitant prices. Some of the patients given the contraband penicillin died; others were maimed or brain damaged for life. The penicillin was diluted with milk and was both weak and contaminated. After an intensive investigation the Bremen thief had been caught and sentenced to life imprisonment. I looked over at the baron reigning like an uncrowned monarch behind his table. I had been impressed with him, had wished I could meet him. Now I wasn't so sure.

When I turned back the woman was watching me, waiting for a sign of interest. Her look quickly turned to coquetry, but I had seen that other look, the flat, animal patience of something that has to stalk its prey to survive. I got up from the table and gave her a German ten-mark bill, saying, "I will probably see you here tomorrow night, but now I have to leave for an appointment."

She asked, "What time will you be here tomorrow?"

"Around nine or ten o'clock," I lied, and made my way through the tables toward the door. It seemed the kindest way to reject her. I thought I would try one or two other cafés now, before I started worrying about a place to sleep.

Halfway to the door I stopped short. A beautiful blonde had just come in, and following her was a tall, familiar figure —Jeno! My good friend Jeno, who had been my roommate and black-market partner in Bremen! I knew he had been transferred to Austria, but I had forgotten all about him. He saw me an instant after I saw him.

"*Servus, servus, hover.* Greetings, greetings, dear friend," we said simultaneously, embracing and kissing each other on both cheeks.

"You crazy bastard! Where are you living now? What are you doing in Vienna?" Jeno asked.

At the same time I said, "I should have known you would show up here when I heard those Hungarian gypsy violins!"

I looked at the beautiful girl clinging to his arm. "This is my girlfriend, Marika," he said. "She lives a few blocks from this café. You must stay with us while you are here. Marika, this is my friend Vanya. You remember, I've told you about him."

She took my hand firmly and said, "Oh, Jeno talks about you so often! I hope you're going to stay in Vienna for a while." She had direct, dark-blue eyes, a deep, sexy voice, and a radiant smile. It was obvious from the way she held Jeno's arm and looked up at him that they were very close.

The prostitute had disappeared, and my table was still empty, so we sat down. The same waiter reappeared and took our orders, glancing at me without curiosity.

There was a lot to talk about. I answered Jeno's questions about where I was living now and what I was doing in Vienna. He told me he wanted to emigrate to Argentina and was waiting for his application to be approved. His dark eyes twinkled with withheld information, and I knew that later, in private, he would tell me about his black-market activities.

When we finished our coffee Jeno said, "Come over to Marika's apartment. You must stay with us tonight, and every night you are in Vienna."

Marika lived in a spacious, attractive apartment in a handsome building, and it puzzled me how she could afford it until Jeno explained that her father owned the building.

We opened a bottle of wine, and I told them what I had seen in the café and what the prostitute had said about the baron's involvement in the penicillin racket.

"Ah, the baron," Jeno said. "He is very well known, and it is whispered that he is one of the biggest black-market operators around Vienna. Because of the penicillin rumor, the authorities watch him closely, but he has so much money that he always knows beforehand when his living quarters or the café will be raided. He usually operates from the café, and rumor has it that he owns the place. He is supposed to have warehouses full of food and cases of American cigarettes. At least, that's what they gossip about him."

I thought that there must be a number of barons on the black market of Western Europe, men who had made kingdoms out of the anarchy and misery of the times. Maybe they had only been born too late to be crowned rulers. For them there was no shortage, but an abundance of the best of everything.

After a while Marika went to bed, leaving us to talk in the Hungarian she couldn't understand. I asked Jeno how he managed in these jobless times.

He said, "Most of Marika's friends are, or were, rich people. They give her pieces of jewelry and other expensive things to sell or trade for butter, eggs, meat, cigarettes, and so on. I handle the transactions and live off what I consider to be my share as the go-between. I often marvel at the way the black market cuts through the lines of caste and class."

I told Jeno about some of my black-market escapades around Hannover. He laughed and laughed at the story of my trip to Belgium in the ludicrous guise of an American soldier. I could sense that he felt his everyday transactions were too easy. He was itching to do something big and daring. I had come here for a rest, a vacation, and had promised Jony that I would stay away from trouble. But when I looked at Jeno's shining eyes the itch for adventure became contagious.

The next morning I woke up to a Hungarian gypsy song. It was Jeno, singing as only a Hungarian can, with reckless abandon. It was good to hear.

I went out into the living room, and Jeno stopped singing and asked, "How did you sleep?"

"As beautifully as you sing," I said, and he and Marika laughed.

After breakfast Marika left to see some people with jewelry to sell. Jeno said he wanted to take me around to some of the cafés, to the various black-market gathering places, especially those in the Russian-occupied zone of the city. I was uneasy about going into the Russian zone, but Jeno assured me that the checkpoints were much more informal than in Germany and that people went back and forth freely.

Outside the American zone the famous *Gemütlichkeit* was less apparent in the cafés, and the hungry, neurotic mood of the populace could be felt more strongly. This part of the city was gray, apathetic, quiet. We passed two Russian soldiers arguing loudly over a bet, and the sound of their voices sent a chill through me. That wasn't DP Russian; it was the Russian of the guards at the labor camp and Mine 28. That sound had pursued me through my nightmares for months after I escaped from the Donbas.

Jeno had a few contacts in the Russian zone. We entered a drab café, and he spoke to one of them, a shifty-eyed man who smoked hungrily and had nicotine stains on his trembling fingers. Jeno gave him a pack of American cigarettes and nodded to indicate that I was all right. The man gave me a sour look and took Jeno aside, talking to him in a low voice.

Jeno looked surprised. He motioned me over and said, "He says he knows a Russian officer who is looking for adventure with profit!"

He asked the man for more details, but the contact just shrugged and said, "I will bring him here tomorrow. Come at about this time, and you can talk to him yourself."

Jeno and I looked at each other. A Russian officer looking for a black-market deal? For money, or just for the thrill? We had to find out about this. Jeno turned back to the man and said, "All right, we'll be here at this time tomorrow."

That evening Marika cooked a delicious chicken with red wine and dumplings. While we devoured the chicken we told her about the mysterious Russian officer.

"We are going back tomorrow to find out what it's all about," Jeno said.

"You two had better be careful," Marika said. "You both escaped from the Russians, and now you want to get into a deal with a Russian officer. Suppose he gets caught? It would be the easiest thing in the world for him to turn you in to save his own skin."

Jeno reassured her. "We're not getting into anything. We're just going to look into it. We won't get involved unless the man seems trustworthy and his scheme is sound." But Marika threw him a look that said "I know you."

Her mood soon lightened, however, and we passed the rest of the evening laughing, reminiscing, and telling stories. Finally Marika went off to bed, while Jeno and I sat quietly, each in his own thoughts. We had had some crazy adventures together in Bremen, and now it looked as if we might embark on an even crazier one.

"Well, *hover*, sleep well," Jeno said, getting up to go to bed. "Tomorrow we'll go to the Russian zone and see what that officer has up his sleeve."

We started out early for the Russian zone. It was quite a long walk, and it was sunny when we started, but by the time we got to the café the sky had clouded over, low, gray, and depressing. It seemed like a bad omen.

Inside it was very dim, but we spotted Jeno's contact sitting at a table with a young Russian officer. I recognized the light-green, high-necked Cossack uniform right away. The officer didn't look formidable or gruff, though, the way I had expected. He looked like a handsome, tousle-headed boy. A Viennese girl was with them, and the Russian was kissing her face and hands against her feeble protests. When Jeno's man called us over the Russian took his hands and eyes off the girl immediately. His attention was totally on us.

I said to him, in Russian, "*Kak dela?* How are you?"

At the familiar words his face lit up. "Can you speak more than that sentence?"

"Talk to me about anything you like," I replied.

He grinned. "I am Mischa," he said, and held out his hand.

"In your country I was called Vanya," I said, and we shook hands. Jeno's friend was staring at us, amazed that I could communicate with the Russian officer better than he could.

As we spoke I found myself liking Mischa. I told him that I had spent over two years in Russia as a prisoner in a labor camp, but that a year ago I had escaped.

"You should have escaped much sooner," he said. "Coal-mine work is for the Turks!" Then he became serious. "I am fascinated by the black market. I want to make a big killing, because I am not in the mood to go back home to the 'labor paradise.' I shouldn't be telling you this, but you have told me you escaped from there, and we have to trust each other if we are going to do something together." He looked at me steadily and went on. "I have a feeling about people, and I feel good about you. I trust you."

This was too much too fast. It was unbelievable that we should have struck each other the same way. Here I was in the Russian zone of Vienna, telling a Russian officer that I had escaped from the Russian coal mines. To him it must have seemed just as insane.

The girl tugged at Mischa's arm, irritated that he had lost interest in her, but he shook her off. "I have been thinking over this plan for a long time," he said, "and I know it can be done. I have about three weeks' furlough coming, and I can get a good truck. I want to drive down to Bulgaria, to a factory I know about, and pick up a few million cigarettes. Then I want to drive to Paris and sell them there. They will bring a terrific price, much better than in Austria or Germany, where the Americans flood the market with their Lucky Strikes."

It sounded like something out of Baron Munchhausen. This madman wanted to drive from Vienna across the Iron Curtain and deep into the Balkans, well over a thousand miles, on very dubious roads. There he would "pick up a few million cigarettes"—he had said it so casually—then turn around and drive nearly twice that distance to Paris, find a contact, and sell those millions of Balkan cigarettes on the Paris black market. It was mad, but his spirit appealed to me.

"I speak some French, too," I said to Mischa.

"That calls for a drink!" he said, pounding on the table.

A nervous waiter came running from the back of the café to serve the Russian officer. He brought a bottle and some glasses, and Mischa poured our glasses full of the clear alcohol. Jeno watched in amazement while I tossed mine off. He hadn't understood a word of what was going on.

I gestured toward him and said, "Mischa, this is my friend Jeno, and we must take him along. He will be a good man to have with us. We will be driving through Hungary, and Jeno is Hungarian. He knows the roads and he knows the language."

Mischa nodded. "Whatever you say. One week from today, I want you and your friend to meet me here, in front of this café, at about eleven in the morning. Be ready to go!" He refilled our glasses and raised his. "To success!"

After the third drink the world and the café began to go out of focus. When Mischa saw that I wasn't sober any more he turned his attention back to the girl, and Jeno and I got up to leave. I shook Mischa's hand. "Until next week—*dosvidania*. Good-bye."

Outside, the raw, chilly weather sobered me quickly, and as we walked I repeated the Russian's plan to Jeno.

He gave a long, low whistle. "You never know what you're

going to run into. Do you think he'll really show up for this venture?"

"Look," I said, "he never mentioned money, so it sounds like a fairy tale. But what have we got to lose?"

"Maybe a lot," Jeno said. "You know I escaped from the Communists in Hungary, and I know the last thing you want is to fall into their hands again. Do you think we'll be safe driving around in the Balkans with this guy?"

"Do you think Mischa is a Communist?" I responded. "He probably has a family in the Soviet Union, and yet he tells me he has no desire to go home when the Red Army orders him back there. You know, his uniform could be the best disguise for whatever he wants to do. It will get him the same kind of free passage the American uniform got me in the West, only better, because Mischa is the real thing, and an officer. It's just a hunch, Jeno, but I trust him. And if I'm right, we will be very safe with him. Anyway, we have a week to think it over."

I didn't mention to Jeno that we would be going through or very near to Rumania. I knew that I would be tempted to get in touch with my parents, and I knew that I mustn't. If we went we would both have to put all our old fears and dreams about our homelands out of mind and just stick with Mischa. Hungary, Rumania—those were places on the map you had to cross to get to a cigarette plant in Bulgaria, nothing more.

Over the next few days we speculated a great deal about Mischa. We both guessed that he wasn't as young as he looked. A shrewd mind and a boyish face could be a strategic combination, and I was willing to bet that Mischa got away with a lot in his military life. I was glad for him. Surrounded by automatons and fanatics, at least he was thinking for himself. More power to the Mischas of the world!

As the week wore on our doubts grew, but not enough to change our minds. During that week of waiting life became automatic. Marika cooked dinner every night, and a couple of times some of her friends came over for the evening. They were young and lively, but I was too distracted by the approaching journey to have much fun with them. Jeno and I went for our customary walks around the station and cafés, came home, and sat around waiting for the day of departure.

The day before we were supposed to leave, Marika got frightened. Her Jeno was going across borders, into Communist territory, without a passport, in the company of a Russian officer. Would she ever see him again? Toward evening she even cried a little. Jeno and I managed to calm her and convince her that we would come back. In spite of all our brave phrases, we spent a nervous night, and nobody slept much.

The time came to go. Jeno kissed Marika. We walked out of
the apartment and strode toward the Russian zone.

It took us an hour to get to the café where we had met
Mischa. It was already after eleven. We sat down and ordered
a bottle of wine, and the waiter, recognizing us from the
week before, brought it and withdrew to the kitchen. We
waited and drank. Would Mischa show up or wouldn't he? It
was about noon now. Jeno was quietly swearing to himself.
We called to the waiter to bring us a second bottle of wine.
He sullenly brought us our bill. I was surprised that in the
Russian zone you had to pay before drinking, but then I
realized that maybe the waiter resented us because he had
seen us with a Russian, his traditional enemy. Jeno threw
some schillings on the table and growled at him, and he
withdrew hastily. We were halfway through the second bottle
when we heard a howling engine approach. Mischa!

We ran outside, and there was an olive-green Studebaker truck growling and purring like a big contented cat. Mischa jumped from the cab, his blond hair sticking up like a crest, his face full of mischief and excitement. "Well, *Rebyata,* boys, you are here! I am a little late. I stopped to get some directions, but now we can go."

In the cab of the truck he showed us a menacing-looking machine gun and several clips of ammunition, saying proudly, "With this we will get the cigarettes, and I think no one will stop us."

In the canvas-covered back of the truck were seven big metal barrels. Mischa said, "One is filled with gasoline for the trip, and the others are for the cigarettes."

We climbed into the truck, Mischa raced the motor, and we roared off. Now that we were really on the way, the nervousness that had nagged at us earlier vanished, and we were full of confidence.

Mischa drove very fast, and in the middle of the road. At first I was not interested in the scenery; I was watching the panel on the dashboard with its speedometer in miles per hour, rather than kilometers. This truck had been made in America, where I would someday live. I asked Mischa if I could drive.

"Wait," he said. "I will drive us to Bulgaria and back to Paris. After that, when we are not in such a hurry, you can drive. We will get to the Hungarian border soon. Tell him"— nodding his head in Jeno's direction—"not to worry. After all, he is with an officer of the Red Army!" He winked at me.

I repeated the reassurance in Hungarian.

Jeno swore and said, "Am I glad he said that! Tell him I was seriously thinking about jumping off the truck at the border and running back. After all, I escaped from the bastards only a year ago, and I remember their 'kindness' all too well."

Two hours after we left Vienna, in the midst of flat green farmland, signs along the road announced that we were approaching the border. Mischa pulled over and told us both to get in the back of the truck and lie down between the barrels. We did as he said. We found a couple of heavy blankets and spread them out to make ourselves comfortable. The back of the truck smelled strongly of gasoline. We bounced along, with no sign of slowing down for the border, and soon our tension gave way to drowsiness. The gasoline fumes helped to drug us into a deep sleep.

Mischa shook us awake saying, "We are about two hours into Hungary."

Jeno and I sat up rubbing our eyes. We both had headaches from the gasoline, but we climbed into the cab, and soon the fresh air cleared our heads. It was getting dark, and in the bluish dusk the soft Hungarian farmland sped by on both sides. I thought Mischa smelled of vodka, and, sure enough, in a minute he pulled out a big bottle and offered us a drink.

"Are we going to stop somewhere for a few hours of sleep?" I asked. "Or do you intend to drive straight through?"

"No," he answered. "I don't want to stop until we get into Yugoslavia or Rumania. At the rate we're going, in spite of the poor roads I can last until we get there. You two can sleep in the back. After we get the cigarettes I will sleep for a few hours, and then you will have to watch our cigarettes, me, and the truck." He grinned. The driving seemed to invigorate him.

He told us that the Hungarian border had been easy, a quickly raised barrier and no questions. It was amazing what a difference the right uniform in the right place made in this age of borders and restrictions. What had happened to the time when you could travel as a civilian with just a few stamped pages, a passport?

The road was still asphalt, but much poorer than in Austria. As the truck jolted over potholes and darkness fell, Mischa didn't slacken his speed, and I began to worry a little. He was tipping the big bottle back frequently, his throat working, the vodka gurgling down like water. It was bound to have some effect on him. But I couldn't detect any. He looked straight ahead, eyes wide open, both hands on the wheel, grinning and whistling to himself from time to time, and reaching for the vodka bottle again.

Several hours later, near midnight, we drove through a darkened village, and Mischa pulled up at the one building that had a light burning. It was an inn. He slung his machine gun over his shoulder and got out, telling us not to be afraid but to go in and order three good meals, and leave the paying to him. The inn was almost empty, ready to close for the night, but when the old innkeeper saw a Russian officer he hurried to serve us. Jeno ordered three plates of Hungarian goulash. It was hot and good, and we ate ravenously, two plates apiece. I felt the strength flowing into my body and, immediately afterward, the sleepiness.

When we finished Mischa said, "Go outside and wait in the truck. I'll take care of the innkeeper."

He came out in two minutes. But how had he managed without Hungarian money?

He laughed. "I am a lieutenant in the Red Army, and I promised him that in a few days we would stop by again, eat some more of his stew, and pay him. He has no choice—he has to wait!"

Mischa offered the bottle again, and I took a healthy swig. In a moment the dizzy, warm numbness came. Before I had a chance to fall asleep Mischa pulled over to the side of the road, next to a field, and took a rubber hose from under the seat and a pail from the back of the truck. Letting down the tailgate, he unscrewed a small cap on the lid of the full gasoline barrel and stuck the hose in. Then he blew on the end of the hose to start the gasoline flowing into the pail. Working by moonlight, we filled the gas tank from the pail with the help of a funnel. It took over five pailfuls.

When we were ready to go I crawled into the back behind the barrels, lay down on the blankets, and, swaying and jolting across Hungary, went to sleep.

Jeno woke me, shaking me until I opened my eyes. It was daylight. The truck's motor was quiet, but we still seemed to be moving. I shook my head to clear it. "How long have I been sleeping? Did we have any trouble?"

"Not at all," Jeno said. "Mischa is a miracle. He is tireless and still in a good mood. I think the vodka keeps him awake, but unfortunately it also keeps him drunk."

The truck lurched strangely, and I looked at Jeno. "The crazy bastard got us on a barge," he said. "We're crossing the Danube."

Looking over the tailgate, I saw that we were swaying downstream on the not-so-blue Danube, at least half a mile wide at that point and brownish yellow. With us on the decrepit, dirty barge were two other battered trucks. The captain was an old fellow with a curved handlebar mustache, who sat in the cabin smoking a long pipe, holding a tattered cap in one hand while he scratched his bald head. He looked like an old Hussar fallen on hard times.

"Where are we? Is this the Rumanian border?" I asked Jeno. My heart began to beat fast.

"No, we're west of that, still in Hungary. Mischa thinks we probably won't go through Rumania at all. He says the best route will be straight down through Yugoslavia and then into Bulgaria."

I wished I remembered my school geography better. I felt a sharp disappointment and a simultaneous relief that we weren't going to drive through Rumania.

Mischa knocked on the cab window and motioned to us. Looking in, we saw him stretched out full length across the seat, his boots sticking out the window. He told us to lie down and get some more sleep, and Jeno, who had been awake most of the night, started snoring almost immediately, lulled by the gentle swaying of the barge.

A jolt and a loud crash woke us. As Mischa was driving the truck off the barge it slid sideways on the gangplank, one wheel hanging in mid-air above the riverbank; but the growling, powerful motor pulled us out of danger. Jeno turned over and went back to sleep. I climbed in front with Mischa, who soon picked up his usual pace.

The asphalt roads were behind us. We were on a dirt road now. But it was a good road, smooth and well kept, with a ditch running along each side. The roads in Rumania had had similar ditches, and I remembered how deep they could be, so I kept hoping Mischa wouldn't skid into one. Out in the fields peasant women were working, bent double between the rows. Now and then we drove through a small village, passing peasants dressed in dark, archaic clothing clopping along in wooden carts behind dusty, skin-and-bones horses. They stared after us and our Studebaker truck through the cloud of dust it made. I wondered what they were thinking.

The green fields and the horse carts reminded me of home. How far was I from my home at the knee of the Carpathian Mountains? I had just gotten a letter from my parents, and now I was perhaps no more than a few hundred miles away. What would they do if a truck suddenly stopped in front of the house, and I ran inside to get them and take them with me to the West? Once we were safely back in Buchholz I could find them a place to live near the camp, or maybe Jony could get them into Barracks 1. But what if one of my black-market ventures went wrong and I got thrown in jail? Who would provide for them? Jony had his hands full with a wife and baby. No, it was impossible.

Mischa must have sensed what was going on in my head, for he reached under his seat and handed me the bottle, saying, "Take a big drink. You need it."

I did, but instead of dulling my imagination the vodka quickened it. Now I had even less control over the longing for home that wanted to overwhelm me. To close out those thoughts, I asked Mischa, "Did we drive through Budapest?"

"No," he replied. "And we are not in Hungary any more. By now, we are somewhere in Yugoslavia, and I am getting very tired and very drunk. Wherever we are, in a little while I'll have to sleep for a few hours. If I keep on we might drive into a tree. Getting stuck here in the Balkans would be no good."

"Mischa," I said, "if you see some trees, pull over and lie

down in the back of the truck. I'll watch while you sleep."

The country was hillier now. Coming out of a village in a small valley, we drove up a gentle slope among vineyards. Near the top of the slope was a shady tree.

Mischa turned off the road and stopped under the tree. He gave me the bottle of vodka and said, "If you get sleepy, drink some of this and it will keep you fresh. But don't drink too much or you'll be no good to us. The one thing we don't need is a drunken watchman." Climbing into the back, he crawled under the blankets next to Jeno and didn't move again. He had been driving for over twenty-four hours.

I got out of the truck and looked around. The green hills rolled away like waves. It would be nice to live in that valley. In the fall the vineyards would be full of sweet, juicy grapes. Below, I saw cows and sheep grazing in the pastures behind the village, and smoke rising from the chimneys. The scene looked as peaceful and untouched as if centuries of history had never happened. There was no sign of soldiers, guards, or barbed wire.

I went back, took a big drink from the vodka bottle, and lay down on the seat with my legs sticking out the open window. Max and Jony were a thousand miles away. What were they doing? If they knew where I was and what I was up to, they would give me a good scolding. Other DPs in our camp would have thought I was insane. People wanted to get out of the Iron Curtain countries, not into them. I had had it made! I had escaped the long arm of Russia and stood a very good chance of getting to Canada within the next eight or ten months. Yet here I was somewhere in Yugoslavia or Bulgaria with a mad Russian lieutenant, looking for millions of cigarettes. I knew that I had only caught the plague of the black-market era, but it was undoubtedly a form of madness.

And Mischa. How strange that Jeno and I had put our lives in his hands on such short acquaintance! We trusted him to know where he was going, and he seemed confident. He hadn't stopped once to ask directions; he had just followed a tattered old map. I guessed he had driven this route before, probably in a wartime campaign. Whenever we mentioned money he only said, "Don't worry. We'll never get stuck." We had no idea whether he was carrying any money at all. He seemed to use his uniform to get what he wanted, and of course he was never far from his machine gun, except when he slept.

It was getting dark. The moon came out, and several lights appeared in the village. It made me feel lonely to look at them. Now and then a cloud covered the moon and then moved away, restoring the silvery brightness. I took another drink and, feeling a little sleepy, got out of the truck to walk around. I was tempted to go down into the village, but I couldn't leave my sleeping friends unguarded.

A large cloud blotted out the moon. Now it was very dark, and the truck was only a black outline. I went back, climbed into the cab, and lay down, listening. Only an occasional ping from the cooling motor penetrated the still night.

I woke to the heavy drumming of raindrops on the roof of the cab. Clouds covered the stars and moon, and it was as dark as the Russian mine. The rain awakened Jeno and Mischa, too. A knock on the window signaled me to open the flap dividing the cab from the back of the truck.

"What time is it?" Mischa asked sleepily.

"The middle of a dark night," I answered.

They both came up front. We took the hose out from under the seat, brought the barrel of gasoline to the tailgate, and filled the tank again from the pail. Mischa had turned on the truck lights or it would have been impossible in the darkness and mud. Thick rain lashed down through the lights. This time the tank took seven pailfuls.

We got in, and I was relieved that the motor started right away. The Balkan pastoral scene had been lovely, but only for a rest stop.

The rain streamed down the windows, and Mischa's singing filled the cab. I recognized the song from my days in the Donbas. It was about a weapon called "Stalin's organ pipes" —twenty-four mortars mounted on a carrier. When all the guns were fired at once the noise was supposed to be terrifying. The song was called "*Katchusha*," and Mischa was singing every verse the soldiers had ever made up for it. It sounded very Russian, robust and melancholy all at once. Mischa sang so beautifully that even Jeno, who couldn't understand the words, listened and smiled. The windshield wipers were working full speed, and the truck swerved and slewed, but Mischa always wrenched it back into the middle of the road.

When Mischa had sung himself out he took a long pull from the vodka bottle, and Jeno started on his Hungarian gypsy songs. As he finished each song Mischa would let go of the steering wheel and clap enthusiastically, nearly running us into the ditch, but he always grabbed the wheel just in time. "Now sing that song again," and he would harmonize with Jeno. It sounded very good. Then back to the vodka.

In the warm, enclosed little cab, battered by night and rain, we spent a wild night singing, drinking, and making sure Mischa kept the truck on the road. We wound through fields and valleys, and the rain poured down in streams. The headlights shone only ten feet ahead and showed nothing except mud and rain. But the American Studebaker seemed indestructible, and our driver appeared to be guided by some drunken sixth sense that was nothing short of miraculous.

Toward dawn I asked Mischa to stop so I could climb into the back and sleep a while. We had spilled some gasoline filling the tank, and the smell was strong in the air. Despite the clonking of the empty barrels, I fell into a deep, dark sleep.

Someone was calling me. The truck had stopped. I opened my eyes and saw bright daylight and Jeno standing over me rolling one of the empty barrels to the tailgate. I looked out and saw that we were in a yard. A man was rolling the barrels into a shack. Across from the shack was a long, low building that seemed to be busy inside. Through a big window I could see several women working at a table. A strong smell of tobacco assailed my nostrils, and my stomach lurched with nausea. The man handling the barrels looked like a pirate in a nightmare. He wore a black patch over the place where his right eye had been, and from under the patch a long white scar reached to his chin. His nose looked as if it had borne the brunt of many unpleasant discussions.

I got down from the truck and immediately wished I hadn't. A few lungfuls of fresh air, and the yard began to turn around me. Sky, buildings, barrels, and the man were revolving like a carousel. My head throbbed painfully, and my stomach went round with every turn of the world. I staggered a few steps and vomited until there was nothing left to come up. With every spasm pain stabbed in my head. I staggered back toward the truck.

Just then Jeno stuck his head out, and when he saw my face he was alarmed. "Do you feel as bad as you look?"

"I don't know how I look," I said. "But help me up on the truck. I have to lie down."

I crawled back on the blankets, between the barrels, and buried my head in my arms. I thought I would die. But I wanted it to be on the hill where we had rested yesterday, not here in the yard of a Bulgarian tobacco factory. The one-eyed pirate with the broken nose seemed to know that I had escaped from Russia, that I had crossed borders without a passport to get here. I didn't know how many borders we had crossed, or how many days and nights we had been driving. I just felt as if I had always been running and running to escape from camps, barbed wire, guards, soldiers, black marketeers, police, and MPs.

Maybe I could last a little longer, until we got back to that hill. Then I could die in peace, and Mischa and Jeno would have to carry on alone with the truck and the cigarettes. But how would Jony and Max and Vasile find out about my end? They would never know. I never should have left them. I groaned. I was too weak even to vomit again. What a way to leave my friends! I couldn't even put up a fight before I died.

Then the truck started moving, swaying and rolling, picking up speed. I felt as if it were going straight into hell.

Shoving myself to the edge of the rolling and swaying truck, I pushed the canvas aside and sucked in lungfuls of fresh air. It seemed to chase the pain and nausea away.

We were driving on a rough road through hilly country, and the truck jolted and swerved from side to side, but it always came back onto the road. I stayed where I was, breathing the fresh air. After about twenty minutes I no longer felt like dying. The fresh air wanted me to live. Was it the gasoline fumes, the vodka, the lack of sleep, or all three that had hit me so hard?

My old friend hunger started gnawing in my belly. Soon I would have to tell my two companions that I was better and needed food. I saw that the barrels had been tied down, so that they didn't dance around on the truck floor any more. Outside it was getting dark. What day was it? I had lost all track of the time even before I got sick. I dozed off and woke up, and the pain was back. Crawling to the opening in the canvas, I sucked myself full of the fresh Balkan night air; within minutes the headache was gone. I knocked on the window of the cab, and Jeno turned to look at me. The truck slowed down and stopped.

My two friends came around to see how I was. They dropped the tailgate, and I crawled out feeling as shaky and weak as a cat pulled out of a river.

"How do you feel now?" Mischa asked.

"Very weak and very hungry."

"Then you are getting better. We should be back to that hill soon, so let's go on. We can get some food from the village in the morning. We'll rest till you feel better."

I got into the cab, and while Mischa drove Jeno told me that Mischa had given the one-eyed pirate a satchel of watches, cameras, and some money for the cigarettes. I asked Mischa where he got the watches and cameras.

He laughed. "Some officers from my base have been stealing them for over a year, and they had quite a stockpile. So when the occasion was right I just clipped them. They can't make too much of a commotion about something they stole themselves. This is the second time I have been here to buy cigarettes. We came through here during the war, and I remembered the cigarette plant, so last year, when cigarettes were tight on the black market, I came back and got some. I knew what the guy would want for them. The money was harder to get than the cameras and watches, but I was lucky with that.

"A Russian officer I knew in Vienna had a girlfriend whose sister went out with a Swiss businessman. Two months ago, that officer came back to the base drunk and passed out in his quarters. When I helped him to bed I helped myself to his wallet. There were about four hundred American dollars in it. He had probably stolen the money from the Swiss businessman. The next morning he asked me, 'Didn't I have a wallet when you helped me to bed?' 'No,' I said. 'I didn't see one.'" Mischa assumed an innocent expression that made me choke with laughter.

"So now we have six barrels full of cigarettes and three cases of loose tobacco, and you'd better get well, because we're on our way to Paris and it's your job to sell them there."

The dawn was beginning to turn blue when Mischa suddenly said, "Isn't this our hill?" There was the single tree, the slope of vineyards, and down in the valley the sleeping village. We pulled off the road and got out of the truck to stretch. I took a deep breath of fresh air and felt better—and ravenously hungry. Mischa took some tobacco out of one of the cases and went down toward the village to trade it for food. Jeno stretched out to sleep in the cab, and I lay on the grass listening to the crickets and drinking in the fresh, sweet air.

I listened as our truck noisily recuperated from its long run over rough roads. It was letting the pain out of its joints, and some of the cracks and groans were loud, but they grew softer and softer, until finally they died out. Now I could hear an occasional crow from a cock in the village. As it got lighter a few dogs barked, and then a shrill whistle made me sit up. Mischa was coming up the hill with a package, grinning broadly.

171

"After we eat all this," he said as he drew near, "we won't need anything else until we get to Paris."

He unwrapped a huge ham and a large chunk of cheese, and we woke Jeno and began to eat, cutting big chunks of ham and cheese with Mischa's pocketknife. We stuffed ourselves until we couldn't eat any more, drank some vodka, and then ate again, until not a bite was left.

After that we filled the gas tank, and Mischa said, "I won't have to sleep for the next three days. By then we should be in Paris." Shades of Vasile!

I got in the back and lay down, near the tailgate so the gasoline smell wouldn't make me sick again. Listening to Jeno sing over the roar of the running truck, I fell asleep.

"Wake up." It was Jeno, standing outside the tailgate. "I want you to see the Danube. Who knows if you'll ever see it again?"

We were on the same old barge in the middle of the murky river. I longed for binoculars that could see down the Danube and into Rumania as far as my home town. I might not be this close to my parents again for many years.

When we got to the middle of the river Jeno crawled into the back of the truck, and the two of us made ourselves comfortable behind the barrels. Mischa looked through the plastic window and grinned as he saw us barricading ourselves in.

He called back, "As soon as we get off this boat and back on the road, we'll decide on our route to Paris."

Jeno asked me, "Do you know how many cigarettes we got?"

"Sure," I replied. "Six barrels full."

"But how many is that?"

"You were there when they were packed, Jeno," I said. "I guess we'll have to count them when we take them out." I laughed. "This is a new measure for cigarettes. We have so many, we count them by the barrel."

Jeno laughed, too, and said, "Not even the Vienna baron measures cigarettes by the barrel."

172

I asked, "Are they good?"

He took an envelope out of his inside pocket. It was full of cigarettes the one-eyed merchant had given him. Jeno lit one. "They're good cigarettes. You should try one."

I did, and it reminded me of the cigarettes I had tried to smoke as a kid, hiding in the garden or behind the house. I hadn't liked them then, and this one tasted the same. But Balkan tobacco was always good, so these must be good cigarettes. And we had barrels of them!

After we got off the barge Jeno and I lay low until Mischa pulled over to the side of the road and called to us to get out. We were on a highway, but there was no traffic at all. Mischa had his large, tattered map of Europe spread out on the hood, and soon he had planned our route across Austria, Germany, and France to Paris. I climbed in front with Mischa, and we were off again.

The country we were driving through was different now. Behind us lay miles and miles of dense forests, little valleys, and steep hills. Here the country was more open, mostly gentle hills and meadows. This was the *puszta*, where the Hungarians bred their horses. We drove through some little villages with run-down houses and littered yards where gypsies obviously lived. In one of the villages Mischa pulled up at a shabby inn. We called Jeno out of the back of the truck and went inside to get something to eat.

An old man with stained and missing teeth asked what we wanted. He was plainly frightened by Mischa's uniform and machine gun, and Jeno and I, two civilians traveling with a Russian, must have appeared to be traitors or informers. But Jeno spoke to the man in Hungarian, and soon another old gypsy, dressed in baggy pants and a neckerchief and with a violin, came out of nowhere and began playing. Wine and fried chicken were brought out of the kitchen by two gypsy girls, and we found ourselves in the midst of a festive party. Mischa went out and got what was left of his vodka, and the gypsies broke out several more bottles of wine.

Halfway through a leg of chicken, I began to have a funny

feeling about our unguarded truck outside. I went to check. Two gypsies were in the back. One of them was trying to pry open a barrel of cigarettes; the other was stuffing tobacco into his shirt from one of the cases. I jumped into the truck and kicked the second one. He staggered and without a word began emptying his shirt front back into the case.

"Mischa! Mischa!" I yelled, and he came running, machine gun in hand. The gypsy who had been trying to open the barrel was scrambling out of the truck when Mischa appeared. The one I had kicked was still putting tobacco back in the case. I kicked him again, and noticed that he had a knife in his waistband. Mischa hit the other one on the head with the butt of the machine gun, and he collapsed. The man in the truck got a blow from the gun butt when he climbed down.

"Shall I shoot them?" Mischa asked.

I looked at him. He was serious. If I had said yes he would have stitched them full of holes without a word. His face was tense and angry. He kicked the two gypsies viciously, fired a short burst in the air, and stalked back into the inn. It had happened so quickly that Jeno was just coming out.

Inside again, Jeno cursed at the owner, who looked very guilty. The old man said pleadingly, "Gypsies just can't help stealing. They are nomads, and nomads are thieves. They meant no harm."

And then the party went on as if nothing had interrupted it. The old violinist played with such emotion that I saw Jeno wipe tears from his eyes. But I found it hard to relax. I was still worried about our cigarettes. Mischa was getting drunk, and so was Jeno.

By the time all the food and wine were gone Jeno was staggering, and even Mischa agreed we should not go on. I drove the truck behind the inn and, being sober, volunteered to stand watch while the others slept. Mischa and Jeno spread out the blankets and were soon snoring soddenly. I sat on the tailgate watching and thinking about the gypsies. Would they dare come back? I didn't think so, but I couldn't take a chance on going to sleep. If they did come and found all three of us sleeping they wouldn't think twice about cutting our throats, taking the cigarettes, and disposing of the truck. I thought about the gypsy with the long knife, and my eyes stayed open.

Then one of the gypsy girls who had served us came out the kitchen door and gave me a challenging look, whether of flirtation or contempt I couldn't tell. Maybe she could help keep me wide awake. I called to her, in Hungarian, "Come over here and talk to me for a while. I'll give you some tobacco."

She came over and sat on an empty case next to the truck. Her name was Roszika, she said, and her father was the violin player.

"What did you do during the war?" I asked.

"Oh, I was very little then. I remember my father had to work in a factory. He tried to run away once, but they caught him and beat him and took him away. Once, in the evening, he played the violin in the barracks where the workers lived, and a German officer heard him as he walked by. My father was taken out of the factory, and from then on he played for the German officers. That was fine, because sometimes they gave him chocolates and he used to give them to me."

"How did the Germans treat you?" I asked.

"Once when they brought my father home one of the officers liked me and wanted to take me with him, but my mother said I was too young."

"How old were you then?"

"I was twelve."

"Now you are sixteen or seventeen."

"How do you know that?" she asked, with a blush.

I looked at her full, ripe body without answering. She wore bright-red lipstick, and her cheeks were reddened by layers of rouge. She smelled of garlic and badly needed a bath.

"Will you take me with you?" Roszika asked boldly.

"No. We will cross many borders, and you would need a passport."

"Ha," she laughed. "No gypsy ever had a passport, and we cross any border."

She got up and spun around so that her skirt swirled, baring her thighs. She knew she was desirable. She had the blackest eyes I had ever seen, and a full, red, teasing mouth under a high, arched nose; her skin was a smooth olive color. She was trying to lure me away from the truck, offering to make love to me.

"My father knows I am out here, and he is watching us, but I know a room where my cousin sometimes makes love, and we·can use it."

Despite the garlic, it was inviting, but I thought about Jeno and Mischa, sleeping and vulnerable, and the gypsy's long knife. "I can't leave here," I said.

Roszika pouted and even raised her skirt a little, but when she saw I wasn't weakening she stuck out a saucy tongue, twirled around, and walked away angrily.

Now I was sure that the gypsies were still trying to get the cigarettes. They were waiting in hiding for me to abandon the truck so they could overpower Jeno and Mischa. Then they could ambush me. This thought drove all the tiredness from me, and I even faked sleep hoping the dirty bastards would try something. A yell from me would awaken Mischa and Jeno instantly; they would dive out of the dark truck, and the gypsies would be in trouble. But I waited in vain.

Toward evening my companions woke up, and we refilled the gas tank and drove on. Now it was my turn to sleep. I was very tired, and the swaying truck rocked me like a cradle. Once or twice I opened my eyes and saw daylight, and then turned over and went to sleep again. The next time I woke up it was getting dark.

"Welcome back," Jeno said when I knocked on the window to the cab. "You slept all last night and all day today, all the way across Austria and Germany. We crossed the border into France about an hour ago."

Our tank was nearly empty again, and when we stopped to refill it I blinked around at the unfamiliar twilit countryside of eastern France. Jeno climbed into the back to sleep, and our tireless Mischa continued driving.

"Don't you want to sleep for a few hours?" I asked him.

"No, I will sleep after we sell the cigarettes."

"Did you have any trouble at the border?"

"They wanted to know where I was going. I had my machine gun on my back, and I said in Russian, 'Open the frontier!' Your friend was hiding in the back with you, and I just drove through. It was surprisingly easy."

After two hours more, we stopped again. Mischa wanted to urinate and to sit and rest awhile. Aches and groans came from the overworked truck. I felt sorry for it.

Mischa saw me listening and laughed. "You worry about everything. You'd better start worrying about where to look for a contact, so we can sell the cigarettes and tobacco. After that, the truck can rest, and we can sleep, look at the French girls, and drink some of their wine. After the cigarettes are sold we should feel like capitalists." He looked at the map again, and we drove on.

In my mind I went over my simple French and knew it would be sufficient. The truck kept grinding along getting us closer and closer to Paris. It was dark, close to midnight, and Mischa drove as fast as the roads allowed.

We were approaching the outskirts of Paris. Farmland gave way to little houses with gardens, to a dark factory district, and then to *pensions*. Now we had to stop every once in a while to ask directions. I wanted to get to the Place Pigalle; from all I had heard about it, Pigalle was the right place to make a contact. Driving through the Balkans had been easy compared to Paris, especially since Mischa didn't know his way around the labyrinth of tiny streets. But we had floated on barges over the Danube and had survived gypsy bandits and patrolled borders, so I was sure we would find someone to buy our cigarettes.

At last we found the Place Pigalle, a little before dawn. The night clubs and strip joints were quiet, but I was sure they hadn't been for long. Mischa parked under a street light, close to the curb. I climbed in the back to wake Jeno up, and he got in front with Mischa, who was so exhausted that he leaned against Jeno for support. I put one of the cigarettes in my pocket for a sample and took off to find a contact.

I saw quite a few dark-skinned Algerians, who looked as if they would be very much at home in a black-market crowd. Since they worked at night, they were probably procurers; they were dressed in dark turtlenecks, tight jackets, and berets, and looked as if they avoided the sun. My clothes were out of place here. As one Algerian stepped out of a doorway I went up to him. He looked at me as if he wanted to strike me, and I realized that he thought I was a beggar.

Before I could say anything he spat out contemptuously, *"Qu' est-ce que tu veux?* What do you want?"

"Do you know who would buy a million cigarettes? *Sont de Balkan.*"

He looked at me incredulously, as if I were a lunatic, and walked away, glancing back twice and shaking his head. Had I frightened him away with the amount? Or had he not believed me? Maybe he hadn't understood my high-school French. It probably bore little resemblance to the Parisian underworld argot.

Soon I saw another prospect, coming out of a side street. He had just slapped a girl and she was crying, but he kissed her and she went away—a pimp practicing his profession. I went up to him and repeated my question. This one understood.

"Are they Pall Malls or Chesterfields?" he asked.

"No," I said. "They are cigarettes from the Balkans."

"Ah, *sont comme les Gauloises.*"

I had never heard of Gauloises, but I said yes.

"How many do you have, and how much do you want for them?"

"I have about one million of them."

Laughing, he made an obscene gesture and walked away. I tried to stop him, but he snarled at me. I was getting disgusted with these Algerians.

As I turned back toward the truck another young Algerian came out of a doorway. I intercepted him and asked, once more, "Do you know anybody who would be interested in buying cigarettes?"

He was immediately alert. "Yes," he said. "My father would. Wait here. I'll call him."

He sprinted back into the house and returned with an older Algerian. I asked the man to walk a little way with me; I had something to show him. We walked toward the truck, and I gave him a cigarette.

He lit it, inhaled twice, and said, "*Sont mieux que les Americaines.* They are better than the American ones."

At the truck, I told Mischa and Jeno I had a contact. I took the Algerian around to the tailgate, pointed at the barrels, and said they were full of cigarettes. He looked at me with disbelief, but he didn't walk away. Without a word he grabbed my arm and dragged me after him.

Turning into one of the narrow, cobbled side streets, we went quickly through a dark hallway, up some steep stairs, and through several locked doors, which the Algerian unlocked and locked again behind us. Up three more rickety flights, through another door, and then all the way down to a basement. Several rats jumped up and scurried away. I kicked at one, but missed. My guide knocked on a final door, and we entered.

The first things I saw were machine guns lying on a table and hanging on the wall. Half a dozen Algerians were lounging on mattresses on the floor. They were a dangerous-looking bunch, dark and lean, with bright, crazy eyes. Also on the table were several bottles of wine, a Turkish coffeepot, and a few big, half-wrapped chunks of cheese. Strings of onions, figs, and dates hung from hooks in the ceiling, and a sweet, heavy stench saturated the air—hashish or opium. A tall, middle-aged man, probably the chief, was sitting at a desk, and he eyed me suspiciously. A younger man jumped up from the floor and came over, and they spoke in their guttural native tongue.

After a few seconds the young one turned to me. "Do you have another cigarette?"

"No," I said. "I don't smoke."

The one who had brought me said, "I tasted them, and they are very good."

They switched back to their own tongue, while those on the floor listened and looked me over as if they would enjoy having me for breakfast. Then they began quarreling violently, and I was afraid they might grab their guns and start shooting. But as swiftly as the quarrel had begun it calmed down.

The leader said, in French, "Yes, we will buy. But we have to see them first."

Then, as one, they all got up, hid pistols under their coats, and we went outside, by a much shorter route. I walked with the guide who had brought me. The rest fanned out along the street; no one would have suspected they were following us.

At the truck, I said to Mischa, in Russian, "I think we've got a buyer, but he wants to see the cigarettes. He has several men with him, all armed. They are scattered over the street. They are professionals."

Mischa had been drowsing, leaning on Jeno, but he was wide awake in a second. He slid out and stood holding his machine gun in front of him. Three of the Algerians were now at the tailgate, and Mischa's appearance, in uniform, with machine gun, made an impact like a sledge hammer. With his left hand Mischa reached into his pocket, brought out about ten cigarettes, and gave them to the tall Algerian who appeared to be the spokesman. To me, he said, "Tell them to smoke these."

A dozen or more Algerians had formed a semicircle around us, and I couldn't understand why such a scene wasn't causing any commotion on the street. Maybe it was too early. The Algerians passed the cigarettes around and lit them.

"Take their leader into the truck," Mischa said, "and tell him to open a barrel. Show him the tobacco, too."

I jumped onto the truck, followed by the Algerian. He tried to open one of the barrels, but he needed something to pry the lid off. One of his men handed up a screwdriver. He got the lid off and stood staring at the densely packed rows of cigarettes.

Then he whirled and snapped, "Let's go back to the office."

To hear him call their hideout an office struck me funny. He had me ask Mischa to come along, but Mischa shook his head.

"Jeno and I will stay with the cigarettes. You go and see if they've got enough money. You know the prices."

"I do," I said. "But we have no idea how many cigarettes we have."

Mischa scratched his head and said, "We'll have to count at least half a barrel."

I told the Algerian that Mischa would stay with the truck. "Now that you've seen the cigarettes, we want to see the money."

On the way back the Algerians spoke to me with respect. The leader kept saying, "It would be easier if you knew how many cigarettes you had. We'll have to count them. We have about ten million francs."

Ten million francs! That was worth a million marks, or somewhere between a thousand and ten thousand dollars at the variable black-market rate. What a stupendous amount! My thoughts were racing. What could be done with all that!

Back in the cellar, the leader showed me a drawerful of franc notes, riffling his hand through the money, turning the bundles over. I saw that some were five-hundred-franc notes, some were one-thousand, and some were five-thousand, the highest denomination available. These guys must have robbed a bank!

"Show us how to get the barrels into the cellar," I said. "In the meantime you can start counting the money."

The leader sent his young assistant along with me, the one I had spoken to on the street. His name was Rashid, and I guessed he was about my age. On the way back to the truck we talked. He was very friendly now, and I told him where we had come from and how we had gotten the cigarettes out of the Balkans. He told me to drive a hard bargain with Pierre Gossarah, the leader, because cigarettes were hard to get in Paris. The tobacco was worth a good deal of money, too.

"How much should we charge for the cigarettes?"

"For ten packs of American cigarettes you should get nine hundred or, at the very lowest, eight hundred francs. And for those cases of tobacco, at least sixty or seventy thousand francs a case."

"But these are not American cigarettes," I said. "Won't that make a difference?"

"No less than seven hundred and fifty or eight hundred francs for ten packs." Then Rashid asked, "Are you planning to make another trip like this? If you are I will give you the address where you can reach me, and we will give you the best deal in Paris." He gave me a card with his address.

Rashid told Mischa to drive the truck into another side street. It was very narrow, and Mischa cursed and had to back up several times before he got the truck right next to the cellar door. The Algerians swarmed out like ants. Mischa stood by with his machine gun watching them unload the barrels and cases. Once everything was inside he locked the wheel, and he and Jeno followed us into the cellar.

Now the bargaining started. I had told Mischa ahead of time the current price of cigarettes on the black market, and I made sure he remembered while acting as his translator. The Algerians were negotiators of the first order, but Mischa was cool and steady, and he held his own. The bargaining went back and forth, hot and cold.

Then came a moment when I noticed a subtle but deadly change in the atmosphere. The Algerians on the floor hadn't moved; they just kept watching us, their black eyes glittering. But the air had become so tense and charged that I knew it for a certainty—they wanted to kill us, shoot us down right here and take the cigarettes. They would get away with it, too, because no one was looking for us. Nobody knew where we were.

I saw one of the Algerians slowly begin to reach for the machine gun nearest him, his face expressionless, his eyes fixed on us. I turned toward Mischa, and softly, very softly, he said, "I know, and I am ready."

And he was. His machine gun was pointing at them, and he was no longer the lovable Mischa I had come to know on the trip. All the life and laughter and mischief had vanished from his face. It was a face of granite, and his voice was charged with danger.

He said to me, "Take their guns, all of them, and bring them here. Let Jeno hold them."

I went among the Algerians—not too close, so they couldn't grab me—took three small machine guns, and brought them to our side of the room. Then I went back and collected eight revolvers and automatics.

Mischa walked over to the one who had reached for the machine gun, and in a flash he whipped the barrel of his machine gun against the side of the man's face. The Algerian fell to the floor. Then Mischa came back, and their leader started talking again as if nothing had happened. Within minutes the sale was agreed upon.

The fallen Algerian picked himself off the floor and sat on a chair in the corner wiping blood from his face. Mischa told Jeno to stay with the weapons while he and I started counting the cigarettes.

We opened the first barrel, and there they were, layer upon layer of them. After a few minutes of counting a strong odor of gasoline began to permeate the room, mixing with the sickly sweet smell of whatever the Algerians had been smoking. The days of driving without any real rest, the tension, the hunger were finally getting to us. My head threatened to split. I looked at Mischa, and he winked at me, but I saw the exhaustion on his face. When we couldn't count any longer the Algerians took over—they were double-checking. We had gotten through about ten layers of cigarettes, and we calculated from this that there were close to half a million in each barrel. We had over two and a half million cigarettes! The Algerians were impressed. Figuring fast, I told them we would take all the money, and they could have all the cigarettes and the three cases of tobacco.

They figured for about ten minutes and then agreed. We were so tired by now we could hardly stand up. They packed the bundles of money in a small suitcase. Mischa and Jeno gathered up the pile of weapons, and Mischa had me tell them that we would leave the guns outside the room.

We slipped out and shut the door. At the end of the corridor we dropped the guns, ran for the exit, and scrambled into the truck. I was afraid the motor might not start, but, thank God, it kicked right over and started growling belligerently. We pulled out onto the main street and drove away, fast. I had the case full of money, millions and millions of francs. I had never seen so much money.

The sun was up, gilding the streets at an early-morning slant, and Paris was beginning to come to life. Butcher shops and vegetable markets banged open their storefronts, and a few trucks passed us. When we had put a safe distance between us and the Place Pigalle Mischa's grim face softened. He looked over at me and Jeno, and we started to laugh. We were in Paris, and we were rich—unbelievably rich!

"*Nu, rebyata,*" Mischa said, "I think we take a rest in the best hotel in Paris!"

We slowed down and soon spotted our first policeman. We stopped, and I leaned out and asked for the address of the best hotel in Paris.

He looked into the cab, saw Mischa's uniform and the machine gun, and frowned. "Where are you from?"

"From the Russian military," I said, on the spur of the moment.

"Ahh," he replied. "*J'ai compris.*" Smiling, he gave us directions to the Claridge Hotel on the Champs Elysées.

We drove and drove, stopping to ask directions every few

blocks, till finally we came out on the broad and famous boulevard and found the Claridge Hotel.

We groaned to a stop in front of the splendid entrance, jumped down, and strode in past a flabbergasted doorman. The Claridge hadn't seen guests like us since the war, and maybe never. During the Occupation officers in uniform must have come here, but Jeno and I looked like refugees. Our clothes were a shambles, passable in any DP camp but not here in Paris. Even the first Algerians had looked as if they wanted to spit on me.

On the way to the desk I whispered to Mischa, "We might not be allowed to stay here. This is supposed to be the best hotel in Paris."

"I am an officer of the Red Army," he declared loudly, "and we will stay here!" All eyes in the lobby turned to us.

Across a cool marble counter, a man in a black suit arched his eyebrows ever so slightly and asked, "What can I do for you?"

"Vanya," said Mischa, "tell him I am an officer of the Red Army, and I want the best he has to offer."

The clerk turned quickly into an office behind the desk and reappeared with another black-suited man, probably his superior. This one bowed to us, a uniformed bellhop appeared out of nowhere, and we were asked to follow him. We did, into an ornate elevator, down a heavily carpeted hall, and into a paradise of carpets, mirrors, plush beds and chairs.

I sank into the soft couch while Mischa and Jeno explored the room. Then we discovered an enormous bathroom with a tiled tub fit for a Turkish pasha. Mischa wanted to take a bath immediately. Throwing the suitcase of money on the bed, he undressed while water steamed and thundered into the tub, and soon we heard him singing *"Katchusha"* in the bathroom.

No one complained now of headache or fatigue.

When Mischa was finished I took a bath. Hot water—for the first time in over three years! It was pure delight to rub the journey out of my skin, to rub deeper, down, down to

185

the layers of grime and weariness Russia had ground into me. After about twenty minutes, I had to give Jeno his turn.

Coming out of the bathroom refreshed, I saw several buttons next to the bed and pointed them out to Mischa. He pressed all of them, and within minutes several uniformed servants were at the door asking what they could do for us. Mischa asked me to have them clean our clothes as fast as possible. Taking Mischa's pants and jacket off the bed, the valet uncovered the bundle of notes. He gasped, gave us a distraught look, and hurried out.

Then we went to bed.

Half a day had passed—to us it seemed like half an hour—when the doorbell woke us, and the valet stood timorously holding our clean clothes. He asked for a few hundred francs; Mischa grandly tossed him a five-thousand-franc note, and he bowed his way out of the suite.

Now Mischa yawned and said, "Boys, I am hungry. Let us eat."

We agreed and pressed the buttons again. The servants came running. Soon all kinds of food arrived in silver dishes on a cart covered with a white cloth: steaming stews, cakes, fresh bread and fruit, glistening black caviar, and two dozen cold chocolate éclairs. Some of the food we didn't even know how to eat.

Another waiter rolled in an ice bucket with several bottles of champagne. Corks popped, the liquid foamed out, and soon Jeno and Mischa were well on their way to drunken high spirits, ordering even more to drink, both champagne and cognac.

Then Mischa announced that he wanted some girls. Another bell was rung. Thousands of francs changed hands, and shortly three very elegant *poules* appeared. They wore nylon stockings, short tight skirts, and black lace blouses, and their perfume was enough to take your pants off. Bright-red lipstick, strong perfume, the dainty, painted faces—next to them we felt like strong, dirty, hungry, tired animals.

Soon the girls were running around the room with less and

less clothes on, laughing and squealing. I had had two glasses of champagne, and my head was spinning. I was afraid to get any drunker; I thought somebody should be guarding the money, or we might wake up in the morning as poor as we had been yesterday. Taking the case of francs into the big bathroom, I shut the door and tried to count the money, but there was too much—it made my head spin even worse. So I took the case into the bedroom and shoved it under my mattress. It raised the head of the mattress and made a perfect spectator's seat. With a plate of éclairs on my night table, I settled down to watch the two clowns perform. And perform they did. All three girls were fucked that night—Hungarian and Russian style.

Three or four hours later everyone was snoring, sodden with cognac, champagne, and love-making. Two of the girls slept with Mischa, and one was sprawled across Jeno. I reached under the mattress and, holding the handle of the money case, fell into a light sleep.

The girls, late sleepers by profession, were awakened by us early risers. They grumbled, untidy, puffy-eyed, and hung over. Each of them got thirty thousand francs, and then they were discharged.

We decided to spend the day sightseeing, mostly for Mischa, who wanted to see the Eiffel Tower and other Parisian landmarks. In our clean clothes we looked somewhat more presentable. Mischa grabbed a handful of five-thousand-franc notes, a bottle of champagne, and, of course, his machine gun. Downstairs at the desk he paid 200,000 francs on our bill. I was carrying the money case.

Our old friend the truck still stood out in front. The hotel staff hadn't dared to move it. I told Mischa we should feed it well and bathe it; after all, it had served us nobly through the mad journey. Mischa just laughed and said, "All it wants is gas, and we've got plenty of that. Stop worrying about the truck."

We waved down a taxi and told the driver to take us to the Eiffel Tower. The elevator to the top wasn't open yet, so while we waited we strolled around the plaza looking at the people. They stared back at us. Paris was waking up slowly. People here were better dressed than in the cities in Germany, and, of course, we saw an occasional American tourist—to us they all looked like millionaires.

We were beginning to attract a crowd. Mischa was waving the bottle of champagne in one hand, and in the other hand several folded five-thousand-franc notes stuck out from between his fingers. His machine gun was slung across his chest. Declaiming in Russian, he made a grand gesture, and five-thousand-franc notes fluttered to the ground. Pigeons clattered away. Some of the onlookers crossed themselves, and five or six raggedy kids dived after the money.

I was nervous. I didn't want to leave Mischa, because with him I needed no identification, but his antics were uncomfortably conspicuous. I told him I was going back to the hotel to get some more sleep, and that I would take care of the money. I worried a little about Mischa and Jeno—neither of them spoke French—but with their thousands of francs and Mischa's machine gun they should be all right.

At the hotel, our suite had been cleaned, and I decided to take another long bath. Still astonished by the luxury of soap and hot water, I soaked and thought about my DP camp and the canteen, about Vasile and his camp. Here I was in the best hotel in Paris, in luxury my friends back there couldn't even imagine, with francs to burn. If I hadn't had Mischa and Jeno with me, from my world, I would have been terribly lonely. This was too rich for my blood. What kind of a millionaire did you have to be to afford a place like this legitimately? Maybe I just didn't remember any more how people lived. I had been in camps so long. Climbing out of the tub, I dried myself and stretched out between soft clean sheets, but I couldn't fall asleep.

I looked around the room, and my eyes came to rest on the buttons. I was tempted to press one of them, but I didn't have the courage. Suddenly I was frightened. What right did I have to press a button, to make someone come running to see what I wanted? I turned over and buried my head in the pillow, shutting out all the luxury, and soon escaped into a deep sleep.

My friends woke me hours later. They had two girls with them, and a waiter was setting up a table loaded with food and champagne and all the things the French are famous for. Soon another party was under way. I thought about asking the waiter to bring me a good-looking girl, because Mischa and Jeno rang for him every half hour for this or that, but I decided against it. My French wasn't good enough to communicate with a French girl, and to get together with someone I couldn't talk to, for such an obvious purpose, was not my style. It went on as it had the night before.

In the morning the girls were again paid and dismissed. Jeno felt like taking a walk, Mischa wanted to sleep for an hour or so, and I climbed into another bath. I loved the sparkling white bathtub. The clean, hot, sweet-smelling water felt delicious. I couldn't wait to tell Jony, Max, Vasile, and the rest how my vacation had turned out. Perhaps now was the time for a *real* vacation, maybe to the south of France, to the gambling tables. With all this money, I could finally buy some new clothes. I was wondering how long the money would last when there was an urgent knocking on the bathroom door, and the hasty entrance of Jeno jolted me out of those south-of-France dreams.

"Get dressed fast, and come with me," he said.

I dried myself, dressed in a minute, and followed him out.

On the way down in the elevator he said, "Wait till you hear what this Hungarian I met has to say."

We hurried through the lobby and outside. Next to our truck stood a man dressed in a shabby, heavy suit. Without introduction he began talking. "Like I said, you should pay me for the information I am about to give you. Every gangster in Paris is looking to shoot you guys. You sold some Algerians millions of cigarettes, and they flooded the black market with them, and most people throw up when they inhale them and others faint. They have a strong smell of benzine. And these gangsters are really looking to kill you."

I told Jeno to give the man some money, and we raced back to our suite. It was obvious what had happened. The cigarettes that had been packed tightly in the empty gasoline drums had absorbed the benzine fumes—the same fumes that had made me sick—while the cigarettes Mischa and Jeno had smoked and given to the Algerians to sample had been carried in their pockets. Those were all right, but the ones packed in the barrels were poisonous!

We woke Mischa, and I told him in a few words how our transaction had backfired. With his quick mind, he understood at once, and within two minutes he was dressed and reaching for his machine gun. Jeno and I threw all the money in the case, and we took off.

We went straight through the lobby, and while Mischa paid the bill at the desk I asked the doorman whether anyone had tampered with our truck.

"No, no, m'sieur."

I gave him a five-thousand-franc note while Mischa pulled the gas barrel to the tailgate. Jeno had the rubber hose ready, and within five minutes our tank was filled. At any second we expected to see a mob of Algerians swarming out of a side street with guns and knives. Mischa's eyes roved restlessly over the street.

He gunned the engine, and we searched for a road east, asking directions only of respectable-looking people strolling on broad, sunny streets. We drove and asked some more, until finally we were in the outskirts, on a road that looked like a main highway. The sun was behind us; we must be heading east. It was an unspeakable relief to get out of the maze of little streets. Still, those Algerians were desperadoes. If they learned which highway we were on they would follow us. No border would stop them from getting their money back, and their revenge.

We sped along, grateful for the open highway and our powerful truck. Every once in a while we glanced back, but we didn't see anyone following us. We were just beginning to relax when an American MP jeep flew past us, siren wailing. Mischa pulled over and screeched to a stop. He jumped out, the machine gun on his back, and walked toward the American soldier grinning. They met halfway. Mischa slapped the soldier on the shoulder and showed him some papers. Whatever he had from the Red Army was probably in the Cyrillic alphabet, so the American wouldn't have been able to read it, but Mischa kept talking and smiling. Finally he adjusted the machine gun on his back, stuck out his hand, and shook hands with the American. Then he got back into the truck, and we were off again. In our rear-view mirror we saw that the jeep stood there for a while and then turned around and drove off.

Mischa saw how tense Jeno and I had been. He laughed and said, "Don't worry. These Americans, they are our friends. And, anyway, I have the machine gun."

After four or five hours of driving through the French countryside Mischa wanted to buy a few bottles of cognac to fortify himself. So we stopped in Metz, and Jeno and I got him a case of the best.

This time we didn't drive directly toward the border, but went in a southeasterly direction. Mischa had oriented himself with his map. He and Jeno would drive straight on to Vienna, leaving me off somewhere in southwestern Germany, where I could get a train north to Hannover.

At our next gasoline stop Jeno and I got into the back of the truck and lay down. I thought wistfully of the clean, soft beds we had left behind in Paris. We opened one of the bottles of cognac and drank until we didn't know where we were.

Mischa shook us awake. "We are in Germany, and I have a surprise for you. Before we crossed the border I stopped in a village and bought us each several pounds of chocolate candy."

I asked, "How did you get them to understand you?"

He smiled and said, "It wasn't easy, but I said *sho-co-LAHT, sho-co-LAHT* repeatedly. I showed the shopkeeper a handful of thousand-franc notes and gave him some. He went into the back and returned with a box of chocolates. I gave him another handful of money, and through gestures I made him understand that I wanted another. He brought another box and as a reward received more money. What else can I do with the money? You bought me a case of cognac, and I bought you a box of chocolates."

He must have given the man close to a hundred thousand francs. I was holding the most expensive chocolates in the world.

We drove on until a sign told us we were nearing Freiburg. I took a deep breath and said to Mischa, "I'd better get off here to catch a train back to my camp. I have been away too long, and my friends must be worried about me."

"But when will you come back to Vienna?" Mischa asked, almost indignantly. I half expected him to say, "I am an officer of the Red Army, and I order you to come with me!"

I looked at him and said gently, "I will try to come back, but I cannot promise. Make sure you don't get into trouble with the Red Army, and don't let them ship you back to your homeland. Try to find someone else who speaks Russian, someone you can trust. Learn some German. It shouldn't be too hard for you. Then you can make the break."

There were no other cars on the road, nobody nearby. Mischa opened the money case, took out several fat wads of five-thousand-franc bills and gave them to me without a word. I asked him if he had any string, and he came up with a few long pieces. In the back of the truck I made the bills into two bundles and tied them to the insides of my thighs under my pants.

Then I shook Jeno's hand, and we kissed each other's cheeks and told each other to be careful—"*Servus, servus, hover.*" I shook Mischa's hand, and he said, "*Nu, Vanyushka, poka*—take care." Slamming the door, I patted the old Studebaker on the flank, and with a growl of the motor they drove away.

I walked along the side of the road feeling forlorn. The

bundles of five-thousand-franc notes chafed my thighs. I was a millionaire, but I couldn't rejoice about it—not yet. I missed my two friends too much. The great adventure was over.

The next adventure began on the train.

I had walked into the town of Freiburg at dusk feeling uncomfortably conspicuous. There weren't many people on the streets, but the ones I passed stared at me. Although I was dressed like a DP, my pockets were bulging—with French francs, German marks, and Austrian schillings—and I was walking like a saddlesore cowboy so that the hidden bundles of francs wouldn't rub too much. Under my arm I carried a big box of French chocolates. I was a poor millionaire in a hungry world, a world where, outside of the black market, there was nothing for my money to buy.

At the train station I asked a stooped, uniformed old employee whether he knew someone who could change French francs into German marks. He stared at me suspiciously and said, "I have never seen you before. You look like a black marketeer. We have no black market here." I walked away before he could call a cop.

A few shabby-looking loiterers hung around the station,

and I was sure they were waiting for deals. They were black-market types, all right, but this was a fairly small town, not a big city like Bremen or Hannover, so there weren't many of them. They must be local people, known to the police and probably paying them off. I would only attract unwelcome attention if I tried to get into the action.

While I waited for the train I wondered where Mischa and Jeno were now, driving eastward into the night. By tomorrow evening, if they didn't take any impulsive detours, they would be back in Vienna, freak millionaires like me. Mischa might be the richest, as well as the craziest, officer in the Red Army.

The train came, and I found a second-class compartment to myself. I put the chocolates on the luggage rack, out of reach of temptation. How I longed to eat them! But I had promised myself to save them for the two little girls at my uncle's, where I was going to stop on my way back to camp. I gave the conductor my ticket and slept the sleep of exhaustion until the train pulled into Frankfurt early the next morning.

After a wait of about ten minutes there, the whistle blew and the engine hissed, and I felt the train jolt into motion. Just at that moment a tall, gaunt man in a dark overcoat ran past my window and swung himself aboard the slowly moving train. He came into my compartment all out of breath, and I realized with a start that I knew him. His long face, the very white skin with bluish beard stubble, his bushy eyebrows above piercing black eyes were unmistakable, but where had I seen him before? He was staring at me, too, frowning, and as his forehead furrowed in concentration I suddenly remembered him. His name was Orlov, and he had been a big black-market man in the north, around Bremen, at the time Jeno and I were in the camp there. He had disappeared in the Scandinavian countries for several months, and when he reappeared in Bremen he had asked me to help him move some heavy crates in the baggage room of the Bremen station. I had had no idea what was in them. Shortly after that he had vanished again, and now here he was in southern Germany.

Orlov looked at me intently and said, "I know we have met before, but where? Where?"

"I helped you in the baggage room at the Bremen station more than a year ago."

"Of course!" he said. "You are the Rumanian with the bad legs. How are they now?"

"Much better," I replied.

He asked me where I was living, and I told him that I was in Transit Camp Buchholz, near Hannover, and hoped to emigrate to Canada within the year.

"I have a lot of French francs," I said. "Can you use them?"

"I'll take them," he answered, without hesitation. "How many do you have?"

"About two million."

He looked startled. "You aren't the type to joke about deals, but that's impossible."

"Come with me to the toilet and I'll show you."

We pushed our way to the toilet, and I went in, took the bundles off, and hid them under my shirt. I came out and, using the lavatory door as a shield, let him see them.

Orlov whistled. "How did you get so much?"

I had him wait a moment, closed the door, and tied the bundles to my thighs again. Back in our compartment I told him about Jeno, whom he had known in Bremen, our meeting with Mischa in the Russian zone, and our improbable adventure.

When I finished, Orlov said, "I've been around the black market for two years now, and that is one of the best deals I've ever heard of, even though it almost backfired. Luck was on your side, or you would never have gotten out of Paris alive, but those are the risks we take. Well, you're in the big time now! I can take some of the francs, but not all of them."

I got about one hundred thousand loose francs out of my pockets, and he gave me twelve thousand German marks for them.

"At the moment I am working on a funny deal," he went

196

on, pocketing the francs. "There are two Americans in Nuremberg who will pay very high prices for antique ornaments, silverware, gold chalices, things from castles where German nobility lived. I've made some preliminary contacts with a gang, and they have a castle near Bad Schwalbach all lined up to break into. They come very highly recommended, but you know how it is with these gangs. They're not too reliable.

"Right now, I am going to Hamburg on other business, but after that I will look into this antique situation more seriously. I wish you would come in with me. Two of us will make a stronger impression, and I'll be more confident dealing with the gang and the Americans. If you decide to come in on the deal it will be easier to finance the operation together." The sly fox had come the long way around before mentioning my money.

I told him I was very tired, and wanted to get back to my camp and rest awhile before I got into any more scrapes, however profitable they might be.

"Well, think it over," he said. "My business in Hamburg will take about a week, and on the way down I'll stop at your camp and we can talk about it."

As the train pulled into Giessen I shook Orlov's hand and said, "I'll see you in a week. Good luck in Hamburg."

I arrived at my uncle's house in the middle of dinner. At the sight of the chocolates the little girls squealed and tumbled over themselves running to me, and I was glad I hadn't given in to temptation. In the bathroom I untied the bundles of money from my thighs—the skin underneath was red and irritated—and I brought the bundles out to the dining room and put them on an empty chair. Angelika, my uncle, his wife, and the old grandmother stared like a row of owls from the money to me and back at the money. Then the questions started flying, and dinner got cold while I told them the whole story.

My uncle shook his head. "How do you stumble over such deals? You go away for a vacation, and look what you get into. It's unbelievable!"

They fingered the French money as if it weren't real. I

persuaded my uncle to take one of the bundles, of three or four hundred thousand francs. Even if he changed them for marks there was nothing he could buy with them on the open market; he would have to find a reliable local black-market contact, and then maybe the francs would keep the family in butter, sugar, and eggs for a while.

I went to bed soon after dinner and slept as if I had been drugged. Early the next morning I tied my remaining bundles to my thighs again and walked to the station with my uncle hoping to catch an early train. In half an hour I was on the local to Kassel, and in Kassel, using Jony's military pass, I got on an express to Hannover.

At five in the afternoon, when I got in, the plaza in front of the Hannover station was packed with black marketeers. I would have liked to show Oskar all my money, but just the thought of looking for him in this crowd was exhausting. I got on the next streetcar, and an hour later I walked down the road to camp. The fields and trees were a rich green, and through the barbed wire I could see some of the DPs walking around in their shirt sleeves. They looked naked somehow without their dark jackets, like animals that have just shed their winter coats.

The Polish guard recognized me and said, "Where were you? Everybody has been asking for you."

"I was visiting a friend," I said, and went toward Barracks 1.

Jony came running out the door to meet me. "*Hei ma unde ai fost?* Hey, where were you?" he shouted, and we embraced.

I asked him to come into the spare room in Barracks 1. He watched incredulously as I took the fat bundles of five-thousand-franc notes out of my pants. I had to tell him right away where I had been, and with whom, and how we had gotten the money.

"Jesus Christ!" Jony said. "You are the luckiest bastard of a Rumanian I ever knew!" He burst out laughing. "I would be scared to do what you have done. I salute your courage."

I gave him two packets of francs and said, "See what you can do with these. I think they would come in very handy if someone wanted to go to Belgium for coffee." He raised his eyebrows in mock expectation, and I said, "Don't look at me! I'm due for a good long rest."

We went to Jony's room, and I kissed Maria hello. I answered her questions almost timidly, expecting one of her fiery tirades, but instead she started to laugh. "I give up," she said. "You can do anything and you won't get caught. There must be a lucky star over your head. I am glad to have you home safe. Now, go wash up and I'll give you some *ghiveci*."

Jony came with me to the canteen, and Max whooped and grabbed me. "My boy, where have you been?" That question again!

"You tell him," I said to Jony. "I want to freshen up after the train ride."

In my little room everything was just as I had left it. Elegant hotel rooms were fine and good, but it felt better to be home again. I took off my shirt, washed, and brushed my teeth, and then I heard roars of laughter coming from the canteen.

I went back out, and found Max doubled over behind the bar and Jony laughing with him, wiping his eyes helplessly. Between laughs Max gasped, "How I would like to have been with them!" He came around from behind the bar and kissed my cheeks again in congratulation. "Ha, you are like old Manolescu, the Rumanian prince of thieves!"

"Here's something for you to play with, Max." I gave him a handful of francs.

He bulged his eyes out at the money, sending Jony into fresh spasms of laughter.

We went to Barracks 1 to eat, and I told Jony about meeting Orlov on the train and the antiques scheme he had proposed. Jony liked the sound of it and agreed to talk it over with Orlov when he stopped by.

Orlov came early, just a couple of days later. In the middle of the afternoon a guard came for me in the canteen, saying,

"There's someone here to see you." I couldn't think who it might be, but I went out, and there was Orlov, tall, gaunt, and tired-looking, with dark stubble on his jaw and shadows under his eyes. It surprised me that he had on the same kind of clothes I was wearing, the DP's old American army uniform dyed black. He smiled and handed me a package, and we shook hands.

"I've brought you some fish from Hamburg," he said.

I thanked him. "You look tired."

"I could do with some sleep," he admitted, rubbing his face wearily.

I took him to my room and showed him the bucket of fresh water and the latrines just outside the canteen. He lay down on the cot, and in half a minute he was breathing deeply and evenly. I locked the door so he wouldn't be disturbed and went to Barracks 1 to tell Jony he had come and was resting.

That evening after supper we went to the canteen and found Orlov sitting at the bar talking to Max. He had shaved and looked better.

I introduced him to Jony, and Jony asked, "Do you want something to eat?"

Orlov replied, "I guess I'm like any other DP—hungry."

Maria had some *ghiveci* left over from our supper, and she took Orlov's fish and prepared that, too. Orlov ate the *ghiveci* with concentration. He didn't say much, but when he did speak Maria laughed at his dry wit. He knew a little Rumanian, and he soon had her as flushed and discomfited as a young girl. With his long, cadaverous face and his pallor, Orlov wasn't good-looking, but he was a powerful man. He could radiate a force bordering on brutality, and his charm had the same force behind it. Jony was unusually quiet. After coffee Orlov bowed deeply and kissed Maria's hand. She had two bright pink spots in the middle of her cheeks, and Jony was scowling. Then Maria heard the baby cough in the next room and reverted to being a mother. Jony looked relieved. I was amused at his Rumanian jealousy.

Outside, the three of us walked around the perimeter of the camp, along the barbed-wire fence. The spiked strands glinted in the moonlight. The sight of the fence never failed to depress me, even though I knew I could come and go whenever I wanted. I noticed it more now that I had been away for a while.

Orlov thought his plan looked good, despite an unexpected delay. One of the Americans who were interested in buying the antiques was in Austria, and it would be three or four weeks before he got back to Nuremberg. Orlov had three German burglars in mind for the job; they were a team of professionals experienced at breaking and entering. But he wanted Jony and me in on the deal, with a full share in both the expenses and the profits. We would put up ten thousand marks, and so would he, to pay for the three men and a truck to carry the loot from the castle to Nuremberg.

Jony asked one or two questions and was silent for a while thinking. Then he stretched out his hand, and Orlov gripped it. They both grinned. The tension there had been between them at dinner vanished, and the deal was closed.

It was a beautiful night, barbed wire or no. The moon shone on the earth and on the trio of black marketeers. We felt that the moon was an omen—the venture would be a success.

I asked Orlov, "Does the castle we're planning to rob by any chance belong to the Baron von Frankenstein?"

Jony laughed and took a few steps in imitation of the monster the baron had created.

Orlov said, "No, but as a matter of fact the Frankenstein castle isn't far from this one. The man who owns this castle is sinister enough. He is descended from an old noble family, and he was very big with the Nazis. It will be a pleasure to rob him."

That night Orlov stayed in the spare room in Barracks 1. In the morning after breakfast he shook hands with Jony and me. "You will hear from me in three or four weeks. A day or two before we go on the job, I'll be here." Then he was gone.

Once again, there was nothing to do but wait.

A couple of days later I noticed a new face in the canteen, the face of a natural clown. Max was talking with him. I went over to the bar, and Max introduced us. His name was Josif Mihailovsky, and he had just arrived with a group from a DP camp near Munich. He was of medium height, slender and pale, with ears that stuck out, a black forelock, and a perpetual elfin grin on his face. After a few minutes I couldn't help liking him.

During the next few days Josif became friendly with Jony. For a few days he was inseparable from the sergeant of the guards. Soon he took his meals with the sergeant's brother, the chef in the mess hall. He stopped paying for his own beers in the canteen, and almost everyone in the camp started calling him by his first name. In a week everyone knew his story.

Josif was from Warsaw. He had been in prison for robbery,

and when the war broke out he had been released and drafted into the Polish army. Not long afterward he was taken prisoner by the Germans. He escaped, but back in Poland he was arrested again and put into a labor battalion. His job was shoveling coal in the big boiler room of a factory.

After several months, his shoes wore out, and he asked for new ones. They told him to shovel coal barefoot for a few days until the new shoes arrived. He shoveled coal and waited and waited. Days passed, and then weeks. One day some glowing coals jumped out of the blazing furnace and burned Josif's feet badly. A few minutes later, the supervisor he had asked for new shoes happened to pass by on an inspection of the boiler room. When he saw Josif sitting down, he shouted, "Get off your ass and get some coal into that furnace!" Josif didn't move. The supervisor kicked him.

Josif said, "You shovel coal for a while. You are too fat anyway, you son of a bitch."

Josif got a severe beating, and for the rest of the war, as long as the factory kept running, he had shoveled coal in his bare feet, burning them often. He remembered that supervisor's name, Fritz.

One day Josif took me aside and showed me a revolver. "No one in this camp knows I am armed, so don't tell anybody," he whispered. "But if you ever need help, just tell me and I will take care of you."

Two or three days later he asked me if I would take him with me to the black market in Hannover.

"Sure, Josif, the next time I go I'll take you."

"I haven't got anything to sell," he said, "but I have heard that the black market in Hannover is very big and that a lot of people circulate around peddling things."

"That's how it is," I told him. "You will find the scum of Germany and Europe there."

He laughed and said, "I like to watch the Germans peddle their wares and their ration cards. They started the war, and now most of them are willing to pick up cigarette butts. I have been around many black markets, looking for a certain

German. Maybe I'll find him yet. I know he is in Germany somewhere. He was a civilian, so he wasn't taken prisoner. He comes from the eastern sector. I looked for him there, but he had left. He likes the American and English zones better. There's more profit to be made. I have a feeling he is circulating around the black markets, and I want to find him."

"Let's go to the black market tomorrow and walk around the station," I said. "Who knows? He might be there." I wanted to look for Oskar, to tell him about my trip and give him some of the francs for himself and Rita.

Early the next day, standing on the streetcar with Josif, I looked at his impish profile and had to laugh. He really was a born clown. He looked at me, and without asking why I was laughing, he started to laugh, too. We laughed until we had all the other passengers staring at us.

Josif gasped, "Enough—stop laughing, or they'll throw us off the streetcar!" It was hard to stop because he was grimacing, biting back the laughter from his face. Then the laughter faded, and I saw that he was intently studying the German passengers. I suddenly wondered whether he was carrying his revolver.

I leaned over and whispered, "I hope you don't have your gun with you."

He whispered back, "I wouldn't leave the camp without it. We are in Germany. They are sons of bitches and whores, and you have to be prepared for anything."

We arrived at the railroad station. When we got off the streetcar, Josif wanted to get into the dense crowd right away. I took him off to the side and said, "I just met you, Josif, and I like you very much, but you shouldn't carry the revolver. I know you want to shoot the German you are looking for, and he deserves it. But if you catch him and pull the trigger, it will be all over for him. He made you miserable for three years, and you want to pay him back by giving him one instant of pain! He'll be relieved. He won't be hungry any more. Don't you think a good beating would make him suffer much more? If you told him you knew where to find him and could give him another beating whenever you wanted to, wouldn't that be better? If you shoot him, with the smoking gun in your hand you'll be a sitting duck for the law, and you won't be able to emigrate. Then what will you do?"

To my surprise, I saw tears in his eyes. I said, "Josif, I didn't mean to hurt your feelings. I hope I haven't said anything wrong."

"No, you haven't said anything wrong. It's just that no one has ever talked to me that way. People always laugh at me, and nobody ever takes what I say seriously. I want so much to emigrate, to build a new life somewhere. Here." He pulled the revolver out and tried to give it to me.

"No," I hissed. "Be careful so no one sees it!"

Under his coat he gave me the gun. I took it and asked, "Is the safety on?"

"Yes," he said. I stuck the revolver into my waistband and pulled my shirt over it.

Josif smiled uncertainly and said, "You really like me, don't you?"

"Sure," I said. "You can be the funniest guy in the world, and I wouldn't give a million German guards for one Josif. Hide the gun when we get back to camp and keep it for a real emergency."

"I will listen to you from now on," he said. "Let's get into this crowd now, and meet here in about twenty minutes."

"Fine," I answered, and the crowd swallowed him.

I stood there for a few minutes, thinking about the poor guy. His clown face was a mask that hid his real feelings. Suddenly I realized that I had forgotten to ask him whether he could handle this German alone. Fritz might be a big, strong man. I could just see him holding skinny Josif in a bear hug, crushing him. I rushed into the mob to try to catch up with Josif, but I couldn't find him.

I looked around for Oskar. Soon I spotted him near the edge of the crowd, alert and straight in his trench coat, talking to a couple of traders. I walked over, and when he saw me Oskar's face lit up with surprise and pleasure, but he waved his hand to me to wait a minute. The two men were talking to him about eggs, a rare commodity those days. Most of the hens in Germany had been eaten.

As soon as the peddlers left, Oskar shook my hand heartily. "Where were you? Rita asks me every day whether I have heard from you! I was on the verge of coming to Buchholz to ask Jony what happened to you, and now out of nowhere you appear again. Please stay in touch with me from now on."

"Oskar, it does me good to see you again."

"*Junge,*" he said, "would you like to visit Rita at her father's office?"

"No, Oskar, it would embarrass her." I looked down at my clothes, the badge of the DP—the homeless, jobless Eastern European. "But as soon as we have another dance, I'll invite both of you. Now I'll tell you where I've been—I've been to Paris!"

"Come, you must be joking. How could you go there? You have no passport." We walked toward the place where I was supposed to meet Josif, and I told Oskar by what indirect route I had gotten to Paris, what we had done in Paris, and how fast we had left Paris.

"*Mein Gott,*" he said when I had finished, "you are very, very lucky. You will have to tell Rita the story. She will love you even more than she does already."

Reaching into my pocket I said, "Here are some of the francs I have left. You keep some and give some to Rita. I have plenty of marks."

Just then I saw Josif looking for me and shouted, "Here, Josif, here!" He heard me and came over, but when he saw Oskar standing with me he shrank back into himself, his black eyes suspicious.

"Josif, this man is a friend of mine and Jony's." I saw him relax, and he shook Oskar's hand in a friendly way. "I will leave you now, Oskar, but I'll see you again soon. Tell Rita that if we don't have a dance in the next couple of weeks I'll invite you both out to the camp for dinner." We shook hands, and Oskar turned back to his surveillance of the crowd.

I walked with Josif around several side streets near the station, and he told me again how sure he was that he would run into Fritz sooner or later. I felt the revolver against my skin, cold and heavy. I wanted to get it away from me.

"Let's go home," I suggested. "It's a long streetcar ride."

The streetcar was packed, but we found a place where we could lean against the side of the car. After about half an hour we found seats. We didn't talk. I kept thinking about Josif. I glanced at his profile again, and his expression wasn't funny now—it was almost fatalistic.

It wasn't until we had gotten off the streetcar and were walking to the camp that Josif's old mood came back, and he joked as we walked along. Before we got to the gate, I slipped him his revolver and reminded him to hide it well. He promised me he would, and then he went back to his barracks.

There wasn't much to do in camp while we waited for Orlov, and I soon began to get bored and restless. I saw Josif a couple of times, and hung around the canteen with Max, and talked to Cheslav, and ate with Jony and Maria. The atmosphere at Jony's was a little depressing. Jony had been to the doctor for another checkup and X ray, and the spots on his lungs weren't any better. The doctor shook his head and told Jony again to try to get more rest. He didn't show it much, but I knew he was deeply discouraged and worried. He wanted so badly to emigrate, to take Maria and the baby to a safer and healthier world where there was a future—not just this drab, endless present, haunted by the nightmare past and relieved only by laughter and danger.

What was worse, the baby had been coughing, and the doctor told Jony that he should bring him in for a checkup. That frightened Maria, who fought against taking the baby to the doctor for fear of learning the worst. The dreaded word—consumption, tuberculosis—was never mentioned, but it weighed on the atmosphere like a stone. We tried to make Maria laugh at supper, to take her mind off her fears, but when she thought no one was watching, a shadow would cross her face and her lips would move as if she was praying. Once

Jony leaned over to me at the table and said, "If there is something wrong with the baby, praying won't cure it."

After another week in camp I had to get away. I thought of going to see Rita, but I felt strangely ambivalent about her. I tried to puzzle out my reactions. Rita had touched me in a way I was afraid to permit. Caring about a girl wasn't an easy or casual thing for me. Too young to be aware of such things when I was plunged from boyhood into a sudden and somber adulthood, I had seen too much since then of the suffering of the weak and unprotected, had been too lonely. No, I responded to Rita with everything in me or I would hardly have responded at all. Olga, the Paris whores—they had aroused only the most superficial interest and were immediately forgotten. Rita haunted me. I could have fallen in love with her, but to me that would mean taking full responsibility for her—willingly and joyously. And that I could not do.

And then there was Oskar. For all her professed interest in me, Rita was obviously still involved with him. I couldn't blame her; he provided much more security for her than I could. But it bothered me that she should be so casual about sleeping with both of us. And Oskar himself seemed to want me to make love to her. He was always saying, "You like Rita? Take her. I give her to you." It was all too much for me. Better to stay out of Rita's life—and yet I thought and dreamed about her more and more as the days wore on and nothing happened to distract me.

Desire might have won out over all my hesitations, but suddenly I had another idea—one so obvious that I wondered why I hadn't thought of it sooner. I said to Jony, "I feel like reading. Do you know where I can get some books?"

"There's a good little library in the town of Buchholz," he said, and he told me how to get there.

As a kid I had loved to read. I read everything, from adventure stories to heroic poetry to Rumanian translations of Dostoevski and Tolstoy. More than once my father caught me in a tent of light under the bedcovers reading with a flashlight or a stolen, dangerous candle when I was supposed to be asleep. I earned some good smacks that way, but, in fact, he was proud of me and encouraged me to steep myself in books.

Then I was taken away to Russia with three schoolbooks under my arm. In the labor camp, a book—if anyone ever saw one—was an object that could be bartered for food, a source of the cigarette paper the guards were greedy for. Even in the Russian miners' homes I visited I saw very few books. For the miners of the Donbas life was too hard and plain for such luxuries of the imagination. Yet the books I had read at home helped keep me alive. I remembered them vividly, and their worlds became warm havens I could escape into when the reality seemed too cold and harsh to endure.

I hadn't read a book, or thought about reading one, for over three years. And now, suddenly, the desire to read had reawakened. I had plenty of leisure, but, what was more important, for the first time in three years I wasn't thinking constantly about my next pitiful meal. It had taken months of the relative security of eating with Jony before that anxiety subsided enough to leave my mind free.

The next day I walked in to Buchholz and found the library. It was small, but to me it was as vast as the legendary library of Alexandria. There were shelves and shelves of books—the place even smelled of books! An old, familiar, forgotten smell.

The guardian of all this treasure was a thin, balding man in his forties. I went to the desk and spoke to him. He said he was sorry but he could not give me a library card; I was a DP.

I looked at him and said, "What do you want—meat, money, or cigarettes?"

His eyes changed from remote, impersonal regret to a quick interest. Before he could say anything I gave him one hundred marks. He still couldn't give me a library card, but he agreed to let me take any books I wanted. So a DP couldn't even borrow a library book without resorting to black-market bribery!

I found some Jack London novels and a volume of Schiller's

poems, and hurried back to camp, shut myself in my room, and plunged into my books. I hardly knew where to begin. The eerie, frozen world of the Arctic north opened up to me through Jack London's stories, but I liked the Schiller even better. Here was the treasure of the German language locked up safe where all Hitler's ravings couldn't touch it. It was a grand language, light-years away from the muttering and wheedling thieves' lingo of the black market. I could have used a dictionary, but it went well enough without one. When I read the line *"Die Elemente hassen das Gebild der Menschen Hand"* ("the elements hate the work of human hands") or Schiller's description of a storm at sea in "The Diver," for the first time I felt I had found something man-made that had the strength of the wind on the tower in Russia or the terrible grandeur of the way winter came there.

I read until I fell asleep, sated and exhausted. When I woke I went to the mess hall for tea and soup, and then sat down in the canteen and read some more. Everywhere I went, now, I took a book with me.

After five days I went back to the library and got some of the Russian classics in German translation and a book of Goethe's poems. On the way back to camp I felt like a thief who had gotten away with something. I could hardly believe that such riches were free for the taking.

I wasn't bored with camp life any more. Now the days weren't long enough. Time passed swiftly, and I didn't mind the wait to hear from Orlov. I rediscovered the adventure stories of Karl May, one of my childhood favorites. He had written about sixty-five volumes, and the library had forty of them. They took me to every corner of the earth—to the North American Indians, the Amazon jungle, Outer Mongolia, the wild Berber tribes, the Arabs. In each of the tribes there was a hero vividly, irresistibly portrayed. Once again I fell under the spell of Karl May.

One day Robert, the librarian, said, "You walk two or three miles between here and the camp every few days. Why don't you move in to Buchholz?"

"I can't," I said, "because from the transit camp I am going to emigrate to the places Karl May writes about!"

He laughed. "What is your profession? What kind of work can you do?"

"My friend," I said, "I get fed at the camp, but it isn't enough. Occasionally some friends and I engage in black-market activities. Then we live better and eat better. If you ask me again what my profession is, I am a black marketeer."

We talked, and I found that he was a kindly, intelligent man. I told him about my background, about the two years in Russia and my escape, and it aroused his sympathies. From then on I got all the books I wanted. I always returned them, although I was sometimes sorely tempted to hide one under my mattress and keep it. Whenever we got food from Vasile's bazaar I took Robert some, and he was always grateful. We had become friends, so I was no longer bartering for the privilege of borrowing library books.

In my excitement at rediscovering reading, I had retreated into a world of my own. I didn't daydream much about Rita, except when the heroine of a book reminded me of her, and I had almost completely forgotten about Josif. Max told me that he had asked for me several times, and when Max had told him I was busy reading in my room, he had walked away angrily. Finally, Josif had said, "Why doesn't he want to see me?"

Max tried to reassure him, but Josif wouldn't listen. From then on I tried to read in the canteen, but when I didn't see Josif for the next few days, I went back to my room.

One day I went to the Buchholz library to return a science-fiction book, and my friend Robert gave me another one by the same author called *Atomic Weight 500*. When I got to the camp gate, I saw that there was a commotion at the guardhouse. In the midst of it were a sour-faced German policeman and Josif. Josif looked torn and bloody, as if he had been in a violent fight. I knew right away that it had something to do with Fritz.

None of the guards, not even the sergeant, spoke German.

Everyone was talking at once. The sergeant didn't understand what the German policeman was saying, and he and the four guards and Josif were all shouting in Polish. I got them quiet, and the policeman started talking.

Not far from the railroad station in Hannover a British MP had called him, shouting that two men were trying to kill each other. He ran to the scene and found Josif clutching a German by the legs. One of the German's ears was half bitten off; he had a gash across his face, blood was running from his mouth and nose, and he was moaning in terror. He had wet his pants. Josif was shaking as if he had a fever. The MP had been driving by in his jeep when he had seen the fight and called the policeman. Josif had said something about the transit camp in Buchholz, and the MP had put both of them and the German policeman in his jeep. He had driven the beaten German to the hospital and brought Josif and the policeman here.

I translated the story for the sergeant, who listened and then asked Josif what he had to say.

Josif laughed demoniacally and said to me, "I found him! I found him! I went into Hannover early this morning and spent two hours milling around in the black-market crowd. Finally I got tired and headed down a side street toward the station. Then I saw him! I ran after him, and when I got right behind him I called, 'Fritz! Fritz!' He turned around, and when I saw his face I think I went crazy. I hit him. He tried to run, but I grabbed his legs and got him down on the ground and hit him and hit him in the face." Josif flailed in demonstration. "He tried to fight back, and whenever he hit me it felt good! I got to his face and bit him a few times. He tried to get away, but I got him down again. I wanted to get at his throat with my teeth, but I couldn't. Then this German came and separated us."

The sergeant tried to interrupt Josif several times, but he kept on talking. Once he snapped at the sergeant, "Damn you, be quiet," and went on until he was finished.

The German said, "I want to arrest Josif." I asked him

why. He replied, "Because you can't go around half-killing people and biting them—not in a civilized world."

A civilized world! The policeman seemed unaware of the irony of his remark, but I didn't dare translate it for the Poles. They would probably grab the man and drag him into camp, and he wouldn't look much like himself when they brought him out late at night for an unceremonious burial. The policeman was an older man; he probably wasn't a bad man, but he had no idea what he was saying. I reminded him that he was in a displaced-persons camp, and that all the people in the camp were here as a result of Hitler's ideas of civilization. I told him why Josif had attacked the German.

The policeman understood. He apologized, and he even shook Josif's hand. Then he saluted the sergeant of the guards, who looked pleased by the gesture, shook hands with me, and walked back toward the streetcar.

As soon as he had left, the sergeant raised his voice and started scolding Josif for making trouble. Josif turned toward the sergeant, and his whole body began to shake. He pointed a finger at him and said, "*Scurvei sin* (you son of a whore), one of these days you will say the wrong thing to me and I will kill you. You are worse than the Germans!" I grabbed Josif and dragged him away from the guard shack. He struggled a little, but then he let me lead him.

I took him straight to my room, shut the door, leaned against it, and started to laugh. I laughed and laughed, and at first Josif watched me sullenly, breathing hard, but then his face began to change, and in a moment he broke out laughing, too.

"You should have seen Fritz's face," he spluttered between laughs. "You should have seen it. Ohh, it felt so good. It was a hundred times better to beat the shit out of him than to shoot him. I feel like a new man, all thanks to you." He laughed hysterically for over an hour. He described everything in detail several times, and after each time he gave out another salvo of laughter. I was happy for him.

Much later, when Josif had calmed down and gone back to his

barracks, I looked at the book lying on my cot. *Atomic Weight 500.* I realized I had been too deeply involved in my reading. I had spent the last four weeks almost completely absorbed in books. I would have to watch life, even in this camp, so it wouldn't pass me by.

16

It was afternoon, and I had fallen asleep with my science-fiction book on my pillow when I heard a light tap on the door. I opened my eyes, and Jony was grinning down at me. Behind him was the long, dour face of Orlov. I woke up instantly. Orlov, the black-market king, had come, and now we would go into action!

"Tomorrow," Orlov said, "we go down to Frankfurt by train and on from there by truck. I've brought some American canned food with me. First I'd like to eat something, and then—sleep." He gave Jony three cans of Spam from his small suitcase.

Jony left, saying, "Both of you come over in about twenty minutes, and we'll have supper."

Orlov groaned as he sat down on the cot. "I rarely sleep when I'm on the road," he said. "I'd like to have a permanent place, but it's safer to keep moving. I still have a place in Bremen and one in Frankfurt, but I only go there to pick up messages. After this job I'm going to take it easy for a while."

He stretched out on the cot, sighed, and continued. "In Berlin I nearly got caught with about five thousand ration cards on me. It would have meant a heavy jail sentence. To be successful at this you've got to take a lot of risks. And yet, how can a man, an intelligent man, live any other way? On ration cards you live like a pauper, always on the edge of starvation. There are no jobs. If you want to live decently the black market is the only way. I am glad I met you on the train on your way back from Paris. We are both lucky and will survive this black-market era."

He closed his eyes, and after a few minutes his breathing became even. I thought he had fallen asleep and was about to tiptoe out, but he sat up and said, "Let's go get something to eat before I fall asleep."

Maria had put aside her worries, and I noticed that she looked especially flushed and pretty as she served us the fried Spam and fresh vegetables she had prepared. For Orlov she had made plenty of freshly brewed coffee. He loved it as much as Oskar did and drank cup after cup, black and strong.

After dinner Orlov, Jony, and I walked out along the road toward Buchholz in the gathering dusk. Jony had been quiet, and finally he said, "Orlov, maybe you're in the wrong business. The wives of some American officers would keep you in the best of food and drink. Have you ever considered that?"

I wondered if Orlov would get angry, but he took it good-naturedly. "I'd be a liar if I said I hadn't, but it has the stigma of a pimp. Just to keep my stomach full isn't enough. There has to be some pride, some challenge in what I do."

"You're like a lot of us," Jony said. "It's the danger that appeals to you."

The trees along the road rustled in the evening breeze. We sat down under one of them while Orlov told us his plan. We would meet the three burglars in Frankfurt. They had a small truck and a car, and the six of us would drive to the vicinity of the castle and wait until dark. The professionals would handle the castle break-in and pack the loot into the truck. We would drive overnight to Nuremberg, and Jony, Orlov, and I would deal with the American. Jony and I had no questions, so we walked back to camp.

We all went to bed early so that we would be rested and alert for the job, but I lay awake for a while thinking about another Orlov I had recently gotten to know—the Orlov in *The House of the Dead,* Dostoevski's story of his imprisonment in Siberia. That Orlov was a prisoner of tremendous determination, resolved to live and to escape no matter how many lashings he got. I hoped that Dostoevski's Orlov might somehow be the great-great-grandfather of ours. This Orlov, too, had a force of will that I sensed could not be turned aside. It was what Maria responded to in him, together with his saturnine charm. I was pretty sure our Orlov was also from Russia; I had heard him speak Russian only once, in Bremen, but he spoke it like a native. If I remembered, I would ask Orlov in the morning whether he was familiar with *The House of the Dead.*

Jony woke me. The sun was shining with early-morning brightness. "Come on, get up. We'll have a big breakfast and then go."

When we had eaten, Maria said to Jony, "I can't stop you from going, but remember what the doctor said. Try not to wear yourself out." Then she turned to Orlov. "You take care of my two men. See that they don't get into trouble." Jony kissed her, and we left to catch the streetcar.

In Hannover, Jony used his identification card to get us tickets on the military express. We had a clean, spacious compartment to ourselves. I had been over this route many times on the way to my uncle's, but never in such peace and comfort.

We arrived in Frankfurt in the long shadows of late afternoon. Jony and I followed Orlov through the crowded waiting room, through the muttering throng of black marketeers, and out into the city. Orlov strode briskly ahead. In front of a café he turned, said, "Wait here," and vanished.

We waited, standing among the crowded sidewalk tables.

Then Orlov came up behind like a shadow, startling us. "We'll be picked up within an hour," he said. "Everything seems to be *in Ordnung*."

A waiter hurried over, bowing. He obviously knew Orlov and treated him with great deference. Magically he found us an empty table, and in a moment he was back with a bottle of wine, glasses, and silverware. Soon each of us was served a big, steaming bowl of fish stew. The other patrons looked at us with envy.

"If you want more," Orlov said, "just say the word. Let them stare. They started the war."

I asked for another bowl, and then I was thirsty. Orlov snapped his fingers, and the waiter rushed to our table and returned quickly with a pitcher of water. Orlov in this café reminded me of the black-market baron in Vienna. They both expected immediate obedience and got it.

Orlov read my thoughts. "I get most of my messages at this café. The staff is well paid for their services."

We had finished eating by the time a black Opel pulled up in front of the café. A solid, blond young man got out, looked around, and came toward our table smiling. Orlov got up and said, "That's our car. Let's go." The waiter stood by nodding respectfully. There was no bill.

Jony and I got in the back, and Orlov sat next to the young driver. He looked like a farmer's son, broad-shouldered and placid as a young ox, but he drove as skillfully as Tannov. On the outskirts he slowed down and pulled up to a warehouse where a stocky, dark-haired man was waiting. Our driver signaled, and the other man turned and went inside. In a few moments a small truck drove out. Our driver floored the accelerator, and the truck followed. Just before reaching the main highway our driver pulled over and stopped, and we all got out. The truck stopped behind us. The stocky man and another man jumped down from the cab and came over to the Opel.

Orlov made the introductions. The stocky man was Johannes. Karl, our driver, was the youngest. The third man was older: balding, medium height, nondescript. He could have lost himself in any crowd, but when you looked at him more closely you noticed that his eyes missed nothing. He was the leader and, I later learned, the brains of the outfit. His name was Joachim, but Johannes and Karl called him "Major." These were our professionals.

Orlov told them, "These people are in on the operation. They are friends of mine. I want Karl to drive the truck, and Joachim will drive the Opel." He tossed Karl a pack of American cigarettes and said, "Let's get moving." Jony and I got back in the Opel.

Orlov and the Major smoked and talked in German as we drove along. Orlov thought we should reach the castle around midnight and be finished with the loading in two hours. They discussed what was to be done if someone came on us unexpectedly during the burglary, and the Major showed Orlov a pistol he was carrying. "Use it only as a last resort," Orlov said tersely, and the talk turned to money. At the end of their conference the Major began to sing German soldiers' songs, and from time to time Orlov hummed along.

Then the Major turned and glanced at me. "How old are you?" he asked, turning back to the road.

"Twenty."

"Where did you meet this youngster?" he asked Orlov.

Orlov explained that he had known me in Bremen and that now I was in the DP camp at Buchholz. Then he told the Major about my trip with the Russian officer and Jeno to the Balkans and to Paris.

"*Ja,*" the Major said, "you are pretty good. But try to emigrate soon, before you get into serious trouble. The black market is bad for young fellows." I felt deflated.

"You are right, Major," Orlov said. "But who are we to tell him anything? Right now, we're taking him along on a job!"

"I understand," the Major went on. "This is the black-market era. But when it ends at least I have a trade. I'm an engineer and will make a good living. A young man like him hasn't had a chance to learn a trade. He does very well in black-market deals now, but when it is over what will he do?"

219

"He will be somewhere in Canada or the United States," Orlov replied. "And he will survive there, I'm sure of it. After all, he was a prisoner in Russia for two years and escaped in the middle of winter."

The Major turned and gave me a look of respect. Then Orlov told him that Jony had been a Rumanian army officer and was now in charge of the camp canteen at Buchholz. The Major seemed satisfied with our credentials.

Jony had dozed off. In his sleep he looked small and frail, and I realized that lately he had been more tired than usual. I felt protective toward him—Jony, who was so fatherly toward me. How I loved his gay, stubborn spirit. When we got back I would have to take even more of the work load off him in the canteen.

A little later, since Jony was still asleep, I asked if I could ride in the truck for a while. "Sure," the Major said, and we pulled over to the side of the highway. I ran back to the truck.

Karl grinned and said, "What's the matter? Don't you like riding in comfort with the brains of this outfit?"

"My friend is asleep, and Orlov is talking to the Major. Anyway, I like riding in trucks. It reminds me of a long trip I took not long ago with two good friends."

"Climb in."

When we got rolling again Karl and Johannes asked me where I came from and how I had ended up in Germany. I told them about the mines in Russia and my escape.

"I know those winters," Karl said. "They are unbelievably brutal. I was on the Eastern front, and our unit had no winter uniforms. I don't even want to talk about it. You must be very tough to have survived what you did."

His unit had dissolved somewhere near the Russian border in the middle of winter. In the panic and chaos of retreat, he and five other soldiers banded together and stole a semi-trailer. They drove westward, and when they ran out of gasoline they disabled a Russian tank, drained its gas, and kept going.

In the evening, half-frozen, they came into what looked like a deserted village. Then they saw smoke rising from the chimney of one of the houses. Longing to warm themselves, they crept into the house—and stumbled into a nest of Russian soldiers. Luckily the Russians were drunk, and Karl and his companions grasped the situation first. They ran for it, lobbing a hand grenade toward the house as they went, and drove away without waiting for the results.

"That was the worst fear and danger I've ever been through," Karl said. "In comparison, robbing a castle is child's play."

Johannes told me that his home was in East Germany and that he had deserted from the army. Living on the run, he had resorted to theft and burglary to survive. "One job led to another and bigger one. It's very hard to turn back. This is my profession now. Even when jobs become available I don't know if I'll be able to start all over again in some dreary factory job or clerkship. I wonder if I'll end up living outside the law all my life. It's all right when you're young and energetic, but as you get older you must get tired of it."

Karl broke in. "Johannes is a pessimist. We'll all become regular *Spiessbürgers*—model citizens—in the end. It's just the times. No one can live on ration cards, so we help ourselves a little, stretching and breaking the law wherever we can. Like tonight. No one will be at that castle, so we'll just go in and help ourselves. Those antiques will bring a handsome sum, and we'll be able to live better than the law allows. The only other way is to mingle with the traders, but the dirt of those petty crooks disgusts me. I'd rather go out on something big like this—one night's work. Sure, there's more risk, but the next day you're done with it, and for a few months you eat well."

I asked about the Major.

"The Major is a very smart man," they answered in unison.

"He is an outstanding engineer," Karl went on. "He entered the Wehrmacht as a private, and within two years he had become an officer by sheer skill and brains. He could analyze any engineering problem in minutes. During the war, the Wehrmacht authorities flew him to places where they needed bridges built quickly and the like. Now, whenever we go out on a job, Herr Major cases it first, and we know we won't get caught."

They agreed that he was a great man and was like a father to them. None of the three was married. They had met in Frankfurt and considered it their home base, but they roamed all over and had even poached in Berlin for a while. To a man they wanted to get out of Germany, but it was impossible for them to leave the country legally.

It was beginning to get dark. The Opel had led us off the highway at least half an hour ago, and we were driving among farms on a good little road. We had gone through several small villages, and as we approached another the Opel stopped. We pulled in behind it. Orlov and the Major got out and came over to the truck.

"Why did you stop?" Karl asked.

"To rest awhile," the Major replied. "We're not far from the place, and we can't go any closer until it gets dark."

I walked up to the Opel for a look at Jony and found him still sound asleep. I was glad for him.

"He's been sleeping ever since you got into the truck," Orlov said.

"How far do we have to go?"

"Less than an hour."

Karl and Johannes got a blanket out of the truck and spread it by the side of the road. The grass was green and soft, and they lay down ready to take a nap. In half an hour it would be completely dark.

Orlov and I strolled along the road. Sounds drifted up from the village, cows ma-a-a-ing and mothers calling their children, but there was no traffic. Orlov said, "Peaceful, isn't it?"

"Yes, and here we are waiting to break into the local castle. How do we know the owners won't be at home?"

"The Major checked. There's only a caretaker. We'll have to make sure he stays quiet for at least three days, and then we'll notify the local gendarme. He will free the caretaker, and the baron will get a telegram saying his castle has been robbed. It won't be healthy to be around here then, especially if your reputation isn't spotless."

I laughed. "I wish we could stay to watch the fun."

Our walk had taken us to the edge of the village. The people who lived there were mostly farmers, and they didn't look as haunted and hungry as the Germans in the cities. We turned back. The Major and Johannes were filling the gas tanks. I climbed back into the truck with Karl. It was nearly dark.

In a few moments the Major gave the signal, and we started off. The headlights were dim, so I couldn't see much. Beyond the village we drove into a thick forest. I jumped when a branch whipped into the cab through the open window. The moon came out, and it got a little lighter. I looked out the window and saw the trees reaching into the dark sky. The Opel was moving very slowly. We drove through several clearings, and I smelled freshly mown hay. Then the dense forest closed in again, and we drove a little farther and stopped.

The Major came to Karl's window and whispered, "We are about twenty-five yards from the gate that leads to the castle. The three of us will go inside. In about fifteen minutes we should have everything ready, and we'll come back for Orlov and his friends. Then we'll all go in and get to work."

I got out and went to the Opel. Orlov was saying to Jony, "They're going in first, to put the caretaker out of commission. I want to warn them again that I don't want anybody hurt." He went to the truck.

Jony stretched and said, "I was so tired that I slept through the whole ride and woke up just five minutes ago. I feel like going in there myself."

"Let's wait until they're done with the part of the job where someone could be recognized."

"Of course," he said. "That's why they're getting paid." We were both whispering.

We walked back to the truck, and Orlov said, "They've

gone in. Now we have to wait about fifteen minutes. If they're much longer than that I'll start worrying."

I sat down on a big rock next to the road, while Jony and Orlov sat in the car. The moonlight cast dark, wet-looking shadows. Nobody spoke. I heard the cronk of a bullfrog not far away, and then some faint scraping and clanking noises from the direction of the castle. I listened, but couldn't make out what they were. Soon we heard soft footsteps, and the trio filed out of the black woods like Indian scouts.

Karl saluted mockingly, and the Major whispered, "Come on. The caretaker is tied up and blindfolded."

We went single file through the splotches of moonlight and shadow, and Karl led the way to an iron gate set in a stone wall. The dark mass of the castle loomed over us, its squat tower jutting up against the silvery clouds. Looking up, I tripped and stumbled against the Major. *"Vorsicht!"* he whispered sharply, and I kept my eyes on the path.

We went through a heavy, carved door and a foyer, and suddenly I could feel that we were in a huge room. It had that high, echoing hush of Gothic churches. Karl turned on his flashlight to show us how high the ceiling was, and the beam caught and sparkled in the pendants of a magnificent chandelier. Orlov gasped and said to the Major, "We must have that."

As we walked hesitantly across the stone floor Karl's flashlight beam revealed glimpses of tapestries, dark, massive furniture, a big fireplace. One of the men turned on some dim lights in a hallway, and we fanned out to explore the luxurious rooms.

In one of the smaller rooms I turned on a wrought-brass table lamp that reminded me of one my parents had at home. In another room I saw some engravings that looked like original Dürers. Gilt-edged mirrors, delicate china bowls and vases, and the fine old furniture all cried out to me that I shouldn't be here. This wasn't right! We had no right to violate this place. People loved their possessions. How would my parents have felt if robbers had broken into our home? I was sure all these things had been in the baron's family for generations. The huge canopied bed in the master bedroom was the same size as the one my mother and father slept in. The rugs were richly figured Persians. I felt terribly guilty.

Jony was calling. I went back to the main hall and found Karl exploring the walls with his flashlight. Then he walked toward a doorway, and suddenly light blazed from the chandelier. We were in another world. I saw the tapestried walls, the oil paintings, the scrolled and gilded furniture, such things as I had never seen except in movies about kings and queens. In the DP world, living in rough wooden barracks and often eating out of tin cans, you forgot that fine homes existed, much less places like this!

Orlov was muttering to himself, "This swine was high up with the Nazis, and he still lives like this now, while we are forced to grovel in their garbage. To rob him is the least we can do. I wish we could strip him naked and throw him out to beg."

When I heard that I felt much better. This wasn't robbery, it was justice!

Then the Major's voice rang out. "All right, we didn't come here to admire the things, we came here to steal them!"

His men gathered around him. He asked Orlov, "Where should we start?" Orlov pointed at the chandelier. The Major sent Karl into the kitchen, saying, "A stairway in there leads to the cellar. See if you can find a ladder down there."

Karl and Johannes were busy with the chandelier when Jony called from upstairs, "Come see what I found!" I ran up the curving staircase and discovered him kneeling in one of the bedrooms. There was a strong scent of perfume in the room—from the baroness, no doubt. Jony had dragged a strongbox from under the bed into the middle of the room. Glancing around, I saw two paintings of billowy, half-dressed nudes, and on the night table some fine leather-bound books. I wanted to look at the titles, but Jony snapped, "Come on. Help me get this open."

I called down to Orlov for a sharp tool. He came upstairs

225

with a crowbar, and he and Jony went to work on the strong-box. They got it open. Inside were several fat envelopes. They were stuffed with money—American dollars, Canadian dollars, Swiss francs, and some letters of credit. In the bottom of the box we found assorted jewelry and several wrist-watches.

Orlov and Jony took the box and went downstairs again, leaving me to wander through the upstairs rooms alone. I wanted to find something for myself. I glanced through other doors and saw more and more beauty. I felt like a thief. I was a thief, but I reminded myself that there was justice in it.

Here was a small library, its walls lined with fine old books. At one end an alcove displayed a fantastic collection of antique weapons: pistols with pearl inlaid grips, silver-mounted and engraved rifles, old muskets, ornamental swords, even a Turkish scimitar with a jeweled handle. The thieves wouldn't pass this by. Collecting old weapons seemed an appropriate hobby for an Aryan aristocrat, one of the men vulgar little Hitler would have gathered around him, envied and aped.

Through another door I found myself in a small storage room opening boxes and drawers where silver and gold tableware gleamed on blue-velvet linings, amid the smell of camphor. On the floor was a sturdy leather trunk with a padlock. Searching the nearby rooms, I found a tool kit in a closet. I carried it back to the storage room, chose a strong, short bar, and broke the lock on the trunk.

I had found my treasure.

I lifted out one of the golden goblets, heavy, gleaming, encrusted with designs of grapes and leaves. It looked like solid gold, and it must have weighed a full pound. There were forty-five of them. Handmade. Closing the trunk, I hammered in some nails from the tool kit until the lid was tight. Then I hoisted the trunk on one shoulder and carried it downstairs and out to the Opel. I put it in the back seat and went inside to help in the looting of the rest of the castle.

But my mind was on my newfound gold.

I would have to find a hiding place for it. Sometime in the future I could come back for my hidden treasure, and then I would be a rich man. The goblets were not only solid gold; they were also priceless antiques, collectors' items. Only an expert could tell how old they really were. If Jony and Orlov would agree to let me keep the trunk I would ask for nothing else.

Our sweating burglars were hard at work packing and lugging things out to the truck: paintings, lamps, chairs, vases, rolled-up tapestries, cases of old weapons. Orlov was calling out directions from somewhere on the second floor, and the valuables came down swathed in sheets and blankets.

I didn't know how to help, so I wandered out to the kitchen. There on the floor was the caretaker, bound, gagged, and blindfolded. It was hard for him to breathe, and I felt sorry for him. I bent down and loosened the gag a little, and right away he started to yell, "*Zu Hilfe! Zu Hilfe! Räuber!*" The Major, Karl, and Johannes came running, and the Major stuffed the gag back into his mouth, tied it tightly, and kicked him. "Leave the dumb ox alone," he said disgustedly. "This type is his master's loyal slave." They went back to work. I still felt sorry for the bound creature, but I didn't touch him again.

Looking for something to eat, I opened the icebox and found a huge round of cheese. I broke off a chunk and was stuffing my mouth when someone called me. There was some heavy furniture to carry, and I helped with that, still chewing and swallowing the cheese. When we finished packing the inlaid chests and cabinets into the truck I went back for more. It was very good cheese, and I ate pounds of it. There was nothing else in the icebox and only a few cans in the pantry. The baron obviously hadn't been here for a while.

I went to see what we were stealing now and was called on to help carry paintings from upstairs down to the truck. I looked into closets, and the wealth of clothing there was staggering: street suits, dress suits, sports jackets and trousers, light coats and warm cashmere topcoats. I tried on one of the sports jackets, but it was much too small across the shoulders; disappointed, I tossed it on the bed. The hardships of the black-market era just did not exist for these people. Slowly but surely we were stripping the castle of its valuables; we would make a dent in the baron's wealth. But then I thought of the millions he must have in his bank vaults, where no one could touch it.

I went into a sitting room and stopped abruptly. I was staring into the painted eyes of a stern, haughty-looking man in a military uniform. Here was the master of the house, the owner of all those old guns and sabers. The disdainful, aristocratic face leaped out of the vivid portrait as if it were alive, and the steel-blue eyes seemed to follow my every movement. A builder of dynasties! The hard pride in that face would have to be reckoned with. He would have had slaves, prisoners of war working for him. Behind him in the portrait was a statue of an officer on a rearing horse. Probably his father. Such things were handed down from father to son.

I heard a movement behind me and spun around. Orlov had come in. He looked at the portrait, and then, very deliberately, he bent down, picked up a woman's shoe, and hurled it at the baron's face. The glass shattered, but the arrogant gaze was unchanged. It would take Vasile to get that look off the man's face. He could do it.

The baron's gaze had shaken me a little. I went into the kitchen again and down the stairway to the cellar, half-expecting to find a dungeon with ancient skeletons chained to the wall. Instead, I found a cool wine cellar with rank on rank of bottles—German, French, and Italian wines. What a time we would have had keeping Max out of here! More boxes of loot lay stacked in the cellar, probably booty from the war years. All stolen, and now we were stealing from him! But we wouldn't be able to take any of this. Our truck was already loaded to capacity, and it was time to leave.

The others came down into the cellar to pick out some wines. Orlov selected two bottles, Jony took one, and the three Germans helped themselves. In the kitchen I showed them the cheese, and everybody broke some off and ate a quick meal.

The Major took the gag out of the caretaker's mouth. He started howling immediately, but several kicks silenced him. The Major untied his feet and shoved him up the stairs. After a few moments I could hear faint, muffled cries and bangings in the far reaches of the second floor. The Major, who had come back down alone, grinned. "I found a strong closet and locked him in. He'll tire himself out trying to break out of there. The police will let him free in a couple of days, when we send our anonymous message."

We left the castle and hurried through the gate. I didn't look back. If someone came here at night and heard the exhausted wails of the caretaker he might well think the place was haunted. Jony, the Major, and I got into the Opel with Orlov. The other two Germans climbed into the truck, and we started off. I sat in the back seat holding on to my treasure.

Nobody said a word. The road was dark, and the trees crowded close and thrust their branches at the car windows. Beyond the beams of the headlights there was nothing but blackness and a solid wall of trees. The forest was a perfect place for an ambush. The baron might be lying in wait around the next curve with a detachment of ex-SS men, his fanatical personal guard. They would catch us and quarter us like butcher's meat. My imagination was playing fearful tricks on me, and I started every time a branch brushed against the roof of the car, but as soon as we turned onto the paved road the gruesome possibilities receded. We picked up speed, putting miles between us and the spellbound baron who glared out at his pilfered castle from his imprisonment in paint.

Soon the bottles were opened, and we began to joke and laugh, releasing our tension. For the Germans the job was over; the rest of us would drive to Nuremberg, and there it would be Orlov's job, and mine and Jony's, to sell the loot to the Americans.

It was time to claim my treasure. "I found this trunk in

the castle," I said to Orlov. "I would like to keep it as my share of the job, if that is all right with you. I won't ask for anything else."

"That's fair enough," Orlov answered. "You found it, so you may keep it." He never did ask what was in it. The haul from the castle was so rich that he must have figured the contents of one trunk wouldn't make much difference one way or the other. To me it made all the difference in the world.

A little later I asked whether I could ride in the truck. I liked the two young German thieves. "Sure, sure," Orlov said, and the Major said it was all right with him, too. They pulled over, and I got out and ran back to the truck. There was plenty of room, and Karl and Johannes were happy to have me ride with them. We passed around a bottle of the baron's vintage Burgundy. Karl said he had been fighting drowsiness, but now it would be easy to stay alert. We joked and told stories for a while, and then Karl started singing German dance-hall songs.

Day was breaking already, and I realized that we must have been in the castle for several hours. The rattling of the truck made me sleepy. Johannes had dozed off, but Karl was wide awake, singing a song about the tropics and palm trees. I didn't want to go to sleep, because the country we were driving through was so beautiful: rolling farmlands alternating with thick, dark forests. In the open country the road was lined with trees. The sun was rising.

We passed a sign saying we were fifteen miles from Schweinfurt. The Opel pulled over, and we stopped behind it. The Major got out of the Opel and Karl got out of the truck, and they conferred for a few minutes. Then Karl came back, woke Johannes, and they both shook hands with me and said good-bye. Orlov and Jony got out of the Opel, the Major got in it with Karl and Johannes, and they drove away.

I asked Orlov, "Where are they going?"

"The Major is taking Karl and Johannes to Schweinfurt to catch a train back to Frankfurt. We'll wait for him here."

We sat in the grass by the side of the road next to our innocent-looking truck with its load of contraband. Only two or three cars passed. The sun was getting hot. In a little while the Opel came in sight and pulled up by the side of the road. The Major got out and said, "All right, let's go. I'll drive the truck. *Kleiner*—little one—you come with me." It was comical for him to call me that, because I towered over him, but he clearly felt taller in years and experience.

Orlov and Jony drove ahead in the Opel, and the Major and I followed. I felt relaxed in his company and soon dozed off. When I woke we were going slower, obeying the speed limit like good citizens. There was more traffic on the highway now, and signs said we were approaching Nuremberg. We stopped at the first roadside inn we saw, and Orlov went in to phone his contact.

Ten minutes later he came out and leaned in the truck window. "We can meet our man the American in about two hours," he said. "I have the address where we're supposed to wait for him. Major, you know Nuremberg better than I do, so let's change places. You drive the Opel, and I'll follow in the truck."

Once we entered Nuremberg it took the Major less than ten minutes to find the street we were looking for. It was in Erlenstegen, a quiet residential section. We parked the truck and the car in front of a house, and Orlov and Jony went in.

They came right out, and Orlov reported, "An American colonel rents this house, and according to military regulations we're not allowed to park here, but we can stay as long as one of us is here to move the car and truck if a policeman or an MP comes along."

The sun beat down on the truck cab, intensifying the heat. I slept for a while, but woke up sweating and got out to stretch my legs and find some shade. The Major was asleep behind the wheel of the Opel. Jony and Orlov were sitting on the front steps of the house.

I sighed and asked, "How long have we waited?"

"Over an hour, but he should be here any minute," Orlov

replied. Suddenly he jumped to his feet. "What fools we are! This colonel might come home with a whole jeepload of MPs and confiscate the truck. We're sitting here like pigeons."

We moved as if someone had jabbed us with a live wire. Waking the Major, we started the engines and drove a mile or so back the way we had come. Then we stopped for a conference and decided that Orlov and Jony should drive the Opel back to the house while the Major and I waited with the loaded truck.

We set up three alternatives. The Major and I would wait for two hours. If Orlov and Jony weren't back by then, we would turn around and drive to Frankfurt, antiques and all. If we saw them driving slowly toward us it would mean that the American was with them, ready to look over our cargo and negotiate a price. If they came back with a jeep following we would make no sign that we knew each other, and the Major and I would head for Frankfurt immediately.

Orlov and Jony drove off. As soon as the Opel was out of sight the Major smiled grimly and said, "They won't take this stuff away from us so easily. I have a surprise for them." He reached under the seat and brought out a small machine pistol and a revolver. He handed me the revolver, and I felt its cold, businesslike weight.

"This is very foolish," I said. "I don't think we'll have any trouble. But if it comes to shooting, we can't fight the American army. It's broad daylight! For us to start shooting would be insane."

"No, *Kleiner*," the Major said darkly. "If they want to take this load away from us they'll have to pay a high price. I'll handle it, don't worry."

But I did worry. I had two hours to worry in. This Major's nondescript appearance obviously hid more than brains. He had the makings of a desperado. And I had the feeling that it wasn't only the money; he had engineered this job, and he didn't want to see it ruined. I guessed he would feel the same way if one of his best bridges was about to be blown up.

Finally we saw the Opel driving toward us, very slowly. I

kept looking to see whether an MP jeep turned into the street behind it. There wasn't one, and I felt an immense relief. The Opel stopped across the street. Orlov and Jony got out with a dark-haired young American in a rather elegant suit. They came over to the truck and climbed into the back without ceremony. We heard them rummaging around and talking. The American spoke fairly good German. Then they went back to the Opel and sat talking for twenty minutes. They were haggling over the price.

At last Orlov came to the truck window and said, "We'll drive back with him. As soon as we leave take the truck onto a side street where it will be out of sight. The Major is to stay with the truck, and you come back to this street and wait for us. Try to make yourself inconspicuous. When we come back, you run and tell the Major to bring the truck out, but not until I tell you everything is all right."

The Major drove around the smaller side streets until he found a garage with an alley next to it. Getting out, he knocked on the door of the garage, looking for the owner, but no one answered. The Major backed the truck into the alley beside the garage, where it couldn't be seen except by someone standing right in the entrance to the alley.

"*Kleiner,*" he said to me, "go, now, and get lost on the street. Come and get me when they're ready."

I walked back slowly, as if I had nothing else to do. It was a hot afternoon, and there weren't many people on the street. Not far from where I was supposed to wait was a little wooden building with a sign saying it was a carpenter's shop. Since the shop was closed, I sat down in its shade to wait. After a while I felt drowsy, so I stretched, shifted my position, and kept on watching the street. Flies nagged at me. I waved them away, but they kept coming back. I chased them until I caught one. Then I saw the Opel. An army truck was right behind it! Instantly I was wide awake, oblivious to the flies, the heat, everything but trouble.

The two vehicles approached slowly. They stopped right at the spot where the truck had been. Orlov got out of the car and looked around. I was about one hundred yards from him, but he hadn't seen me. I crouched in the shadow of the carpenter's shop, thinking maybe they had guns on Orlov and Jony, and there were soldiers in the back of the army truck waiting to confiscate our load! Orlov returned to the car and said something, and Jony got out. He looked around. I saw him glance my way, and then he walked casually toward me. He didn't make any sign to Orlov, but when he was a few feet from me he stopped and said, in a low voice, "Is anything wrong with the truck?"

"No," I whispered fiercely. "But what about the army truck?"

Jony turned and yelled to Orlov, "He's here," startling me half out of my skin. He turned back to me. "Go get the Major. Everything is fine."

Relief flooded through me. Running back to the Major in his alley, I reported what had happened. When he heard about the army truck I had to reassure him several times before he would drive back.

As we pulled up across the street from the Opel two American soldiers jumped down from the army truck. They climbed right into the back of our truck and began unloading the cases, paintings, and sheet-wrapped objects, under the direction of the well-dressed young American. Orlov came to the driver's side of the truck and spoke briefly with the Major. Then he got into the Opel again with Jony. I saw four good-sized boxes in the back seat, stacked on top of my trunk, and guessed that they must be full of cigarettes. I looked at the Major. He was grinning.

The young American was evidently a connoisseur, from the way he inspected and loaded the valuables. It took him over an hour to finish. When he was done we nodded good-bye to him.

He waved back and shouted to Orlov, "I'll see you next month sometime!" Then he climbed into the army truck, and it drove away swaying with its load.

Orlov came over to the truck and gave a carton of cigarettes to the Major and several packs to me. "Congratulations," he said. "Everything turned out very well. Vanya, you were wise to be so cautious. Now, let's get back to Frankfurt."

Unloaded, the truck felt peculiarly light. On the highway the going was smooth, and I soon dozed off. A sudden jolt woke me. It woke the Major, too. He had fallen asleep behind the wheel, and we had swerved and hit a boulder at the side of the road. Looking sheepish, the Major quickly got the truck under control, and neither of us slept again.

As we entered Frankfurt I asked the Major to drop me, with my trunk, at the railroad station. An idea was forming in my mind about where to hide my treasure, but I didn't say anything to the others.

I shook hands with Orlov and the Major, and the Major wished me good luck. "*Junger Mann*," he said, "go to another continent and make a new life for yourself. Let this trunk help you."

Then I shook Jony's hand and said, "Take it easy and enjoy the spoils. I'll be back at Buchholz in a day or two." I picked up my trunk and walked into the station.

There was a small town not far from Frankfurt where my uncle had worked in a hospital for a while. He had taken me there once, during one of my first visits when I was in Bremen, and I remembered that there was a thick forest beginning right behind the railway station. It had occurred to me that I might be able to bury my treasure there. It would be easy for me to find it again, but the forest was dense and wild enough so that nobody else was likely to.

I didn't have long to wait for the local train, and when it came I hoisted my trunk aboard and sat on it near the door. The trip took about an hour.

Clambering off, I looked around. The town was small and sleepy, just as I remembered it. There was no traffic at all, and hardly any activity around the station. But I needed a shovel. I shouldered the trunk and walked slowly toward a street lined with shops. It was the middle of the afternoon.

Coming to a tool and repair shop, I set the trunk down and

went inside. A young fellow in a dirty apron asked what he could do for me. I told him I needed a shovel to bury a dog for a patient at the local hospital. While I talked I dug into my pocket and brought out a pack of American cigarettes. His eyes lit up when he saw them.

He looked around and said, "My boss isn't here, and we don't have a shovel to sell, but I can lend you ours." He went into the back of the shop and returned with an old but sturdy shovel.

I gave him the cigarettes, and he stared at me in disbelief. "The whole pack?" he said.

"Take them. The patient deals on the black market. He's got plenty of cigarettes. I'll return the shovel in two or three hours."

He gulped and looked around again. Then he said, "If I am not here when you return, just lean the shovel against the door, and don't tell anyone you gave me the cigarettes, *ja?*"

I took the shovel and went out, hoisted the trunk again, and walked back to the station. There I sat down and looked around. Nobody was watching me as far as I could tell. I waited half an hour. Then I picked up the trunk and the shovel and walked slowly around to the back of the station, across a little meadow, and into the forest. The minute I was hidden by the trees I stopped and looked back. I put the trunk down, sat on it, and watched the station for a while longer. I had to be sure that no one knew what I was about to do.

As I sat there I thought of the books I had read as a kid about pirates and their buried treasure. Gold spilled on the bottom of the ocean, sunken ships of the Spanish fleet, gold bullion, Treasure Island. Now I had a treasure of my own. I was rich, and not on black-market goods. I had gold in a doubly valuable form. A skilled goldsmith had made each of those goblets by hand, slowly and with patience. There was no way I could take them with me when I emigrated to Canada, but years from now, when I was a Canadian or American citizen, I could come back here and claim my treasure. I felt like opening the trunk again just to feel the weighty metal and feast my eyes on its gleam.

The afternoon passed and evening came. As the shadows lengthened I grew hungrier. I hadn't seen anyone looking toward the forest from the station. Turning, I searched for a tree that was marked somehow, one I would be able to find again. A few yards from the denser part of the forest, standing among bushes and young trees, was a fine old beech. That was it. I counted five paces from the beech toward the edge of the dense grove and started digging. The ground yielded easily to the shovel. Before long I had a hole about six feet deep and long enough for the trunk.

I kept looking furtively around, even though I knew I wasn't being watched—my instincts would have warned me. I lowered the trunk into the ground and quickly shoveled in loose earth until the hole was filled. The soil that was left I scattered through the bushes. Then I measured the five paces again. When I was sure of the place I walked a little way off and sat down. In my mind I went over what I had done. Was the trunk safe enough? I decided I had made it as safe as I possibly could. It was dark by now, and I was tired and very hungry. I coudn't remember when I had eaten or slept last, but my treasure was safely buried.

Back at the beech tree, I counted off the five paces one more time. In the dark I felt the rough ground under my feet and knew I was standing right on top of the trunk. I wished it would rain and wipe away the last traces of my digging. It was cloudy, and the moon shone through the clouds from time to time. I sat down again, just to be near my treasure for a while, and fell asleep.

Raindrops woke me. I picked up the shovel, said good-bye to my gold, and hurried toward town. Down the main street, I leaned the shovel against the door of the repair shop and went back to the station. A bleary-eyed attendant told me that the next train to Frankfurt wasn't until morning. It was only 1:00 A.M., so I lay down on the bench and slept again.

A peculiar grunting woke me. It was the attendant starting his morning shift and making his morning noises. The sun was shining in the station window. I bought a ticket, and when the train came in I got on. I was in Frankfurt in less than an hour, in time to catch the morning train to Hannover. All the way home I thought about my treasure and its hiding place. It made me feel happy and safe.

When the train got into Hannover I went straight to Oskar's. Now I wanted to see Rita. My hidden gold sat in the ground like an anchor in a stormy sea, and I walked with the weight and confidence of it. I felt ready to celebrate.

To my surprise, Jony was there. He had arrived not long before and was waiting for the taxi to take him to Vasile's bazaar and then back to camp.

Oskar and I embraced, and he said, "Jony told me about your latest deal. I smell success, and money."

"Where's Rita?" I asked.

Oskar laughed and winked at Jony. "Patience, *Junge*. I will go and bring her here."

"Ask her to come shopping with us," Jony said, "and then come and stay with us at the camp for a day or two. He will take good care of her." He pointed at me. "He is in love with her."

"*Ja, ja,*" Oskar said. "She is in love with him. I'll go and get her now. But first come upstairs with me, and rest and take a shower while I'm gone. I have lit the heater already, and within ten minutes you will have hot water." He led the way to his bare but pleasant living room and then left to get Rita.

Jony asked, "Did everything go all right with hiding the treasure?"

"It went fine. But please don't mention it to anyone, all right?"

Jony laughed and said, "Your secret is safe with me."

"What did Orlov say before he left?"

"He said he was on his way to Switzerland, but that he'll stay in touch with us. He's really amazing. For him, all Western Europe is the black market—Berlin, Bremen, Hamburg, Frankfurt, Vienna, Zurich. I'm sure he's even had dealings in Paris. Yet he dresses like an ordinary DP! He's even bigger than Alfred, but Alfred plays the part more. He's a bit of a dandy."

I said, "I think Orlov keeps himself inconspicuous because results are more important to him than style. With him, all the fire is on the inside. You can see it in his eyes and feel it in his presence."

Jony told me that the Americans had paid a fantastic price in marks and cigarettes for the loot. Orlov had given the three Germans their agreed-upon fee, plus a handsome bonus. He had thought it very generous of me to give up my share, in spite of the mysterious trunk I had kept for myself. Jony's share was close to four hundred thousand marks, some dollars, and four cartons of cigarettes.

"I consider your share to be part of that," he said firmly. "Until you leave for Canada you will eat with us, and whenever you need money just ask for it. When I go shopping at Vasile's camp you come with me, or tell me what you want and I will bring it to you."

I couldn't think of anything more fair, and I told him so.

"The American colonel and that well-dressed civilian

really made the deal, and the big money," he went on. "They got an incredible weapon collection and some very valuable paintings, not to mention the furniture and tapestries. I saw the look they exchanged when they saw the stuff. They made the real profit, not us. In a matter of months we will eat the money up, and we took all the chances robbing the castle. The Americans are taking advantage of us, but what can we do? Today it's them. Let's hope tomorrow it will be us."

Jony stretched out on the couch, and I went to take a shower. I startled myself in the large bathroom mirror—wild hair, a gaunt face, and a lot of downy fuzz that needed shaving off again. Why did Rita like me so much? All my ribs stuck out, and my legs were skinny and scarred. But there was enough muscle in my shoulders and chest to make up for it a little.

When I came out of the bathroom I woke Jony and said, "Take a warm shower. I'll keep an eye on the money. Of course, I trust Oskar, but one of the waiters or customers might sneak up here."

Jony showered, and we dressed and were going downstairs with the money and cigarettes just as Oskar and Rita came into the restaurant.

Rita caught her breath, and her face turned pink. She ran up and kissed me. I put my hands in the silky dark-blonde hair, and we kissed for what seemed like a long time. Then I pulled her head back, and we looked at each other and burst into embarrassed laughter. I picked up her light weight and swung her around, vaguely aware that Oskar and Jony were watching with fatuous grins on their faces. I didn't care.

"What are you doing here?" she gasped when I put her down.

"See if you can get off for the afternoon to come shopping with us."

Rita turned and looked at Jony, as if to ask him whether I was serious.

He said teasingly, "Why are you looking at me? He wasn't asking me."

She turned back to me so violently that her hair swung across her face. "Oh," and she tossed it back, blushing fiercely, "of course I will get the afternoon off. But I am so mad at you!" she stormed. "I haven't seen you for over six weeks, and I think about you most of the time. Then, when I'm sure you've forgotten me, out of a clear blue sky here you are, fresh and full of life, and you ask me to go shopping!" She whirled and ran up the stairs.

I was about to follow, but Oskar said, "Relax. She's just going to telephone her father that she's taking the afternoon off."

She came down in two minutes looking radiant in her fresh white blouse and smooth-fitting brown skirt. She took my arm, smiling up at me with those deep dimples and clear gray eyes, and I had to admit that Jony was right. I was in love with her.

"Are we going to the bazaar?" she asked. "How wonderful! Oskar talks about it as if all the riches of the world were there, and now I can see it for myself."

While we waited for the taxi driver I gave Rita a carton of cigarettes and asked her to give a few packs to Oskar. She was overjoyed, but she protested, "You are always giving me things, and you never let me do anything for you. You don't even tell me where you're going."

"Rita," I said, "you know what kind of a life I lead. You know I live in a DP camp. I have no civilian clothes, I live from day to day, and I might emigrate soon to another country. Let's not get more of each other than we can handle."

"Here is the first lover's quarrel," Jony chided. "And you haven't even been together for twenty minutes!"

"Oh, you men!" Rita said. "You make a joke of everything. I am mad at him, but because—because I like him so much, I can't stay angry, and you laugh at me."

On the way to Vasile's camp, Rita leaned against me, her

delicate profile turned toward the window. The breeze blew strands of her hair against my face, and I kept looking at her, feeling a surge of protectiveness and warmth each time. I wanted to surprise her, to buy some sugar and pork back and butter for her parents.

Vasile was at the camp gate, with his usual black pants and shirt and mane of untamed black hair, leaning against the guard shack in titanic ease talking to one of the guards. When he saw us he shouted, "Hah! Jony! *Dracule*—you devil!" And we drove through, Rita clinging to my arm. Vasile's shout had scared her.

Before the car even stopped Vasile had the door open and was starting to pull me out. Rita shrank back in the corner.

"It's all right," I said. "Come and meet Vasile. He'll be gentle with you."

She got out of the car like a deer ready to run and stared wide-eyed at Vasile. He looked hairy, powerful, and sweaty, and quite predatory as he stared back at her with his hawk nose and fierce black eyes.

"Rita is my girlfriend," I said simply.

"Fine," Vasile said, and stepped closer. He took her hand in his. In his strong paw her hand looked like a baby's. Even from where I stood I could smell the garlic and liquor on his breath. He looked at Rita with his black eyes shining and said, in broken German, "Love a strong man, and you will be protected."

Rita smiled timidly. Vasile embraced me, patting me on the back with his usual punishing gusto, and then turned to Jony, but Jony dodged. "The last time you patted me you nearly broke a few ribs!"

"Where have you two been?" Vasile roared. "You must have done a good job somewhere. You look successful. I can smell it." Without waiting for an answer he bent, looked into the car at Oskar, and bellowed, "Why don't you come out where I can see you?"

Oskar hopped out, and Vasile asked, "Was that your place where we dropped off a bag of sugar about two months ago?"

"Yes, sir," Oskar replied. "And I haven't thanked you for it yet. If you will come to my restaurant sometime I'll make a special dinner for you."

Vasile looked pleased. "You deserved the sugar," he said royally. "Go to the bazaar, now, all of you." Glancing in at the driver, he nodded his head and said, "You, too."

We walked toward the humming crowd at the bazaar. Rita was shaking her head. "I've never met anyone like him. Oskar didn't exaggerate. He is incredible!"

At the bazaar the poor driver gazed around ecstatically, dazzled by the sights and smells. Rita gripped my arm. "This is impossible," she said, staring at the mounds of food. Spread out there was more food than her family could have bought with ration cards in three years, and many things they could never have found at all in the stores.

"Now you have met Vasile, and this is his kingdom," I said. "He brought all this together and keeps it running by his own sheer strength. He has an iron will and the energy of ten men, and he rules by fear and generosity."

I bought two pounds of butter, salted pork back, two pounds of sugar, potatoes and some other vegetables, several bars of soap, two tubes of toothpaste, and a large bag of candy. Then I guided Rita away from the brawling Eastern European market place, from the traders' gibberish and conglomerate bad breath.

When we got to the car she said, "Do you realize that you spent at least a thousand marks at the bazaar? Do you know how many months I have to work to earn that much money?"

"Yes," I said. "But in your kind of work you don't take any chances. When we go out we take big risks, so the rewards are much bigger."

Jony and Oskar came back with their packages, and I left Rita in the car with Oskar while Jony and I went to the guard shack for our ritual drink with Vasile.

Jony told Vasile about the castle robbery, and Vasile said, "Good, good. Take all you can from them. Just be very careful and never get caught."

The liquor we were drinking was more like raw alcohol. Vasile tossed it down and said, "This is still from the sugar we took from that UNRRA thief! I think the still gave me enough to last until I go back home to Corsica sometime next year, and I drink enough for several men. You"—he turned to me abruptly—"have found a nice girl. You'll need a woman as you grow older. She's a little young, but she looks fine."

Vasile's view of things was like that—simple and strong. Emigration, jobs, all that to him was faint-hearted nonsense. A man needs a woman. You love the girl? Grab her and take her home with you. Live by your wits and your strength. What is the problem?

For Vasile, back home in Corsica, perhaps there would be no problem. He could master the anarchy of the black-market era, but it was in one of those rugged little pockets of the old life, like Corsica or parts of the Balkans, that he really belonged. Such places were getting rarer and rarer, though, and when they finally joined the twentieth century once and for all Vasile's breed would become extinct. Perhaps by now it has.

Jony gave Vasile one of the envelopes he had taken from the strongbox in the castle, one with some letters of credit in it. Then we drank another toast to Vasile's health and left.

After we dropped off Oskar and his packages I asked Rita where she lived. "I want you to take home the things I bought for you now, so you don't have to carry them on the street-car in the morning."

Unbelievingly, she asked, "All those things you bought are for my family and me?"

"Yes. Just tell the driver where you live."

"He knows."

Within minutes we were in front of a nice apartment house. Rita took some of the packages inside and came back for the rest.

"Come inside and meet my mother. She wants to thank you."

"No, Rita," I said. "Look at my clothes."

"Go in," Jony snapped. "You can always apologize for your clothes, but show your face and accept thanks."

I went with Rita into the clean and modest apartment. In the kitchen a slender, graying woman in her forties stood with her back to us opening the paper with slow, unbelieving hands and staring at the butter and sugar. She unwrapped the salt pork and murmured to herself, "*Mein Gott,* this is wonderful!"

Rita said, "*Mutti,* here he is."

Her mother turned and looked at me. Then she said, to Rita, "He is a fine-looking young man, and I don't care what the neighbors say about DPs. They don't come any kinder. God bless you, young man." She gave me a firm, warm handshake.

"I've been out working," I apologized. "Please excuse my clothes. Enjoy the food, and give your husband my regards." It embarrassed me to see how grateful she was. I felt myself turning red and said, "We have a car waiting outside. Next time we'll stay longer."

Rita kissed her mother, and we left.

At camp, Jony took his packages to Maria, and Rita and I went straight to the canteen, impatient to be alone together. But Max was behind the bar, and when he saw us he came out, kissed my cheeks and Rita's hand, and wanted to hear all about the robbery, Orlov, the thieves, the money.

Rita and I glanced at each other. "The job was fantastically profitable, Max," I said. "Here are fifteen packs of cigarettes for you. We should be able to take it easy for the rest of the year."

He thanked me and was about to ask another question, but he stopped and gave us a shrewd look. "All right, get out of here, you two. Let me enjoy my cigarettes in peace."

I took Rita's hand and grinned my thanks at Max, and we went into my room and closed the door.

We looked at each other for a long moment, prolonging the expectation, and then we were together. Our mouths and bodies remembered each other quickly, and all my hesitations and worries were swept away in the joyous hurry of their reunion.

We were on the verge of falling asleep when a loud knock sounded on the door and Jony called, "Supper's ready!" We both jumped up guiltily and started to laugh. After washing off the sweat of love-making with cold water from the bucket, we got dressed and went over to Jony's.

We sat through dinner in a dream. Maria served us from the stove, her cheeks rosy with the heat and her own happiness, and we wolfed down the delicious food almost automatically, aware only of each other. After dinner we thanked Maria and went off to the canteen. I relieved Max so he could have his supper, and Rita sat at the bar with her chin in her hand watching me and laughing lazily. We shared a bottle of wine. By the time Max came back we were in even more of a daze than before, and he laughed and shoved us out, saying, "We'll talk tomorrow. You must be *very* tired."

We woke up and slept and woke again, explored each other's bodies in recurring eagerness, and let our hunger slowly play itself out. It was more than physical hunger; there was a strong emotional satisfaction, for me, in holding her in my arms. I couldn't worry any more about whether I could afford this. In Russia love had been an unthinkable luxury, but once the belly is full the hopes and dreams reawaken, and they, too, need to be fed. There was sadness in the knowledge that we couldn't think ahead, because in a few months I might leave for another continent. But we were both determined to make the most of the time we had, and that gave our love-making a special intensity. We would nourish ourselves on it, feast on it, and slowly recover together from the starvation of the war years.

That was how the peaceful late summer of 1948 began. After a delicious breakfast at Jony's I walked Rita to the streetcar stop, kissed her, and promised to come into Hannover the next weekend. And so the pattern of my days was established. During the week I plunged back into my reading, hardly taking time out for meals. My German vocabulary improved daily. I walked to Buchholz every other day, taking Robert, the librarian, cigarettes or food from Vasile's bazaar, and he helped me with German and continued to feed my omnivorous appetite for everything from Goethe and Gogol to the Western novels of the American Max Brand. We talked at great length, and Robert shared with me his knowledge of books and his passion for strong literature. When absorbed in reading I was hardly aware of the time or the day of the week. Sometimes I took a book out into the fields beyond the fence and read and dozed in the grass, listening to the insects and breathing the sweet drying scent of late summer. I didn't have to worry about food or money. The pay-off from the castle robbery, carefully managed by Jony and Maria, kept us well supplied with food from Vasile's bazaar.

Weekends I spent with Rita. We had agreed to meet every Saturday afternoon at Oskar's restaurant, and Oskar presided over our affair like a benevolent uncle. If Rita still slept with him, I didn't want to know it. I was too happy to let jealous suspicion spoil our present pleasure, when there could be no future and no promises.

Sometimes we wandered around Hannover, but there wasn't much to do. At every turn we came up against the privation and abnormality of the times. We felt it in silly little ways: we wanted to go swimming, but I had no idea where to find such a thing as a bathing suit, and if there was a pool open somewhere nearby, neither information nor transportation was available. The city had one operating movie house, and we went there twice, but it was often closed for no apparent reason. With all the money I had, there was nothing to do with it. We usually went back to camp early, talked and joked with Max at the canteen, and ate with Jony and Maria. Then we would make love half the night and sleep late on Sundays. We were hungry, healthy young animals, and the pleasure we took in each other was our chief entertainment. In such times you are thrown back on the basics: food and laughter and love-making are all you have, you are lucky to have them, and God help you if you get bored with them.

This period was much more of a vacation than my hectic trip to Vienna, the Balkans, and Paris. Both Rita and I gained a little weight, and I was almost positive that I would be able to pass the medical examination that was coming up in a month or two. I could feel myself growing calmer, less raw and on guard. Some Sundays, after a lively night with Rita and a big breakfast at Jony's and Maria's, I felt almost stupid, I was so sleepy and content.

I knew this was a natural healing process, and I knew I needed and deserved the rest. Yet it bothered me a little. I had a growing feeling of unreality, as if I were living in a cocoon that held the noise and dirt and suffering and struggle at a distance but also took the sharp edge off reality. And on Saturdays, when I went into Hannover to meet Rita, I would find myself drawn to the black-market crowd. The traders both repelled and fascinated me. Maybe I had to make sure I wouldn't forget the era we were dragging through, or the trading, chiseling, milling masses of a lost generation.

One afternoon I got caught up in the circulating mob. I bought some ration cards, and then sold them on the opposite edge of the weaving, restless crowd. Next I bought some English cigarettes, and a few minutes later sold them for five marks more than I had paid. I bought a pack of American cigarettes and was waiting to sell them when it dawned on me what I was doing. I was caught up in the black-market treadmill. I put the cigarettes in my pocket and walked on to Oskar's to meet Rita, feeling uneasy and ashamed. I didn't tell anyone what had happened, and from then on I tried to stay away from the crowd of traders.

But when I thought about it later, I realized that the black market *was* the reality of the times. Diseased as it was, it was the life and pulse of Europe. It was like a great beast, smelling of fear, with all the strength and cunning of desperation. It had the terrible vitality of an animal struggling to stay alive. I understood it in my bones.

Summer gave way to Indian summer, and a chilly tang in the air turned the leaves yellow and drove me into my jacket in the evening. The prospect loomed of still another winter in a camp, of huddling around stoves in thin wooden buildings and watching the gray faces of DPs settle into an even deeper apathy. It was not appealing. I had only a few more weeks to wait for my medical examination, and when I visited my uncle he took my blood pressure and said with approval that if I could just stay out of trouble a little longer I would easily pass it.

One evening in the canteen I overheard a Polish DP talking to Max about a letter he had gotten from a friend in Canada. The friend had emigrated about five months ago and was working in a lumber camp. He lived in a bunkhouse in the forest and ate hearty meals in a mess hall. The letter gave his wages, the prices of butter, sugar, and chocolate bars, and even an entire day's menu, from breakfast through supper: hot cakes with maple syrup, eggs and bacon, fried potatoes, hash and rich beef stew and apple pie. My mouth flooded with saliva as I listened. To us, sausage, pork back, potato *ghiveci,* and bread and butter were luxuries; this man was describing paradise. The contrast between a week's wages —thirty or forty dollars—and the price of a chocolate bar —five cents—astonished me. In Germany, a week's wages for an ordinary worker—if he was lucky enough to have a job—might have bought one or two chocolate bars on the black market, if they were available. And thirty dollars on the black market was a small fortune. I calculated in my head and discovered that in Canada a week's wages would buy six hundred candy bars! That was the place for me. Besides, I liked the idea of doing healthy outdoor physical labor.

Max asked the DP wistfully, "Did your friend write how much the whiskey costs in Canada?" The DP shook his head, and I laughed at Max's one-track mind. "I would like to work in a small town near the lumber camp," Max said. "I'd have the bar shining when the laborers came to town to spend their money and get drunk, and I'd tell stories and make them laugh, like I do here."

"But, Max," I said, "maybe there it will be harder to make them laugh."

"Nonsense," he replied. "People are the same the world over. Sure, they have different customs and traditions, but, after all, the only real North American is an Indian. The rest came from Europe. Once I was in the bar, I would feel their pulse like a doctor, and in one evening I would know what they like to hear. The next evening I'd have them howling. There are a lot of French-speaking people in Canada, and I speak French well, so all I have to do is learn English, and I'm beginning next week. One of the secretaries from the Canadian immigration office is going to teach me."

"How will you pay for her time?" I asked.

"I'll teach her German, French, or Polish, or"—he winked —"anything else that appeals to her!"

I began to think more and more about what it would be

like to live in a lumber camp in Canada. The bite in the air was making me restless, and I knew that Rita, during our weekends, could sense that my thoughts were sometimes far away. It hurt her, but she understood and accepted it; we had agreed at the beginning not to let our dreams run away with us and not to start hoping for more than we could manage. Our love-making already had a nostalgic quality.

I felt less like reading as the time for the medical exam drew closer, but one morning, while I was sitting in the mess hall drinking coffee with some other DPs, another diversion presented itself. Someone started talking about the hand-wrestling matches he had seen in southern Germany. Soon two of them were at it, left hands clasped, elbows on the table, arms and shoulders straining. Another pair tried it at another table, and the spectators began hooting and howling encouragement. It got so noisy that the chef came into the hall and threw us out.

The combatants were dejected, but then one of them noticed me and asked, "Could we continue in the canteen?"

The idea had already occurred to me. "Yes, we can," I said. "But only until noon."

I unlocked the canteen door, and within thirty seconds hand wrestling was going on at three tables.

It intrigued me. I offered to try it with Marion, a Polish DP who had just won a match.

He smiled and said, "Sure."

I sat down to face him, and he gave me his hand across the table. It was a big hand, and it shook a little from the exertion of the other matches. "Do you want to rest first?" I asked.

"No," he said. "Let's start."

His hand tensed as he applied pressure. It seemed hard, but as I gripped it I felt with surprise that my shoulder had a lot of power in reserve. I held my hand as it was, upright on the table. Marion looked at me and put on more pressure. His face grew tense. I saw that the other DPs had stopped and were standing by our table watching quietly. They knew that we weren't putting forth our best efforts yet. More pressure came into my opponent's arm, but I held steady. Slowly I increased the power of my grip, and then I realized that I was only toying with him. I increased the pressure again. He tried to hold his arm in place, but slowly it went down and he gave up.

He swore and said, "You never wrestled before? *Scurvei sin sdarovei.* Son of a whore, he is strong!"

Everyone was still standing there watching us. Marion asked, "Do you want to try your left hand?"

"Sure, but my left hand is stronger than my right."

He said "I don't believe it," and so we were at it again.

Now I knew what it was all about. His left hand wasn't as strong as his right, and I won that one quickly. I saw out of the corner of my eye that Jony and Max had come in and were watching. We matched right hands again, and I let Marion put my hand down until it nearly touched the table. He tried with a tremendous effort to put it all the way down, but, instead, his hand rose until our forearms stood straight up again. Then his hand went down and down, and he gave up.

A DP standing by sidled up to me and said, "In a camp near Berchtesgaden there was a Pole they considered the hand-wrestling champion. Maybe he'll turn up here, and we'll really have a match."

Jony asked me, in Rumanian, "Was the guy you just wrestled very strong?"

"He is pretty strong, but I am stronger. My left shoulder was developed shoveling coal."

As we left the canteen I said, "I've got a couple of weeks until the medical exam, and now I have something to do. I hope I'll be able to find somebody to wrestle with every day."

"I never thought about it," Jony said, "but you are very strong. The hard work you did in Russia is paying off. Those Polacks will spread rumors, and soon they might even ask their hand-wrestling champion here for a match. They are dying for some excitement."

I knew my muscles would be very stiff the next morning, but I liked the hand wrestling. Reading was fine, but this was physical, and it relieved the pressure of the restless energy that had been building up in me.

After that, there was hand wrestling almost every morning in the canteen. My shoulder was stiff for the first few days, but soon it felt stronger than ever. I was surprised at my own strength. I hadn't suspected that the months of shoveling coal from crippling positions had given me such powerful shoulders. DPs I had never spoken to before, but had only seen around the mess hall or canteen, came to challenge me. Some were powerful men, but no one could beat me. I had become the unofficial hand-wrestling champion of Buchholz.

Just before the medical examination was scheduled a new transport of DPs arrived in camp. About twenty of them were in the canteen getting drunk one day, and it came out that among them was the DP from Berchtesgaden who had been the best wrestler in the camps of southern Germany.

Max boasted to them, "We have a very good man here, and I think he can beat your man."

I was in my room reading when I heard the loud voices from the canteen. I recognized those of several guards from the gate, including one I had wrestled with. Soon they were in a heated argument. One of the voices was high-pitched and sounded a little hysterical. I was curious, so I got up and went into the canteen.

Max shouted, "Here comes our man. Make room for him!"

"Be quiet, Max," I said.

Nicco, the guard I had wrestled with, was at a table with the new hand wrestler, a powerful-looking man with a good-natured Slavic face. The high-pitched, hysterical voice belonged to a little guy who hung behind the big fellow the way a pilot fish follows a big, sleepy shark. Nicco and the DP locked hands and started wrestling. Within two minutes Nicco had lost with both hands. I watched the big guy. He had barely grunted; the little pest behind him was making all the noise. The big Slav gave me a confident look, as if he knew there was no doubt about the outcome of a match with me. That look annoyed me.

Max pounded me on the back. "Come on. Show them we have somebody who can beat them."

Nicco whispered in my ear, "He is very strong."

The canteen got quiet. I shook myself loose from the others and walked a few paces, stretching my hands and flexing my shoulders. For the first time it occurred to me to wonder whether the exertion of hand wrestling could drive my blood pressure up. I cursed myself for not having thought to ask. I had been getting plenty of rest, but would that make up for it? Well, it was too late now.

Jony came in, and Max whispered to him. Jony came over and said, "Try him. It can't hurt you."

I sat down with the Slav. On my side of the table were the DPs from our camp, on his the new DPs. We looked at each other and matched forearms. His arm was bulging with muscle and was very heavy. But there was no way back, so we began. The right hand first.

We were locked for a while; then he increased the pressure slowly. The son of a bitch was strong.

The little guy behind him jumped up and down shrieking, "That's it! That's it! Give it to him, give it to him. You've got him! A little more . . ."

I tried to shut out the irritating voice. I saw that the Slav was holding on to the table with his left hand and that this helped him increase the pressure on his right. The veins were bulging in his neck. I held on as long as I could, and then I was down. His side roared and clapped.

I shook his hand and said, "You are very good. But now let's try the left hand."

"Fine," he said. We matched left hands and began.

This time I held on to the table with my free hand, as he had. Again we were locked, until he increased the pressure. I let him think he was slowly winning. Suddenly I gave it everything I had, including all the help I could get from my right hand holding on to the table. He put up a strong resistance, but I had him going down. If I stopped for a moment I would lose. I called on my last reserves, and he went down with a clunk.

As his hand banged down on the table I felt a searing pain in my right hand. I looked at it and saw blood gushing out. The little guy with the hysterical voice ducked quickly behind the Slav. He had tried to cut off my right hand!

A terrible commotion broke out. The Slav reached back, yanked the little guy around, and tossed him to our group the way he would have thrown a towel or a rag. Max and Jony grabbed him, and Jony took the knife away. Nicco gave him two powerful slaps while he shrieked, "I saw him cheating! He wasn't supposed to hold on with his right hand."

The Slav's voice boomed, "I did the same thing, you bastard! It was a fair match."

Jony was pale. "Is the hand cut off?" he asked.

I was numb with shock, but I held my wrist as tight as I could and flexed the fingers. The blood kept pouring out. "Jony, don't worry," I said. "I can still flex my fingers, but a vein must be cut. Let's go to the doctor and get the bleeding stopped."

By now the canteen was very crowded. Several guards dragged the little DP away.

We rushed to the doctor's office, and he and a nurse got busy stopping the bleeding. While they worked Jony told them what had happened. When he finished the doctor said, "You are a very lucky young man. You have lost a lot of blood, and that guarantees that your blood pressure will be way down, just in time for the examination. If you had planned this it couldn't have worked out better."

We went back to the canteen. I had a clumsily bandaged right hand and felt a little weak, but otherwise I was fine. The big Slav had waited for me. He asked worriedly, "How is the hand?" and Jony and I assured him that all was well; I had lost a lot of blood, but the cut would heal quickly.

The next day I passed the medical examination.

19

At the emigration office they took my papers and told me I would be shipped out in about two months, shortly after New Year's Day, 1949, to a lumber camp in Ontario, Canada. As I walked out of the administration building I felt light-headed and dizzy, only partly from the loss of blood. It was dizzying to realize that I actually was leaving soon, emigrating to a new life. The familiar horizon of low buildings, smokestacks, and barbed wire that had bounded my world for so long was finally lifting. In its place was empty space—the unknown.

As my hand healed the restlessness grew fierce. It had a focus now, and the two months that separated me from my goal seemed maddeningly long, longer than the ten months I had already been in Buchholz. Now that I knew I would be leaving I was impatient to get on with it. I didn't want to examine my feelings about leaving Rita and my friends, or about putting an ocean between me and my parents, or about exchanging a world whose rules I knew for a new and strange one. What was the use? What counted was that thirty to forty dollars a week and the fierce drive to get out of starving Europe. Part of me was already gone. I walked around camp like a sleepwalker, with my eyes open but not really seeing.

Max, too, had learned that he would be allowed to emigrate sometime in the next few months. He was happy about it, but it didn't really change anything for him. He had jumped into a lot of strange waters and had always bobbed right side up, like one of those roly-poly toys. Wherever he was he would find girls to charm and drunks to amuse. In German, French, or English, he would still be Max. He lived in the present.

We had some money left from the castle caper, but it was dwindling, and Jony said that soon he would have to start looking around for another deal. He had been coughing more as the weather got colder, and their baby had lost weight, too. Things didn't look good for the Mateescu family. They had done all they possibly could for the baby and for Jony's health, considering that they lived in a DP camp. But Jony needed a long rest in a healthy climate, and that was out of the question. Here, no matter how much he tried to rest, he was under the constant strain of being responsible for the canteen, for keeping us all fed, and, most of all, for Maria and the baby.

I knew the strain on him would be greater yet after I left. That was another thing it was pointless to think too much about. We rarely talked about my leaving, and in spite of everything Jony managed to keep his spirits up and to be his usual lively self—just a little thinner and paler.

About a week after the medical exam he and I went shopping at Vasile's bazaar, and there I was given a last black-market assignment that came very close to destroying all my hopes and plans.

That afternoon, hopping off the streetcar in Hannover near the trading crowd, we found Oskar and invited him to come with us to the bazaar. My hand was still bandaged and Oskar looked at me with concern.

"It's nothing serious, Oskar," I reassured him. "And thanks to it I passed my medical exam. I'll probably be able to emigrate in two months or so."

Oskar grabbed my good hand and said, "*Junge,* how wonderful! But what will we do without you? Little Rita will be desolate. But you will go off to make a new life in a rich country, and that is the main thing. All our thoughts will go with you. Now, come on back to the restaurant and have some coffee and kuchen to celebrate while I call the taxi."

I hadn't seen Rita for ten days, and in the car I asked Oskar how she was.

He rolled his eyes. "She talks about nothing but you. Shall I tell her you'll see her this weekend? It will make my life much more peaceful."

I laughed. "Max says we're finally having a dance this Saturday, so why don't you both come?"

"*Ach,* that would be nice."

We drove through the gate of Vasile's camp and parked behind the guard shack. While Oskar and Jony walked toward the bazaar I went into the shack. Vasile was sprawled out on a bunk sound asleep, his loud snores filling the little room. I had never seen him sleeping. One of the guards nudged him awake, and he stretched and came over to me laughing and grunting. He needed a shave and a bath, as he always did.

"What the hell happened to your hand?" he asked, with a huge yawn.

"Nothing much. Jony will tell you about it."

"Let's go to the bazaar," he said. "I want to check up on some of my traders."

The bazaar was thick with jostling, dickering DPs, but we saw Jony at the sugar stand and pushed our way over. When the people in the crowd looked up from their trading and saw Vasile they hurriedly made way for him, parting like the Red Sea. Jony saw us and shouted to Vasile, and I left them talking for a few minutes while I looked around for Oskar. I found him, almost buried under his packages, and then I heard Jony and Vasile calling me.

Vasile was laughing, and the trading around us hushed. He roared, "Why didn't you kill the bastard with the knife? If I had been there I would have wrestled the big ox and afterward beaten them both to death. Hahh—now I am in the mood to shake down some of my bazaar thieves!" He slapped one of the traders on the back, and the poor fellow nearly collapsed.

Vasile asked me, "What do you want to take home?"

"Oh, some sausages, pork back, sugar, candy."

At the nearest sausage stand Vasile grabbed two handfuls of sausages and thrust them at me. The startled Polish dealer cursed under his breath, and Vasile growled and stepped toward him. The Pole snatched up another sausage and, trembling, held it out to Vasile like a vampire's victim holding a cross out for protection. Vasile grabbed the sausage and piled it on top of those I already had in my arms. Then he dragged me to the sugar stand, grabbed a ten-pound bag, and added it to my load. I tried to protest, but he silenced me with a growl. I got a big hunk of pork back the same way, and a sack of hard candy. My arms were full, so I went back to the car and dumped Vasile's gifts inside.

Back at the bazaar Jony and Vasile were arguing about money. Vasile didn't want Jony to pay for anything, and of course Vasile won the argument. We helped Jony and Oskar carry their bundles back to the car, and then we left Oskar with the driver and went into the guard shack for our drink.

Vasile poured three glasses of the burning liquor and proposed a toast to my future. Then he looked at me and at Jony, and sent the guard out of the shack. He reached into his shirt and pulled out a small, stained leather bag on a thong around his neck. He took it off, opened the bag, and poured the contents into his cupped hand.

I caught my breath. The stones sparkled and danced in the hard brown palm of his hand, even under the dim bulb of the guard shack. They were diamonds, cut, brilliant, full of restless fire. They were of many different sizes and shapes, but the largest ones were as big as a wild strawberry—maybe four or five carats.

"These are around my neck day and night," Vasile said, and his eyes shone. "There are thirty-nine of them, and when there are fifty I will consider my account with the Germans settled and will go home to Corsica." He poured the glittering stones back into the little bag and put it around his neck again, under his shirt. "Now I want you to do something for me."

He made another toast, refilled our glasses to the brim, and then told me what he had in mind. A trader he had been dealing with, whose specialty was saccharin pills, had just emigrated to Australia. The trader had made many trips into the Eastern Zone of Germany to sell the pills, bringing back a lot of money every time. Vasile knew his contact in the Eastern Zone, but there was no one he really trusted that he could send in as a courier.

"So," he said, "you must go for me, next month, just before Christmas. You will get a very good price for the pills. I will arrange everything. I can even tell you what road to take, the same road my trader used for two years. You'll just have to walk about ten miles out of Braunschweig. You cross the border in the middle of the forest, where it's not too well guarded. You meet the contact in a small village, he gives you the money, and you give him the saccharin and come back here."

My thoughts were whirling. The last thing I wanted was to go back into Russian territory. It had turned out all right with Mischa, because he was a Russian officer and a rebel, but who wanted to tempt fate twice? Besides, back then in Vienna I had been reckless, a DP in a world of DP camps and black markets that seemed to stretch from horizon to horizon. I had had nothing to lose but hunger and boredom; emigration had been a distant dream. Now it was almost within my grasp; now I had everything to lose. After all I had lived through, to be caught by the Russians and shipped back to Mine 28—it would kill me.

Jony was frowning, and I knew he didn't like the idea, either. Yet I already knew I would go. I had to. This was Vasile, and if he asked me to do something I couldn't refuse. I took a deep breath and said, "You can count on me. I will go."

He slapped me on the back. "You are a good man. I knew you would do this for me." We had another fiery drink, and then we left.

In the car, on the way back to Oskar's, Jony was quiet and tight-lipped. Finally he said, "I told him you had passed the examination. I told him you were supposed to emigrate after the New Year. And yet he wants you to take this terrible risk."

"Stop worrying," I said. "You know that for him I have to do it. You would do the same. I don't think he would send me if it was really dangerous. After all, the last courier used that route for two years and never got caught. I've gotten through worse things than this. I'll be all right." I wished I was as sure as I sounded.

Jony said slowly, "You're right. I would do it, too, if he asked me. And he would do anything for me. He wouldn't let me spend any money today. He just said, 'You have a family, and you don't have the opportunities I have. I am your friend, so I will help you, and it won't cost me anything.' I took out some money to pay for something, but Vasile grabbed my hand like a vise and put the money back in my pocket. That's how he is. And that's how we have to be with him."

We dropped Oskar off at his restaurant and reminded him to come to the dance on Saturday night with Rita. Then we drove back to camp.

That week I rested and read, trying not to think any further ahead than the dance. Saturday night came, and the canteen was crowded with DPs. I said hello to my old friend the piano player and told him it looked as though I would be shipping out for Canada soon. He looked wistful and said that the band still hadn't gotten permission to emigrate; their papers were tied up somewhere. "I will miss your music," I said, "so try to emigrate soon. Maybe someday I will hear you play in Canada."

Oskar and Rita came in and found me, with my one good hand, helping Max behind the bar. I hadn't seen Rita since the medical exam, and we were suddenly shy, as if the knowledge that I was really leaving made us strangers. Halfway through the dance she said she was tired and wanted to lie down for a while, so I took her to my room and went back to help Oskar behind the bar—Max had long since abandoned his post for the dance floor.

After a while I saw Max staggering out of the canteen, and I followed along to help him. He put his arm around my neck. "I have a girl waiting in my room. Shh-shh," he said loudly, putting his finger to his lips in a comic parody of secrecy. By the time I got him to Barracks 1, I was carrying almost his entire weight. We could hear the music from the canteen through the corridor's open window, and I asked him if he could still dance. He took his arm from around my neck and did a few reeling but recognizable steps. I was amazed, but a moment later I had to catch him or he would have fallen. He knocked on his door. It opened, and there stood the young wife of one of the DPs. She was one of the girls he usually danced with. Max staggered inside, and she closed the door. I wondered what she would tell her husband in the morning.

At the canteen, the crowd had thinned out, and the band's playing was softer and better. I opened a bottle of wine and took it to my room.

Rita was crying quietly, her face buried in the pillow. "Hey," I said, and took her by the shoulders. She resisted, but I pulled her gently up to a sitting position. Her hair was tangled, and she turned her face away, but I saw by the moonlight coming through the window that it was wet and despairing. I felt helpless and clumsy.

"Shh," I said. "You knew this was going to happen. Didn't I tell you at the beginning that we shouldn't get more of each other than we could handle?"

"I know," she said. "It's just that I'm going to miss you so much—I have to get it out of my system now. Then maybe it won't be so bad later."

I held her and stroked her awkwardly until her crying quieted down. "We still have a month together, Rita," I said. "I'll drink a glass of wine to that."

She laughed through her tears, and I gave her a glass of wine. We touched glasses in the dark and sat close, listening to the music. After a while the beat of the music began to get confused with the beat of my blood. Soon we were lying down, still listening to the music, stroking each other. We kissed, undressed, and made love for a long time in the moonlight from the window. As we drifted into sleep I realized that the canteen was quiet. We hadn't noticed when the dance ended and the music stopped, as if our love-making had taken up the theme and continued it long beyond the last notes of the professor's piano.

Rita spent the next weekend with me, and the next. She didn't cry again; in fact, she was almost too resolutely cheerful, and I realized with a pang of regret that she had made her decision to give me up. By now, my wrist had nearly healed, and there was only a scab where the gash had been. It would leave a big scar, but it wouldn't be my first, and scars, like bad experiences, fade a little with time.

During the week I had a talk with Nicolai, the big Slav hand wrestler. The accident had made us friends in a way. He was shipping out in a few days, also to Canada. He was one of the lucky ones. An uncle of his had a farm in Saskatchewan, and he was going there to work. I wished him luck. Soon I would ship out, too, to a completely new life. That is, if nothing went wrong with this next venture, carrying saccharin into the Eastern Zone for Vasile. I dreaded that, but I had to do it.

I was already getting ready, though I didn't know exactly

when Vasile would call on me. Another transport of DPs had come in, and from one of them I bought a Canadian army leather jacket for eight hundred marks, to replace my frayed old field jacket. I asked Jony for some oil and oiled my shoes well. I couldn't risk their squeaking when I stole across the border into East Germany.

We had the first snowfall of the year, big, wet flakes tumbling out of a gray sky. Two days later Vasile came to our camp, and all afternoon the canteen rang with his boisterous laughter. That night I left with him for his camp.

Toward noon the next day we tied three thousand saccharin pills around each of my ankles. Then Vasile wrapped the ankles with tape, I pulled my socks up over the tape, and my pants covered the socks. Vasile gave me my instructions. The man I was to meet in the small village in the Eastern Zone was called Konrad. I was to give him the saccharin and another small package, which Vasile told me to carry in my back pocket. He didn't tell me what was in it, and I didn't ask. He asked me how much money I had with me. I counted it—about two hundred marks. He gave me another five hundred.

A truck from his camp took me to Hannover, where I was to catch a train eastward to Braunschweig, just this side of the border. I thought it would be a good idea to buy a pack of American cigarettes—they worked like magic when a fast bribe was needed. Despite the warmth of the massed bodies, everyone on the black market was shivering with cold, and soon I was shivering, too. I went inside the station and bought a ticket on the local.

The train was terribly crowded. It had been dark since about four in the afternoon, but there were street lights in Hannover, and the station had been bright. As soon as the dimly lit train left the city I realized how dark it really was. The bodies huddled in the dim light, the stink of misery, the cold, all added to the ominous feeling I had about this job. After the train had stopped in several small villages and discharged some of its load, a cold half-moon appeared and brightened the night a little. We pulled into the small town of Braunschweig, and I got off.

Vasile had told me to follow a certain road from the train station. That was easy—it was a paved road—but the going got harder when I had to turn off the road and take the path into the forest. The snow must have been on the ground here longer than two days; it was trodden down and crunched underfoot with each step. I was to walk about ten miles through the forest, and then I would be in the Eastern Zone.

I walked quickly, stopping from time to time to look around. It was dead quiet, except for a rustling overhead when the wind stirred the tops of the pines. The path was narrow. After a while it turned steeply uphill and the snow got deeper. My ears were very cold, and so were my hands, though I kept them jammed deep in my pockets. I walked uphill for a long while, going over Vasile's directions in my mind. He had told me that after climbing the hill the path would go down through a valley and end. I would go straight on across a meadow until I saw the lights of a village. The big building at the end of the main street was the inn, where Herr Konrad would be waiting for me.

I walked fast, until I panted like a steam engine and my breath made clouds of steam in the thin moonlight. I thought I must be making as much noise as a bear running through the forest. If Russian guards were patrolling the border they couldn't help but hear me. I stopped for several minutes, until my breathing was quiet again. Then I went on at a slower pace, trying to walk quietly. But the cold made the snow crunch and squeak with every step; there was no way to avoid it. To me, frightened as I was, it sounded as loud as gunfire. I was very angry at myself. There had been no reason for me to take this stupid risk. I could have explained to Vasile why I was afraid to go into the Eastern Zone. He would have understood. But if I turned back now, having come this far, he would think I was a coward.

I tried to make less noise by walking to one side of the path, but I only sank into the snow, and the hard crust crunched anyway. I was still going uphill, though less steeply; but now the path leveled off, and soon it began to go down toward a clearing. Vasile had said that there would be a meadow and then the village where I was supposed to meet my man. Maybe I was going to make it, after all.

Then the voice rang out. *"Gde te idiosh?* Where are you going?" When I heard that, everything in me collapsed. It was over.

It was the arrogant voice of a Russian soldier.

If I ran he would shoot. When he questioned me and I couldn't identify myself properly, he would arrest me. I was caught. I would be shipped back to the Donbas. And all for some miserable saccharin pills.

For that one moment I felt black despair. And then, miraculously, my wits came back. On the second step after I heard that voice I stopped—and started cursing in Russian. I cursed like an angry coal miner who spits all the venom out of his system and then goes on cursing for the sheer joy of it. As if the specter of the Donbas were inspiring me, I came out with a stream of curses that any Donbas miner would have been proud of. I suggested what should be done to the mother of all three persons of God, and to the blood and the holy soul of Christ. I cursed the name, the mother, and the marrow of (I thought fast) that son of a whore, my aunt's brother who lived in Berlin. Then I heard the soldier chuckle. My heart began to beat very fast with hope.

"Where did you learn to curse so well?" he called out. I turned toward his voice. He was leaning against a tree about ten yards away, his rifle in the crook of his arm. I couldn't see him clearly, in spite of the moonlight; he was standing in the shadow of the tree.

I said, "I worked in the Donbas during the war. And this accursed brother of my aunt lives in Berlin, and I was supposed to go and see him for her, and now I've gone and gotten caught." I started cursing again.

He chuckled. "I see that you have a nice leather jacket. I want you to know that your cursing saved you, it sounded so good to me. But I want your leather jacket. Take it off and throw it this way."

I took the jacket off and threw it to him, but the icy wind hit my skin like a slap, and I knew I would never make it if I went on in just my shirt. "I'll freeze like this," I said. "It's only right that you give me your coat. The leather jacket is much warmer."

He grunted and stood still for a moment, and suddenly I realized that he was very drunk. He was thinking. I could almost see how slowly his brain was working, and it gave me courage. He staggered toward me. I hoped he would come close enough to be within reach of my hands, but he wasn't quite that drunk. He stopped at the next tree, shrugged out of his coat, and threw it at me. I caught it and put it on, knowing that by morning the lice would be crawling all over me. But at least I wouldn't get sick from the cold.

He took a bottle out of his waistband and said, "Take a drink of this. It will help against the cold." He tossed me the bottle.

I caught it, pulled out the cork, and gulped down several burning mouthfuls of vodka. The warmth spread quickly through my chest and belly. For a moment I thought of throwing the bottle in his face, but I decided that would be stupid. The light was bad, and my aim would be poor, so why take a chance? He was letting me go, and he had only taken my jacket.

"*Dosvidania*. Good-bye," he said, and waved. "Maybe I will see you when you cross over again."

I started walking. Now I wasn't worrying about the noise my steps made in the snow. I just walked fast. I had left the forest and was crossing the meadow when I noticed that something heavy in the pocket of the coat was bumping against my leg. I reached in and felt a leather satchel. Walking faster, I took it out and opened it. The satchel was full of wristwatches. The soldier had forgotten they were in his pocket. I started to run.

Just then I heard him shouting, "*Stoi! Stoi!* Stop!" A shot snapped behind me, and another spat into the snow off to my right. He meant business, but so did I. I was going like an Olympic sprinter.

All my fatigue and tension were swept away by a surge of adrenalin. I felt as if I could run for hours, as if I could outrun his bullets—especially as drunk as he was. The cold air ached in my lungs and the vodka glowed in my belly. I raced across the last ten yards of the meadow and came flying into the village as one more shot cracked and the forest rang with a last, far-off howl of outrage.

It was after midnight, and the streets were completely deserted. I ran down the main street looking for the inn where my contact would be waiting. At the end of the street I saw it and ran up to the door gasping for breath. Before I knocked I felt both my ankles to make sure the taped saccharin was still in place, and then in the back pocket of my trousers for Vasile's package. Everything was there.

I banged on the door several times before a voice came toward it mumbling, "What do you want?"

"I am to meet Herr Konrad," I said.

The door opened with a grating protest, and a shapeless old woman muffled in scarves and blankets led me into a dimly lit barroom. It was empty except for a well-dressed, dignified-looking man in his fifties who sat serenely smoking a pipe. When he saw the Russian army overcoat he turned away.

"He has asked for you," the old woman said.

He half turned toward me. "Why are you wearing that coat?" he asked, quietly and bitterly, without looking at me.

"It isn't mine," I said. "I got it coming across the border, a mile or so back, in the forest." I told him about the encounter with the soldier. Then I bent down, untaped the saccharin, and gave it to him. I took the package out of my back pocket and handed him that, too. He seemed to sigh with relief, and I felt much the same way.

I sat down, and Herr Konrad asked me how Vasile was. "Is he still like a rough monarch?"

"Yes," I said, "he is that. If anything, he is stronger than ever." I asked him whether Vasile ever dealt on the black market in Berlin. Was he known there?

"*Ach, ja,*" Herr Konrad said. "Everybody important knows that Herr Vasile is looking for big diamonds. He has quite a reputation, and he is feared and respected."

I asked him whether there was some other route I could take across the border. "That soldier will be looking for me, and if he catches me I'm in for some rough treatment."

Herr Konrad laughed sympathetically and asked me to show him the watches. I took out the satchel and handed it to him.

He pulled out the watches, counted them, and examined a few. Then he said, "You have thirty-six here, and several are very good Swiss watches. Vasile could sell them for you and get a good price. The Russian must have stolen them or taken them off people."

I repeated the saying we had had in Rumania during the Russian occupation that followed close on the heels of the German occupation: "Bad as it was with *Der, Die, Das,* it's worse with *Davay chas*"—Russian for "Give me your watch." Very few Russians had wristwatches, and those they had were crude and poor, so they were always the first thing the occupation soldiers demanded.

Herr Konrad gave a short laugh and nodded recognition. "I'll get you an old German who knows the border like his own hand. He will take you across before morning."

I gave Herr Konrad two of the watches. "That's for getting me the guide."

Before starting to count out money on top of the bar, he called to the old woman, "Bring this young man some hot tea, and then go get the old man to come here. Tell him I have to get somebody important across the border before morning."

She disappeared through a door. In a few minutes she came back with a steaming cup of tea, and then she took a coat from the wall, hung it around her shoulders, and went out into the cold.

Herr Konrad had finished counting the money, and then I had to recount it. There were four piles of twenty thousand marks each, mostly in twenty-mark bills. I counted till I was dizzy. It seemed to be exact.

Konrad said, "Please forgive me for my initial suspicion. It's just that I had never seen you before, and the Russian coat gave me a shock. In these times, it is so hard to be sure of anyone or anything. When you get back to Vasile's camp just make sure you get out of that coat and clean off the lice. You will have plenty of them. I know those border guards. They don't change their clothes often, and they usually sleep in them. But, young man, the exchange is still in your favor. Those are fine watches."

As we drank our tea together I wondered what Herr Konrad had been before the war. A professor, maybe. He was very well-spoken and had the air of cultured authority that comes from years of lecturing to students and receiving their respect. He struck me as the kind of man who would meet a grave crisis with a well-turned philosophical phrase.

The old lady came in mumbling something, followed by a very old man who seemed to be all beak nose and beard. When Herr Konrad told him he was to take me over the border the old man just nodded and sat down. In an old, quavery voice he asked for a cigarette. Konrad shook his head and gestured with his pipe, and I remembered the pack of cigarettes in my pocket. Taking it out, I offered it to the old man.

He tried to get up quickly, but I put my hand firmly on his shoulder, pressing him back into his chair. "Keep them."

"*Das ganze Paket?* The whole pack?" he asked hesitantly.

"*Ja, ja,*" I said.

His eyes were grateful, and Herr Konrad nodded his approval.

Then the old man said, "We should go now, so that we can use the darkness for a cover."

"*Ja,*" agreed Herr Konrad. "One thing more—tell Herr Vasile I'll have something big for him in February."

A big diamond? I wondered, but kept my curiosity to myself and said I would pass on the message. We shook hands, and the old man and I stepped out into the night.

It was even colder than before. The old man led at a surprisingly fast pace. Every once in a while he slowed down and stopped, wheezing in a way that worried me, but he seemed to be listening as much as resting. Then he set the pace again. We were going around the village, following a different route from the one I had come in by.

We crossed a narrow bridge over a small river. By the faint light of the moon I could see that the river was frozen. Soon the forest closed in around us. The old man lit a cigarette and slowed down. He was straining to hear the slightest sound. I tried to talk to him, but he held his finger to his lips and kept walking. He seemed to be a very tough old man.

As we came to the crest of a hill he pointed to a distant light and whispered, "That is the Russian border shack. A highway goes right past it."

I whispered back, "If it's that far away, why do we have to be so quiet?"

He put his finger to his lips again and whispered, "*Hünde* —dogs."

The hair on the back of my neck prickled. If I had known that on my way over . . .

We kept walking slowly on. I longed to go faster, but I stayed close behind the old man. At this pace the cold got to me. I wanted to know the time, but I wasn't wearing a watch—just carrying thirty-four of them.

I tapped the old man's shoulder and asked quietly, "How far yet?"

"Another hour, maybe," he replied softly. "Do you have another pack of cigarettes?"

"No," I said, "but I will give you a wristwatch, and with it you can get yourself more cigarettes." I gave him one of the watches, a good one, and he bobbed his head and said, "*Danke, danke,*" several times.

Finally we came out of the forest onto the road. It was beginning to get light. "We may be in time for you to catch a train right away," the old man said. "There is one due soon." We reached the town, and the old man led me to the station.

A train would arrive in about half an hour, according to the attendant. It was a little warmer in the waiting room than it had been outside, and we both sat down. I could already feel the lice crawling and tickling on my body. I bought a ticket to Hannover. Keeping back about twenty marks, I gave the rest of my money to the old pathfinder who had led me across the Russian border.

He said, "This is like Christmas for me—the cigarettes, the watch, and now over four hundred marks! And when I get back Herr Konrad will also give me something. *Ach, ja,* there are some good people left." He added that Herr Konrad was a very big man on the Berlin black market.

As the train whistle sounded the old man got up. "I hope you will come over again. I will take you back and forth safely. Just send word to me."

We shook hands, and I said, "Be careful going back." He just smiled and shuffled out of the station.

It was late afternoon and getting dark by the time the train rolled into Hannover. I had slept most of the way. Now I had to find Oskar, so that I could get his friend the taxi driver to take me to Vasile's camp. It felt so good to be in the Western Zone again, out of reach of Russia, far from that frozen border with its drunken guards and its dogs.

Oskar was as surprised to see me in a Russian overcoat as he had once been at my showing up in an American army uniform. And when I told him the story he was very angry at me for the chance I had taken. I gave him a wristwatch, to distract him, but he kept scolding until the taxi arrived.

In the car I immediately fell asleep. The driver woke me, and there was the familiar gate of Vasile's camp. I asked him to wait and went inside.

Vasile was sitting at the table inside the guard shack eating sausage and drinking whiskey. He hollered, "You must have stolen that coat from some Russian! Come, sit down and tell me."

First I gave him the money. He began counting it right

away, and he counted fast and expertly. I told him the high-lights of the trip, and when I got to the part about the watches he laughed and laughed, slapping his knee with delight. I gave him two of the watches, and then I repeated Konrad's message.

Vasile picked up the bundle of money, counted out two thousand marks, and shoved them over to me. I pushed them back, but he angrily picked up the money and stuffed it into my pocket. There was no arguing with him. I would give the money to Jony.

Before I left I had one thing to ask him. "Vasile, what was in the little package I gave Herr Konrad?"

He looked at me steadily and said bluntly, "Opium."

I tried not to show the shock I felt that in these hard times there was still room for drugs. "Would you have told me if I had asked you before I left?"

"Why not?" he replied. "You are my friend."

I went back to the taxi, said, "Buchholz," and fell asleep again. The driver woke me, and I gave him one hundred marks and walked through the gate in my Russian coat, to the guard's amazement.

I went to the canteen, and Jony shouted, then embraced and kissed me. I told him and Max what had happened, and I pulled out a handful of watches and displayed them on the bar. Then I took Jony into my room. I told him about the package of opium I had taken across the border with the saccharin, and he said, "It will help Vasile get his fifty diamonds, so he can go home to Corsica."

I kept one of the watches and gave Jony the rest. "Sell them. They should keep you going for a while."

"*Mercy ma.* Thank you," he said simply, but it was enough.

Before he left Jony admonished me. "That was your last caper on the black market." He said it with finality.

I slept for twenty hours and woke up itching and scratching. Taking the Russian coat behind Barracks 1, I poured gasoline over it and burned it. Jony gave me some disinfecting powder, and after I undressed in the washroom he took my pants, shirt, mattress, and blanket to the disinfecting room. I took a cold shower, shook the powder all over my body and rubbed it in, and that was the end of the Russian lice, those old acquaintances from the East.

Christmas was only a week away now, and the next day we took Oskar's taxi and went to Vasile's camp for a big shopping trip. The bazaar was very crowded, and I was happy to discover that there was a large assortment of candy on the stands for the holidays. Vasile had even managed to find some chocolates. It didn't make any difference to me that I was about to emigrate to the land of five-cent chocolate bars. My hunger for the stuff seemed bottomless.

I was hovering over the candy stand trying to decide when Vasile slapped me on the back and said, "My good friend, how are you? Come, let me pick up some things for you."

I protested, but he insisted. He started by grabbing handfuls of candy and filling a big bag with them. As we walked along I was afraid to look at anything, because if I showed any interest Vasile would go over, grab whatever it was, and give it to me. I did get some things for Rita and a large bag of food for my uncle's family for Christmas.

Then Vasile said, "Now take something for yourself, my friend."

I said, "Could I buy a shirt like yours?"

"Of course—you may have one!" he shouted, and led me away from the bazaar toward the barracks directly behind it. We went into a big room just inside the entrance. In spite of the clutter of boxes and crates, it was much more handsomely furnished than most DP barracks rooms. From a suitcase Vasile took two black shirts and gave them to me. They were his own. He waved my thanks away. "That's not necessary. Did I thank you for going to East Germany? No, because I do whatever I can for you, and I expect the same from you."

Years afterward, when I was a prize fighter in Chicago and later a coffee-shop owner in New York City, I still wore black or dark shirts and pants like Vasile's.

We met Jony at the guard shack, drank to the holidays, and we left.

I had decided to spend Christmas at my uncle's, so the next morning I packed an old suitcase, took my bundle of food, and caught the train to Giessen. It had snowed again. The fields going by the window were white, and the people on the train huddled in the warmest clothes they had been able to find—often just layers of rags. Near all the train stations where we stopped were children and old women searching with skinny hands for lumps of coal to burn in their stoves or fireplaces. Hunger was plain in their faces.

My uncle's family hadn't heard from me for months. They were overjoyed that I had passed the medical examination and intrigued by the saccharin story. I told them about everything except the opium. Although they were as hungry as everyone else in Germany, I knew that smuggling drugs into the Eastern Zone was something they wouldn't understand. Nor would they understand the unquestioning loyalty demanded by my relationship with Vasile.

With the food I had brought and a little tree from the woods outside town, we managed to make ourselves a decent Christmas. But I ached with missing my parents. I had a letter from them, and as usual it brought both sadness and happiness. They missed me terribly, too, and wrote of the wonderful Christmases we had had together, before the war shattered everything. Now my sister was dead, and they knew I couldn't come home. I wrote them the good news about my emigration and promised to write again, as soon as I had an address in the New World.

Greeting the New Year was a brawling, drunken orgy at the canteen in Buchholz. Fights broke out, triggered by alcohol, rivalries, petty jealousies, and drunken disagreements. I think Jony and I were the only sober ones there. I had hoped that Rita and Oskar would come, but they came the next day instead. We wished each other a happy New Year, and Rita gave me two books as Christmas presents. Oskar left after dinner, but Rita stayed the night.

It was our last night together. I promised to let her know

when I would be leaving, but as it turned out I didn't have time. So that was our good-bye, that cold gray morning at the streetcar stop. I took the memory of Rita, and the two books she gave me, to Canada with me.

Max was shipped out of Buchholz a week later. I left three days after Max, early in the morning. Jony walked me to my bus and promised to give Vasile, Oskar, and Rita my best. We said good-bye gravely, but hoping we would meet again someday. It was not to be. Jony died in Germany, of tuberculosis, a little over a year later—six months after his baby son. Max I was to run into one day in 1960, in front of Saks Fifth Avenue in New York. But I would see Max once more before that.

The bus took me to yet another kind of camp, an embarkation camp called Fallingbostel. Here, DPs from various transit camps gathered before being sent to their ships. As I got off the bus my heart leaped with glad recognition. There was Max, strolling around with a stick tucked under his arm like a retired general. When he saw me he shouted and ran to me. We embraced, happy that we might sail to the New World together.

We were together for two days, and Max was like a solid, familiar island in a sea of confusion and change. Then I was sent, without Max, to Bremerhaven, surrounded by strangers —DPs I had never seen before. They were to be my shipmates for the voyage to the New World. We were herded aboard a shining ship and down below into crowded bunkrooms—the barracks all over again, except that the stability of the earth was gone, and in its place was a faint unsettling motion. It was later to build into a pitching and rolling that would make many of my bunkmates violently sick.

We sailed several hours later, into the darkness of evening and a new life. The deep baying of the ship's horn said good-bye to hunger and rationing, to camps and black markets, and to my friends and my buried gold. From now on it would come back to me only in dreams, like my years in the Donbas.

Toward morning I went on deck to escape the stifling atmosphere, the groans and sickness of the hold. It was chilly and windy, and nobody else was out. I liked that kind of weather. I stood at the railing and looked out over the waves, feeling the sea wind on my face and wondering how my twenty-first year would turn out.

EPILOGUE

In 1954 I was a soldier in the American army, stationed at Metz in France. The first weekend pass I got, I asked the supply sergeant for a trenching tool and a small shovel and boarded a train for Frankfurt. I hadn't forgotten my buried treasure.

It was not the Germany I had known. Everything was clean and neat, and the people looked reasonably well fed. Rationing had ended; most of the rubble had been cleared away, and new buildings were going up everywhere. The *Wirtschaftswunder*, the economic miracle of postwar Germany, fueled by German energy and American money, was under way. There was no black market around the train stations now.

I got into Frankfurt late at night and waited several hours for the local train to the little town where I had buried my trunk six long years ago. I had changed as much as Germany had. I was forty pounds heavier. I had been a logger in Sault Sainte Marie, Canada, I had boxed in Minneapolis, Chicago, and London, and I had discovered cornflakes. I remembered myself, a skinny DP kid in a stolen uniform, masquerading as an American soldier in a wild gamble to smuggle coffee out of Belgium. What would that kid had thought if he had known that one day he would come back to Germany as a real American soldier?

The train came, and I got to the little town at six o'clock in the morning. Just as it had been before, the station was nearly deserted. A new road led around the station, and I followed it, my heart beating fast. Any minute now I would see the familiar tree that marked my treasure. I turned the corner of the station. There at the edge of the forest stood a new apartment house.

It took my breath away. Just about where my tree had been was the front wall of the building. It was a good ten minutes before I could think further. I wondered if I should ask when the apartments had been built. I could even ask whether a trunkful of golden goblets had been found—as if anyone would tell me! Or maybe the trunk was still in the ground, and it would take dynamite to liberate it. But that would get me into big trouble with the German authorities. It had been their gold before I stole it, and now it was theirs again. It was my fault. I should have gone deeper into the forest to hide it. I felt weak.

Staring at the new building, I walked slowly toward it and stopped. An older man came up from the basement and gaped at the American soldier who stood there smoking a cigarette (I smoked now) and gazing forlornly at the foundations.

"How old is this building?" I asked.

"*Na ja*," he said, "about three years. Are you looking for someone who lives in it? I know everybody here. Maybe I can help you."

"No, no," I said in German, and I turned around and walked back to the station.